Asian
Transitional
Economies

Challenges and
Prospects for
Reform and
Transformation

D1797470

The mission of the **International Center for Economic Growth (ICEG)** is to enhance the capacity of indigenous policy research institutions to develop sound economic policy analysis and to deliver it effectively to the policy process. ICEG works with a network of such institutions in developing and transitional countries to promote sustainable economic growth and human development and thus improve the lives and opportunities of the world's citizens.

ICEG, founded in 1985, is a non-profit international policy programme of the Institute for Contemporary Studies. ICEG has built a network of 340 policy research institutes in 117 countries to create an international dialogue for the exchange of experiences and scholarly information.

Inquiries, book orders, and catalogue requests should be addressed to ICS Press, 720 Market Street, San Francisco, California 94102 USA. Telephone: (415) 981-5353; fax: (415) 986-4878. Book orders within the contiguous United States: (800) 326-0263.

The **Institute of Southeast Asian Studies** was established as an autonomous organization in 1968. It is a regional research centre for scholars and other specialists concerned with modern Southeast Asia, particularly the multi- faceted problems of stability and security, economic development, and political and social change.

The Institute is governed by a twenty-two-member Board of Trustees comprising nominees from the Singapore Government, the National University of Singapore, the various Chambers of Commerce, and professional and civic organizations. A ten-man Executive Committee oversees day-to-day operations; it is chaired by the Director, the Institute's chief academic and administrative officer.

The **ASEAN Economic Research Unit** is an integral part of the Institute, coming under the overall supervision of the Director who is also the Chairman of its Management Committee. The Unit was formed in 1979 in response to the need to deepen understanding of economic change and political developments in ASEAN. The day-to-day operations of the Unit are the responsibility of the Co-ordinator. A Regional Advisory Committee, consisting of senior economists from the ASEAN countries, guides the work of the Unit.

Asian Transitional Economies

Challenges and Prospects for Reform and Transformation

edited by
Seiji Finch Naya
Joseph L.H. Tan

**INSTITUTE OF
SOUTHEAST ASIAN STUDIES
SINGAPORE**

**INTERNATIONAL CENTER
FOR ECONOMIC GROWTH
UNITED STATES**

Published by
Institute of Southeast Asian Studies
Heng Mui Keng Terrace
Pasir Panjang
Singapore 119596

Cataloguing in Publication Data

Asian transitional economies: challenges and prospects for reform and transformation/edited by Seiji Finch Naya and Joseph L.H. Tan.
1. Asia — Economic policy.
2. Asia — Economic conditions — 1945–
3. Investments, Foreign — Asia.
4. Vietnam — Economic conditions.
5. Laos — Economic conditions.
6. Myanmar — Economic conditions.
7. Mongolia — Economic conditions.
I. Naya, Seiji Finch.
II. Tan, Joseph Loong Hoe.
HC412 A843   1995   sls95-67266

ISBN 981-3055-09-X
ISSN 0129-1920

Typeset by International Typesetters Pte Ltd
Printed in Singapore by Chong Moh Offset Printing Pte Ltd

Contents

Introduction

Seiji F. Naya

The seemingly inexorable spread of economic reform movements from centrally directed to market-oriented systems into some of the more isolated and lesser-developed economies of Asia has been the subject of an eighteen-month study under the direction of the International Center for Economic Growth (ICEG), in collaboration with the Institute of Southeast Asian Studies (ISEAS), Singapore, the publishers of this volume.

The countries under study are a diverse group, bound mainly by their efforts in varying degrees to liberalize and open up their economies. They are: Vietnam, probably the furthest along towards the market economy and increasingly the target of foreign venture inquiries, but still bound by an adherence to socialist doctrine; Laos, a land-locked neighbour, but with external exposure through cultural and commercial ties with Thailand; Myanmar, resource-rich, but mired in self-imposed isolation for half a century; and Mongolia, far to the north and still struggling from a history of Soviet dependence.

For purposes of this project, this group has been termed the Asian transitional economies (ATEs). While unique and distinctive in terms of culture, historical heritage, and resource endowment, they do share certain commonalities that stand as obstacles to reform and development progress. To start with, they are among the poorest of the poor and classified among the world's least developed countries. Generally, the instruments of macroeconomic control are rudimentary or non-existent, and the physical, institutional, and human resource infrastructures are grossly underdeveloped.

Yet they have one common attribute that may prove most conducive to their development aspirations; that is, good neighbours. Despite their recent isolation, the ATEs have long-standing historical and cultural ties with some of the highest performing Asian economies. From this factor and current observation, they are becoming more convinced that the movement towards market-based, outward-oriented regimes provides the best means of uplifting living standards in the transitional period and sustaining economic growth over the long term.

From the ATE perspective, it may be said that market-oriented, outward-looking policies are the *necessary* conditions for economic growth. But are they *sufficient*? This project addresses this question. Key researchers or research institutes in each of the four countries prepared papers under broad themes set forth by ICEG, with support in each case by external specialists.

This volume includes the four main country papers, together with an integrative chapter by Professor Mohamed Ariff of the University of Malaya, who served as joint co-ordinator of the research programme with Dr Joseph Tan of ISEAS. It also includes keynote presentations by specially invited outside economic development specialists, which were given at an international conference in Osaka, Japan, from 30 October to 1 November 1994.

Since Professor Ariff has so skilfully and comprehensively presented and interpreted the main findings of the project in his chapter, we will not attempt to go over similar ground. Rather we will seek to draw out some of the highlights of the international conference, which provide additional insight on the challenges and opportunities facing the ATEs and also other economies that are encountering transitional reform experiences.

Conference themes and questions for deliberation were set by opening keynote speakers. Asian transitional economies now have more choices, according to Shinichi Ichimura, Osaka International University vice-president. South Korea chose to follow the Japan model. India opted for the socialist model, while others were perhaps coerced into following the Stalinist model. The end of the Cold War resulted in increasing economic globalization. China was able to recognize this, and its market reforms followed.

The East Asian economic miracle, featuring accelerated outward-oriented growth in South Korea, Taiwan, Hong Kong, and Singapore, followed by Thailand, Malaysia, and Indonesia, and more recently China, has been widely heralded. Can this be a model for the new transitional economies?

Singapore's Professor Chan Heng Chee, former ambassador to the United Nations and current Director of ISEAS, stresses the view held by most development economists: there is no singular development model. Much can be learned from the successes and mistakes of rapidly developing economies. But the historical context must guide the reform process, and political forces are often determinate. What works? What and when to adopt? What are the social costs? Each country must confront these questions, and answers are not clear-cut. But can it afford not to be on the track?

Peter Petri of Brandeis University echoes these sentiments. The East Asian miracle defies simple explanation. There are multiple means to success. East Asian economies placed early emphasis on macroeconomic stability and discipline. This provided reliable signals for efficient resource allocation, reinforced by external price signals from their outward orientation. Governments intervened strategically rather than massively. Industrial policies were enunciated and development directions set. Missteps were quickly remedied, and distortions not prolonged. Probably the most enduring impact of East Asian governments has been their early and consistent investment in upgrading their human resources.

This is not to say that anything goes, and that everything results in Asian success, as Ulrich Hiemenz of the Organization for Economic Co-operation and Development (OECD) was to point out. Asian performance was both more flexible and more structured than other developing areas. Singapore and South Korea, for example, were quick to adjust their misjudged labour and capital investment policies respectively, but many Latin American countries simply piled one mistake upon another. What the more successful economies were able to demonstrate was adherence to a "minimum critical effort", or their ability to intertwine enterprise and budgetary reform at the micro level with stabilization at the macro level.

Models exist, but transitional economies, as each of their representatives would point out, face both daunting internal challenges as well as a different, probably less amenable international environment. Ironically, these economies are just beginning to open up; at the same time, protectionist tendencies seem to be ascending in the industrialized world. These tendencies are also reinforced by demands for stricter interpretation and enforcement of intellectual property rights, which may retard attempts of less-developed economies to "catch up".

Researchers from the transitional economies all reported macroeconomic progress. Vietnam is currently growing at about an 8 per cent rate, with 10 per cent gross domestic product (GDP) growth expected by 1995, and appears to have reduced both budget and trade deficits and brought inflation under control. As mentioned, it has become the latest Asian investment magnet. Laos, its neighbour, appears to have met the International Monetary Fund (IMF) structural adjustment requirements and has succeeded in reallocating resources from its agriculture sector to infrastructure and human capital needs.

Mongolia also reported progress in structural reform, although its representatives were less sanguine about its sustainability and longer-range effects. The Myanmar report pronounced reform as being irreversible and focused on its attempts to transform an inefficient public sector and encourage outward-oriented private enterprise, although liberalization efforts are still marred by high inflation and government inefficiency.

Each of these papers acknowledged similar deficiencies or obstacles to sustainable reform, the points being summed up best by Stanley Katz, drawing from his service as vice-president of both the Asian and European Development Banks. The transitional economies presently lack the body of laws, regulations, and enforcement procedures to govern and arbitrate market transactions. Financial reform or even financial institutions need to be put in place to handle these transactions without generating inflation. Physical infrastructure, ranging from power and communications to rural water supply, is woefully inadequate. Most of all, the economies and their leadership lack a longer-range perspective on national development objectives and how to reach them.

The latter problem is not peculiar to Asian economies, as Jan Kulig of Poland and Tsuneaki Sato of Nihon University were to point out in their respective comparisons of the European and Asian transitional experiences. Further, as Mohamed Ariff of the University of Malaya suggests, a reversal or alteration of reform direction is not to be ruled out: "transformation fatigue" can set in, particularly if expected benefits are submerged by persisting costs.

However, there is also room for optimism. As we have suggested, Asian transitional economies, in contrast to those in Eastern Europe, are located within or close to a most dynamic area. There can be considerable spill-over effects from the economic growth in the Association of Southeast Asian Nations (ASEAN), and at least for Vietnam, ASEAN membership is entirely feasible. Further, Asian transitional economies are not saddled with large loss-incurring state industrial enterprises, which are most intractable to reform efforts. Then there is the overseas Chinese connection, which has sparked export and investment growth in the neighbouring economies. Even Mongolia, far to the north, has a dynamic economic neighbour in China and has attracted interest from Japan and South Korea.

We conclude this introductory section with what will undoubtedly be an inadequate attempt to properly acknowledge the substantive and financial contributions of numerous individuals and institutions. Dr Nicolas Ardito-Barletta, General Director of ICEG, regrettably was not able to attend the international conference, but his knowledge of reform and transitional experiences in Latin America and Eastern Europe contributed substantially to the project. The beneficial collaboration with ISEAS has been noted.

In addition, the Asia-Pacific Economic Studies programme of the University of Hawaii under my colleague, Dr Shelley Mark, provided essential research and logistical back-up to the project and conference, as did the International Development Centre of Japan (IDCJ). And of course Professor Ichimura and his colleagues at Osaka International University provided invaluable hosting and logistical support throughout the conference. Funding for the conference was from the Pew Charitable Trusts and the Japan Foundation Centre for Global Partnership, augmenting the basic support of the United States Agency for International Development (USAID) throughout the entire project.

It should be mentioned that the conference was attended by not only policy officials from the ATEs, but also representatives of international development and donor agencies, such as the Japan Overseas Economic Co-operation Fund (OECF), Sasakawa Peace Foundation, Canadian International Development Agency, Asia Foundation, and the OECD Development Centre.

Of particular import was the active participation of the Kansai Economic Research Centre, which hosted a full-day symposium and social reception on 1 November 1994, during which conference speakers were given the opportunity to meet and address more than 100 key private sector executives. The occasion was the feature event of the thirtieth anniversary commemoration of this prestigious organization.

The conference also benefited substantially from the participation of the OECF, whose Deputy Director for Development Assistance, Yoshihiko Kono, presented a perceptive paper on "Japan's Financial Assistance through OECF to Transitional Economies" and expressed strong interest in ICEG's overall approach to development and reform issues.

On a personal note, in addition to expressing my deep appreciation to all participants, including many whom I have not mentioned in this section, as ICEG's Asian section advisor and chair of the conference, I would like to say that I was extremely impressed with the seriousness with which countries are trying to reform their policies from central planning to market orientation. It is clear that these economies will face difficult problems, many in the political arena, but I am confident that their transitions are irreversible. I thus conclude with this sense of optimism.

Part 1

Issues and Comparative Perspectives

2

Some Key Development Issues for Transitional Economies — East and West

S. Stanley Katz

In the decades since Messrs Marx and Engels launched what was to become a thriving profession of economic advisers and consultants, scores of books and articles have been written on how to transform a nation's economy from a market-based to a centrally planned system. Very little has been written on how to move in the reverse direction — from planning to free markets, and countries that undertook this kind of reverse-transition have been pretty much left to mark out their own routes to the market-place.

In this regard, the transitional countries of Asia — Laos, Mongolia, Myanmar, and Vietnam — enjoy a significant advantage. Since they are not the first to make this journey, they can analyse the diverse routes taken by predecessor countries, notably in Asia and in Central and Eastern Europe, and decide which features best suit their circumstances and objectives.

The divergent paths to market-based reform and restructuring taken by Asian and Central and East European nations reflect a variety of country-specific economic, cultural, social, historic, and political facts and circumstances. Overarching such country differences is a range of regional distinctions, particularly in terms of the environment and rationale for economic reform and transition. Asian nations, for example, achieved economic independence and began their economic reforms earlier and under less politically charged circumstances than did their Central and East European counterparts. In Central and Eastern Europe, moreover, a job and a modest standard of living were seen as a national birthright; while in Asia, unemployment was epidemic, living standards were low, and expectations even lower. On the other hand, Asian nations did not feel the contempt for government and the need to erase overnight decades of state economic intervention that characterized Central and East European reform efforts.

The point of this brief aside is to underscore the fact that while there are regional considerations that lend content to the 'Asian Approach' and 'Central and East European Approach' labels, each country within these regions that undertook market-based economic reform did so on the basis of specific national needs and circumstances. With this *caveat* in mind, it is instructive to outline the main features of the two main routes to the market-place that reforming countries have pursued — the 'Asian Approach' and the 'Central and East European Approach'.

Alternative Approaches to Economic Restructuring

The Asian Approach

While Asian countries were economically underdeveloped, most did not feel a compelling need, on achieving independence, for radical changes in economic direction or for throwing the public sector out of their nation's economic life. As compared with Central and Eastern Europe, Asia's reforms were long-term and developmental rather than radical and rapid. In that context, Asian nations' development and restructuring programmes were in general set out in a multi-year forward plan prepared at the central government level. Planned objectives were for the most part developmental: to expand jobs, increase agricultural production and exports, develop industry, and replace imports with domestic output.

Except for South Korea and Taiwan and, of course, Hong Kong and Singapore, conversion from state planning to free markets was not an explicit developmental objective for most Asian countries. In some it was in fact the opposite: to expand the government's role in their nation's economic affairs. Only after years of watching their own economic progress lag further and further behind that of their market-based neighbours did many of the lagging countries begin earnest efforts to move to market-based economic systems.

Consistent with Asian attitudes and values, economic development and market-based reform have in general been viewed as a step-by-step, incremental process, to be pursued over a fairly extended time frame. While private enterprise and free markets are seen as driving this process, most Asian countries also expect their public sectors to play an active supporting and moderating role in market-based reform at a macroeconomic level.

The Asian approach to transition has not typically entrusted to the market or to foreign investors responsibility for deciding which industries will prosper and which will not. Rather, they have attempted to formulate macro-level industrial strategies based on projections of market developments and a corollary assessment of which of their infant industries could likely carve out a competitive niche in world markets, and which would not. The first group received import protection, export incentives, tax relief, and other types of financial assistance to help bolster their growth and competitiveness. The second group received help in diversifying or phasing out.

Asian countries have implicitly recognized that foreign currencies are stronger (compared with their national currencies), and most have used foreign exchange and currency exchange rates as tools of economic policy. Exchange rates, for example, have typically not been left to float up and down with the tides of international currency markets. Rather, rates have been set by the country's monetary authorities to encourage exports and saving and to discourage imports. Only when the country's exporters had become established in overseas markets, and foreign exchange reserves had reached comfortable levels, were restrictions on foreign currency transactions eased and national currencies allowed to appreciate.

Domestic prices in Asia's market-based economies have for the most part been set by market forces. Key prices, however, have often been nudged up or down by fiscal means (taxes, rebates, tariffs, subsidies, etc.) in order to ensure that the buy/save, sell/invest signals they emit conform to national priorities — increased domestic employment and production, high rates of savings and investment, relative food self-sufficiency, and the like.

Taiwan's economic development and restructuring programmes exemplify the Asian approach at its most successful. Restructuring first began in the early 1950s — more than four decades ago — and continues to the present.[1] In brief, Taiwan's initial four-year plan, launched in 1953, was designed to improve agricultural productivity and output and to expand savings and exports. The resulting surpluses were channelled to new and expanded light industry. This was followed sequentially by a period of export expansion and investments in export industries during the 1960s. The programmes developed for the 1970s built on the results of prior periods. They were directed to developing a more sophisticated capital- and technology-intensive industrial base, to meeting infrastructure needs, and to stimulating domestic demand. Programmes of restructuring and development for the 1980s and 1990s recognize Taiwan's arrival on the global economic and financial scene and focus on, among other things, strengthening overseas marketing and distribution and the liberalization and progressive internationalization of the Taiwan economy.

Two features in particular define Taiwan's approach to economic development and restructuring. First, it is comprehensive, coherent and sequential. Second, it employs the macroeconomic policy and programme tools available to the public sector, working with and through the private enterprise sector, to develop the public–private synergy needed to advance the country's strategic economic objectives.

The Central and East European Approach

The unexpected collapse of the Soviet economic system at the end of the 1980s compelled the leaders of the newly independent Central and East European states to take over the reins of their economies and to begin restructuring even before the dust had settled in Moscow. As a consequence, these countries' approach to economic reform and transition stands in sharp contrast to the Asian approach.

Having endured decades of invasive government-sponsored economic mismanagement, removing the government's grip on the economy and moving with all possible speed to Western-style free markets were these countries' first priorities. After their long isolation from the West, ignorance of how markets in fact worked was prodigious. Leaders of some countries believed that once they had announced that their economies would henceforth be market-based, foreign investors would come flocking in and prosperity would be just around the corner.

In that environment, it is not surprising that many Central and East European nations opted for the rapid, 'shock therapy' or 'big-bang' approach to economic restructuring. This approach had been urged on them by scores of advisers as the most direct route to the market, and its apparent simplicity had great appeal. All it seemed to require was to put the economy on 'automatic-pilot', let the markets decide supply, demand, and prices, and, *voilà*, economic transformation! Moreover, the government sector would play no part in this economic system; and once launched, 'big-bang' reforms would be virtually impossible to reverse.

The key prescription of the 'big-bang' approach is the transfer of economic decision making to the private sector and the near-elimination of the government sector from the national economy. The ramifications of this seemingly simple formula are formidable and far-reaching. Countries that adopted this approach committed themselves, in principle if not in fact, simultaneously to freeing wholesale and retail prices; eliminating consumer and producer subsidies; opening their borders to foreign exports and capital; making their currencies freely convertible for current and capital transactions; closing down or selling off state enterprises; dismissing redundant workers; and dismantling safety nets at the industry and firm level.[2]

The Record of Predecessor Countries' Achievements

From an overall impressionistic viewpoint, the record of success and failure under these two main approaches is broadly as follows:

Asian Performance: An Overview[3]

The Asian Newly Industrialized Economies. The so-called NIEs or

'Asian Tigers' — Taiwan, South Korea, Hong Kong, and Singapore — were the first to begin transforming their national economies in a consecutive and systematic manner. While each faced different political and economic circumstances,[4] their sustained restructuring and development efforts during the past four decades have paid substantial dividends. Each now ranks near the top of the list of rapidly growing and internationally competitive market-oriented economies.

Other Industrializing Asian Nations. A second group of Asian countries, including Thailand, Malaysia, and Indonesia, began the journey from underdeveloped command-based to developed demand-based economic systems at about the same time as the four NIEs. Only in the past decade or two, however, have their restructuring efforts become more integrated and more effectively implemented. These countries are now making significant progress in changing the orientation of their economies and are experiencing substantial improvements in growth rates, living standards, and international competitiveness.

The People's Republic of China. China's approach is unique in virtually all respects, attempting as it does to marry a centralized political system with an increasingly decentralized, market-oriented economy. Although political controls remain in place, China's rapid and spreading economic development and its corollary improvements in productivity, living standards, and exports are impressive. While the country's experiment with a mixed and decentralized political-economic system seems to be working well so far, China is not likely to serve as a useful model for Asia's smaller transitional countries.

South and Southeast Asia. The record of market-based reform has been mixed in other Asian countries, including the Philippines, India, Sri Lanka, Pakistan, and Bangladesh. Although these countries have formulated development plans and programmes for decades, consistent and well-defined efforts to move economic decision making from the state to the private sector are in most cases of fairly recent origin, and development and restructuring success has been limited. In part this reflects an extended period of misguided pursuit of economic development through a centralized rather than a decentralized approach.

Central and East European Performance: An Overview[5]

Now some five years after the 'big-bang' approach was first put into practice, it remains highly controversial. Its critics see it as the economic equivalent of Sherman's March to the Sea during the American Civil War and consider it both too simplistic and too costly in human terms. Its advocates, on the other hand, claim that there was no other way in the then-existing circumstances and point out that it is working where countries have adopted its prescriptions in full. Whatever its inherent merits and demerits, restructuring results under this approach vary considerably from country to country.

The Czech Republic (once it had shed the slower-reforming Slovak Republic) has parlayed the shock therapy approach into successful economic transition. The Czech economy (including its informal markets) is growing at a reasonable if modest rate. Inflation has been contained, employment is up, foreign investment is increasing, and the entrepreneurial sector is expanding. This outcome has, of course, been shaped in large part by the country's technically skilled labour force and the country's proximity to Germany and other West European markets.

Hungary, which quietly started economic reforms in the financial sector a decade or so earlier, has taken a more pragmatic and selective approach to economic restructuring. The Hungarian economy is increasingly open and market-driven, privatization has been selective, and domestic and foreign investment is increasing. The country has made meaningful strides towards a self-sustaining market system, perhaps as much in spite of, as because of, 'big-bang' prescriptions.

Poland's experience has been rather mixed, with a resumption of real growth but continued high inflation and unemployment, and increasing disaffection with reforms. The country's current political leadership and its labour unions seem less enthralled by economic reform than their predecessors, and a large part of Poland's initial restructuring programme seems to be on hold.

Economic transition in other former Soviet republics and satellite nations, including the Baltics, Romania, Bulgaria, Ukraine, Belarus, and the central Asian republics, which started with a jolt when the Soviet system collapsed, shows poor to mixed progress. Although most of these nations are in principle committed to market-based economies and private enterprise, in practice few have moved very far in that direction. Much of the apparatus and bureaucracy that set the economic rules under former regimes remains in place. Overall reform is moving slowly, and restructuring often takes the form of individual private deals, often with government ministers as silent partners. In general, transition has been slower and more complex than had been anticipated, and support for economic reform is increasingly passive.

Russia[6] is the largest and most economically diverse country to have opted for the shock therapy approach. Given the huge size and geographic complexity of the country and the state's long and pervasive involvement in its economy, it is not surprising that reforms have been uneven, uncertain, and, in some cases, undone. At the outset, the suspension of controls on most internal prices caused cascading inflation, and Russians living on fixed incomes saw their living standards collapse overnight. The relatively free conversion of rubles into dollars absorbed a substantial part of domestic savings and export earnings and created highly profitable black markets in imported goods. These in turn have spawned a new élite that drives Mercedes, drinks Scotch whiskey, and owns London flats. A wide — and volatile — gap in living standards now exists between Russia's new 'haves' and old 'have-nots'.

The economic picture in Russia has improved somewhat recently, although living standards continue to stagnate in real terms. Unemployment remains of epidemic proportions. Inflation has been moderated while the ruble has experienced further declines, a result of printing more rubles needed to keep state-owned plants from closing and spewing millions of workers onto the streets. On the plus side, private enterprises have begun to spring up and increasingly to meet consumer needs. Some factories are being retooled to meet domestic and foreign demand, and foreign investors are showing some interest in the Russian economy.

Key Issues for Transitional Economies

From the perspective of Asia's new transitional economies, this review raises a number of important issues. Two in particular stand out. The first concerns the *process* of transition, the second the *institutions* of transition. More specifically, the question of process involves the tempo and sequencing of restructuring. The question of institutions involves the role of the public sector in the transition process.

The Tempo and Sequencing of Restructuring

Economic restructuring exacts real costs and upsets the established economic and political order. It is axiomatic, therefore, that support for economic reform is inversely proportionate to the pain and dislocation it causes. If support for economic reform is to be sustained, the tempo of change cannot impose unacceptably high economic costs or too rapid structural shift within too short a period of time. Nor, on the other hand, can the tempo of reform be so slow that supporters turn away, frustrated by inadequate results. By these criteria, the initial pace of reform in much of Central and Eastern Europe was too rapid, and in many parts of Asia, too slow.

In fact, the tempo of economic transition is not an independent variable. Besides a nation's readiness to accept change, the overall pace of reform is dictated by the ability of the country's leadership to formulate, organize, and implement a logical and consecutive sequence of macro-level reform strategies, policies, and measures. In too many cases, the wrong sequence has resulted in a waste of valuable time and resources: power plants built before energy pricing policies had been formulated; foreign exchange used for consumer imports when the economy was starved for capital and spare parts; capital-intensive, high-technology industries launched when investments in agriculture and light industry promised greater employment and productivity gains.

The ramifications of an appropriate tempo and sequencing of transitional measures are many. First, it means that a broad, macro-view of the economy must be developed in order to bring into clear and coherent focus the strengths and weaknesses of existing sectors, institutions, programmes, and policies. Next, it means that national macroeconomic priorities must be established with respect, for example, to identifying and supporting sectors and industries with large prospective productivity gains, linkages to other sectors, and potential comparative advantage; to strengthening private sector industries; to stimulating internal savings and private investment; to preserving scarce foreign exchange for high priority uses; and to addressing infrastructure bottle-necks and technology gaps. Next is the need to formulate strategies and establish institutions, policies, and programmes required to pursue the identified economic priorities in a systematic, phased manner, and on the basis of a realistic assessment of available resources.

The need for comprehensive, integrated macroeconomic strategies, policies, and programmes to serve as a vehicle for economic transition leads directly to the second major issue: the role of the public sector in the transition process.

The Role of the Public Sector in the Transition Process

That the development of free markets and a vigorous private sector is the driving force and *raison d'être* of market-based economic reform is beyond question. A reading of the economic history of both newer and mature market-based economies in Asia, North America, and Western Europe demonstrates, however, that free markets and private enterprise do not emerge and cannot prosper in a macroeconomic vacuum. Rather, they require a conducive policy environment and an institutional support system that can deal with the kinds of market imperfections that, especially in the early stages of transition, frustrate the emergence of entrepreneurs and efficient markets.

More specifically, the vacuum created by the abandonment of command-based economics in Central and Eastern Europe has been filled by a truncated version of neo-classical free market economics that holds that private enterprise operating in a framework of market-determined prices all but eliminates the need for public sector participation at the macro-level in a nation's economy. While this view may have great ideological appeal, it is contrary to the real world experiences of Asian countries, such as Japan, South Korea, and Taiwan, and of non-Asian countries, such as the United States, Germany, and the United Kingdom. In each of these countries the public sector has played, and continues to play, a key role in strengthening and supporting the development of a vigorous private enterprise sector and efficient markets.

All but the free market's most ardent supporters acknowledge that some types of economy-wide activities that are required to encourage and support a growing private sector are beyond the time-frame, concerns, and resources of private investors. Responsibility for such activities has therefore been typically taken on, by design or default, by the public sector. The question, then, is not whether to intervene or not to intervene, but rather how the public sector can meet the macroeconomic policy, institutional, and programme needs of emerging market-based economies in a manner that will support, but not pre-empt or crowd out, the private sector.

Public Sector Functions and Responsibilities

The balance of responsibilities between the public and private sectors will differ from country to country reflecting, among other things, the country's resource endowments and its economy history, social structure, culture, and political system. Moreover, the public–private sector balance will shift as the transition to market systems proceeds, with increasing responsibility moving from the former to the latter.

This progressive shift in sector responsibilities notwithstanding, a core group of public sector policies and programmes has become a conventional feature of most, if not all, modern market-based economies. Abstracting from this general proposition, the institutions, policies, and programmes that are considered most important in encouraging, supporting and, as required, modifying the operations of market-oriented economies fall into six main categories.

1. Commercial Laws, Regulations, and Enforcement Machinery. The life-blood of a market-oriented economic system is the ability of individuals and groups to engage in myriad, simultaneous commercial transactions: to buy and sell products and services, to form and dissolve partnerships, to incorporate business firms, to start up or close down small businesses, to declare bankruptcy, to lend and borrow funds, to lease real property, to hire and fire workers, etc. Some of these transactions are evidenced by written contracts, others are unwritten. Each must be based on mutual trust and confidence and invested with unquestioned status and sanctity. These pre-conditions, in turn, require uniform, transparent, and codified commercial and civil laws, codes and regulations, backed and enforceable by a nation's highest public authority. By the same token, the resolution of commercial disputes must also be governed by uniform rules and regulations emanating from the national level; and, if required, by resort to independent, non-political tribunals. Regulation of natural monopolies and the prevention of commercial crimes and misdemeanours are also, by convention and long practice, public sector responsibilities.

2. Independent Central Bank and Integrated Commercial Banking System. An effective central bank is an indispensable requirement of a functioning market-based economy. The central bank in general operates within the framework of governmental policy but is free from day-to-day political influence. Its basic function is to ensure reasonable internal price stability and the soundness of the nation's currency and financial and fiscal institutions. For these reasons, the central bank is typically responsible for setting interest rate policy, determining aggregate money supply and credit creation, exchange rate policy, and other related elements of macro-financial management.

An integrated network of secure and adequately funded commercial financial institutions is also necessary to support the day-to-day operations of the private sector, and the central bank plays a key role in ensuring that this need is met. It is generally charged with chartering and supervising privately owned commercial banks and other financial institutions, for establishing banks' capitalization ratios and reserve requirements, and for helping to organize a nation-wide payments clearing system.

Particularly in the early stages of economic reform, the central bank may play an important role in stimulating savings and conserving foreign exchange, for example, by the selective use of differential interest rates, by organizing a network of national savings institutions, by promoting and supervising the development of money and capital markets, and by managing the country's foreign exchange resources and supervising its foreign exchange dealers. The central bank can, in addition, provide active support for the transition process by providing re-discounting facilities and other services to commercial banks and by the selective extension of credit to priority industries and sectors.

3. Essential Physical Infrastructure. In most transitional economies, infrastructure — power generation and distribution, transportation, communications, water resource management, etc. — is inadequate to meet the needs of an expanding market-based economy. Some of these infrastructure deficits can be met by private investors, with financing from dedicated fees or tolls, by Build-Operate-Transfer arrangements, or by temporary financial incentives.

In cases where infrastructure is too capital intensive or pays off over too long a period to attract private investment, it is most often undertaken at the national level. In the United States, for example, the Tennessee Valley Authority, the Interstate Highway System, and, more recently, the Internet Information Highway are cases in point. Once they are up and running, many of these facilities can be sold to private investors.

4. Extra-Economic Values. In their single-minded pursuit of economic efficiency, markets may not assign sufficient priority to a nation's longer-term, extra-economic values and objectives. These include, for example, maintaining public probity, safety, law and order; protecting the environment and natural resource base; ensuring literacy and education opportunities for all citizens; providing basic health research and facilities; and protecting the welfare of children, the elderly, and the disabled.

In most market-oriented nations, the government sector is expected to ensure that these extra-economic values are reasonably met. To do so requires the public sector to intervene in and modify the operations of markets through taxes, spending, subsidies, and other types of transfer payments. While the modification of market-based decisions is in such cases considered necessary, the pursuit of extra-market values should not be permitted to disrupt the efficient functioning of the nation's private enterprise sector and open markets.

5. International Economic and Financial Relations. The era when nations could ignore the impact of external factors on their domestic economies has long passed. All nations, large and small, developed and developing, are now participants in a global economy. While the myriad domestic and international trade, finance, and investment transactions that constitute the global economy are best left in the hands of private enterprise, the public sector cannot avoid responsibility for dealing, in close and continuing consultation with its private sector, with other national authorities whose actions affect its domestic and international commerce.

In the international arena, this involves participation and negotiations in multilateral economic organizations such as the United Nations, General Agreement on Tariffs and Trade (GATT), and the International Labour Organization (ILO). At a bilateral level it involves dealing with other governments on foreign assistance, Most Favoured Nation status, and specific bilateral trade arrangements concerning, for example, footwear, textiles, and apparel.

From a domestic perspective, this role may involve ensuring that the nation's firms and traders can compete on a level international playing field. Since most firms in transitional economies will be small and new, the government may have to adopt policies and programmes to support their growth and competitiveness by means, for example, of general or selective fiscal measures, incentives for needed foreign private capital and technology transfers, and GATT-accepted forms of infant-industry protection. Similarly, in order to support the development of a viable domestic industrial base, the public sector may find it necessary to channel foreign exchange resources to priority domestic investments, which may in turn involve a period of foreign exchange rationing and restrictions on capital exports.

6. Long-Term Perspective. As exemplified by Taiwan's approach, the government sector is perhaps the only place from which it is possible to view and assess a nation's economic passage from a broad, long-term perspective. Such a perspective is indispensable if a coherent, integrated approach to the transition process is to be formulated and acted upon. This top-down view provides the basis for a sector-by-sector assessment of comparative advantage and for formulating macroeconomic strategies, policies, and programmes, all of which are basic inputs into defining and implementing transition priorities. The later priorities typically include improving agricultural and industrial productivity and output; expanding exports; increasing domestic savings and investment; attracting foreign investment and technology; channelling financial and real resources to the most promising sectors and industries; and establishing long-term health, education, and welfare standards and facilities.

Summary and Conclusions

In sum, Asia's new transitional economies, Laos, Mongolia, Myanmar, and Vietnam, can learn from the experiences of Asian and Central and East European nations that embarked on the process of economic transformation before them. In so doing, Asia's new transitional economies will find it necessary to address a range of policy and programme issues that support and drive the transition process. Two in particular stand out.

The first involves the *tempo and sequencing* of the restructuring process. In essence, a satisfactory *tempo* is one that does not bracket the costs of transition within so short a time period that the public finds them too burdensome and abandons the reform effort. Conversely, economic restructuring should not stretch over so long a period as to make its benefits seem trivial.

The second aspect of this issue involves the *sequencing* of policy and programme actions. Developing a workable sequence of transition policies and programmes is no mean task. It requires, first, establishing a framework for viewing the national economy from an overall perspective and evaluating the relative strengths and weaknesses of its component sectors, institutions, and programmes. Second, it requires setting priorities and developing a transition strategy consistent with these assessments; and, third, designing policies and programmes to translate transition from the drawing-board to reality in logical sequential stages, within a reasonable time frame, and on the basis of a realistic assessment of resources.

Considerations of tempo and sequence lead to a second major issue: the role of the public sector in the transition process. For good reason there is a long history of the public sector in market-oriented countries assuming responsibility for macroeconomic activities of a broad institutional and policy nature. These activities encourage support, and, where necessary, modify the operations of the market-place and the private sector. The public sector's role in the national economy typically encompasses: (1) establishing commercial laws, regulations, and enforcement machinery; (2) creating an independent central bank and an integrated commercial banking system; (3) meeting essential infrastructure needs; (4) ensuring that the nation's non-economic values are respected; (5) conducting international economic and financial relations; and (6) providing a longer-term framework and vehicle for pursuing economic restructuring, development, and transition.

Notes

1. Taiwan's economic reform process is discussed in a series of lectures delivered by Dr Samuel C. Shieh, Governor of the Central Bank of China, Taipei. See, for example, *The 'Taiwan Miracle' in Economic Development — A Lesson for LDCs and Development Economists* (Madrid: School of Economics, Universidad Complutense de Madrid, 1994).

2. A discussion of these reform features can be found in Lee C.H. and H. Reisen, eds., *From Reform to Growth: China and Other Countries in Transition in Asia and Central and Eastern Europe* (Paris: OECD, 1994).

3. See Asian Development Bank, *Asian Development Outlook 1994* (Hong Kong: Oxford University Press, 1994).

4. Hong Kong is a special case. It has long been a free market-based city-state and did not face the range of economic development and transition needs of South Korea or Taiwan. Its authorities did not, therefore, find it necessary to formulate forward-looking development programmes. Although Singapore's restructuring needs were, for similar reasons, of a different character than those of other NIEs, Singapore's authorities did frame and implement a series of economic strategies and programmes.

5. European Bank for Reconstruction and Development, *Transition Report 1994* (London, 1994) presents a current assessment of transition progress in twenty-five countries of Central and Eastern Europe and the former Soviet Union.

6. See M. Goldman, *Lost Opportunity: Why Economic Reforms in Russia Have Not Worked* (New York: W.W. Norton, 1994).

References

Asian Development Bank. *Asian Development Outlook 1994*. Hong Kong: Oxford University Press, 1994.

———. *Key Indicators of Developing Asian and Pacific Countries*. Hong Kong: Oxford University Press, 1994.

Bruno, Michael. "Stabilization and Reform in Eastern Europe". *IMF Staff Papers*, 39.4, December 1992, pp. 741–77.

European Bank for Reconstruction and Development. *Annual Economic Review 1992*. London, 1993.

Goldman, Marshall. *Lost Opportunity: Why Economic Reforms in Russia Have Not Worked*. New York: W.W. Norton, 1994.

International Bank for Reconstruction and Development. *The East Asian Miracle: Economic Growth and Public Policy*. New York: Oxford University Press, 1993.

Katz, S. Stanley. "From Central Planning to a Market Economy: East Europe Should Learn From Asia". *Financial Times*, 24 April 1993.

Kirkpatrick, G. "Transition Experiences Compared: Lessons from Central and Eastern Europe's Reform". In *From Reform to Growth: China and Other Countries in Transition in Asia and Central and Eastern Europe*, edited by Lee C.H. and H. Reisen, pp. 95–118. Paris: OECD, 1994.

Rana, P.B. and Wilmelmina Paz. "Economies in Transition: The Asian Experience". In *From Reform to Growth: China and Other Countries in Transition in Asia and Central and Eastern Europe*, edited by Lee C.H. and H. Reisen, pp. 119–40. Paris: OECD, 1994.

Shieh, Samuel. *The 'Taiwan Miracle' in Economic Development — A Lesson for LDCs and Development Economists*. Madrid: School of Economics, Universidad Complutense de Madrid, 1994.

The Lessons of East Asian Success:
A Primer for Transitional Economies

Peter A. Petri

Introduction

East Asia is an ideal place to develop. Eight of the nine major economies of developing East Asia (China, Hong Kong, Indonesia, South Korea, Malaysia, the Philippines, Singapore, Taiwan, and Thailand) were among the twelve most rapidly growing economies of the world during the 1965–90 period. Had growth rates been randomly distributed across all developing economies, there is roughly one chance in a million that success would have turned out so regionally concentrated. Whether this 'coincidence' is due to common characteristics and strategies, or to interactions with fast-growing neighbours, there is clearly something significant about being East Asian.

The transitional economies of Southeast Asia — the new applicants to the club of East Asian miracles — have an advantage simply due to location. But will their success require following some optimal recipe of East Asian development? From the viewpoint of these economies, the analysis of the basis of East Asian success is not merely an academic exercise, but a critical step in the formulation of policy.

Empirical studies have shown that much of the East Asian growth can be attributed to exceptionally large investment in human and physical capital.[1] The most robust lessons are the simplest: education and investment are critical. But it is also true that the region's total factor productivity (TFP) growth rates are unusual, even after allowing for high savings and education. In a study of eighty-seven countries, Page and Petri (1993) found that Hong Kong, Japan, South Korea, Taiwan, and Thailand were within the top decile of all countries in terms of TFP growth rates, and that Indonesia, Malaysia, and Singapore were also significant achievers. These divergences are important, and perhaps they are related to more complex aspects of policy, including possibly an active government role.

This chapter examines the determinants of success in a broad group of East Asian countries, including the newly industrializing economies (NIEs) — Hong Kong, South Korea, Singapore, and Taiwan — as well as the next-tier miracles of East and Southeast Asia — Indonesia, Malaysia, and Thailand.[2] It also looks at a broad range of alternative theories and confronts these with country experience. The key finding is that no single explanation fits the wide range of East Asian case studies. The region's success stories are simply too diverse to yield any single recipe for success.

There are, nevertheless, important commonalities in the East Asian experience. These boil down to success along three basic dimensions of economic management. Each East Asian miracle involved (1) a stable environment that encouraged investment and enterprise; (2) powerful incentives to guide resources and initiative into efficient activities; and (3) some dynamic engine to provide leadership for high-speed growth. These common requirements, however, were achieved by a wide range of specific institutions and policies.

The policy combinations used to meet these requirements included market-oriented approaches as well as government intervention.[3] East Asian incentive systems ranged from unimpeded competition to vigorous government oversight, and growth engines from small-scale manufacturing to foreign investment. Fundamentally, East Asian economies met the three objectives of economic management with diverse policies, but in each case well fitted to domestic circumstances. They did not usually inherit successful policies, but rather created them through experimentation and reform.

These findings have several implications for the next group of East Asian miracles. First, not one, but several East Asian models need to be studied. The question is not "which is the best", but rather "which is the most relevant" to an imitator's initial conditions and environment. Second, the choices made at any given time are not likely to be right in all respects, and will have to be modified if they do not work. Monitoring and flexibility in adapting to changing circumstances are essential for long-term success.

Theories of the Miracles

There are at least four broad explanations of the East Asian miracles. Neoclassical approaches have emphasized outward orientation and macroeconomic discipline. Structuralist theories have singled out government leadership in industrial policy. Culturalist explanations have focused on governance and societal characteristics, as shaped by the region's Confucian traditions. Finally, it is possible that East Asia's dynamism is at least partly the result of the 'contagion effects' of regional success.

These four theories will be described very briefly below, with special attention given to their underlying logical elements. Based on these descriptions, we will later identify specific causal factors — policies, endowments, external circumstances — that are closely associated with the workings of each theory. The important of these factors will be then checked against country case histories (in the next section) in order to see how well each theory fits experience.

Neoclassical Explanations: Right Fundamentals

> The neutrality and stability of the incentive system, together with limited government interventions, well-functioning labor and capital markets, and reliance on private capital ... have been the main ingredients of successful economic performance in East Asia. (Balassa 1988, p. 288, as quoted in Chau 1993)

The first analyses of the East Asian miracles emphasized neoclassical causes by arguing that the NIEs "got the fundamentals right" in several key policy areas. In this view, East Asian economies succeeded because they came closer than other developing countries to providing (1) a stable macroeconomic environment for saving and investment and (2) a competitive, open economic structure for the spontaneous, efficient growth of enterprise. Modern versions of this approach retain the neoclassical thrust, but place somewhat more emphasis on investment, especially in human capital and infrastructure (World Bank 1991). Thus, East Asia's miracle economies:

1. *adopted an outward-oriented trade strategy* to build strong linkages with world markets and technology. They achieved this with policies ranging from complete liberalization to export promotion designed to offset protectionist biases favouring domestic industries;
2. *pursued conservative macroeconomic policies* to create a stable, predictable environment for investment and trade. Imbalances were addressed swiftly and decisively, keeping inflation low, exchange rates competitive, and debt affordable;
3. *invested vigorously in human capital* to develop an educated and technically competent labour force; and
4. *maintained competitive markets for factors* to facilitate the structural transformation from primary production to manufacturing and eventually to knowledge-intensive industries.

The empirical evidence summarized later confirms that East Asia performed better on these measures of accumulation and allocation that other developing countries.

Structuralist Explanations: Wrong Prices

> ... economic expansion depends on state intervention to create price distortions that direct economic activity toward greater investment. State intervention is necessary in even the most plausible cases of comparative advantage, because the chief asset of backwardness — low wages — is counterbalanced by heavy liabilities (Amsden 1989, p. 14).

Structuralist interpretations of East Asian success emphasize that policy regimes in many East Asian countries departed significantly from market-oriented norms. In the structuralist view, these interventions were key to the region's success, because it would not have been possible to develop infant industries and to upgrade the industrial structure without them. In more sophisticated variants of the argument, these interventions are seen as remedies for market failures in capital markets (Stiglitz 1989) and for externalities in the development of new industries (Pack and Westphal 1986). To overcome these common problems of early industrialization, the East Asian economies:

1. *created élite, autonomous bureaucracies* that could design and implement sectoral policies without becoming the tool of special interests. (The Confucian legacy of meritocratic government may have been essential in this respect.);
2. *targeted sectors that offered strong opportunities* for growth and productivity, based on the experiences of similar, more advanced economies (for example, Japan);[4]
3. *directed resources into targeted sectors* by 'getting prices wrong' with selective trade restrictions, preferential access to credit and important inputs, and government investment; and
4. *avoided big policy mistakes* by limiting the duration of government support and setting performance-oriented criteria, such as export success, for promoted firms.

Despite the far-reaching consequences of these arguments, there is little empirical evidence on the significance of market failures. As for East Asian experiences, relatively few economies examined followed structuralist policies for any significant length of time, and several abandoned intervention, or intervened in ways that cannot be reconciled with structuralist models.

Culturalist Explanations: Confucianism

> Four institutions and cultural practices rooted in the Confucian tradition but adapted to the needs of an industrial society — a meritocratic élite, an entrance exam system, the importance of the group, and the goal of self-improvement — have ... ignited the greatest burst of sustained economic growth the world has yet seen. (Vogel 1991, p. 101)

Chinese culture and Confucian traditions are important throughout East Asia and figure prominently in both Asian and Western interpretations of the miracles. The culturalist approach argues that Confucian traditions have had a large impact on the economic behaviour among agents, and on social organization and methods of governance. Specifically, Confucian cultures may have had an especially high propensity to undertake saving and educational investments, and may have given rise to strong, publicly motivated bureaucracies. Confucian traditions contributed to these objectives because they:

1. *emphasized group values over individual values,* giving rise to cohesive forms of political and business organizations;
2. *developed meritocratic institutions,* creating strong incentives for learning and education;
3. *created mutual obligations between government and the governed,* yielding (relatively) publicly motivated policy making; and
4. *legitimized authoritarian rule,* leading to long-term regimes and stable, consistent policies.

The country experiences suggest limits on the applicability of culturalist arguments. Confucian traditions were strong in the four NIEs, and even extended to Southeast Asia through significant Chinese minorities (Hamilton 1991). But in many successful economies the Confucian influence on governance — supposedly a key reason for its economic effect — was very limited.

Interaction Effects: *Contagion*

Although most previous writing has focused on variants of the above three approaches, the obvious common feature of the East Asian miracles is geography. East Asian development patterns are also more alike than might have been expected on the basis of similarities in resource endowments. This suggests that East Asian economic growth may have been partly induced by regional contacts — including flows of goods, investments, technologies, aspirations, and ideas about governance. Thus, individual East Asian economies might have been much more successful together than they would have been in isolation. Geographical proximity of East Asian countries may have:

1. *encouraged the imitation of each other's policies* by exposing policy makers to successes in similar, nearby economies;

2. *promoted the imitation of technologies and business strategies* by exposing entrepreneurs to the achievements of similar, nearby companies;
3. *expedited international trade* through low transport costs; and
4. *facilitated direct investment,* particularly by smaller firms, through cultural and ethnic ties based on history and migration.

Empirical studies show that physical distance is an important correlate of economic integration, and East Asia is well integrated through trading, investment, and migration relationships (Petri 1992). The contagion hypothesis helps to explain why growth was so spectacular, widely shared, and regionally concentrated, but it does not ultimately specify what caused East Asian growth.[5]

Causal Factors and Country Experience

Each of the approaches sketched so far points to a handful of critical determinants of East Asian success. This section collects the factors associated with all the approaches — altogether ten are identified — and confronts them with country experience.

Outward Orientation

Balassa (1981), Krueger (1985), and other neoclassical writers argue that openness to international trade has been the critical factor in the East Asian miracles. The neoclassical case for outward orientation rests on allocative gains associated with specialization according to comparative advantage, as well as dynamic gains associated with increased competition and access to international technology.

For different reasons, outward orientation is important in the contagion approach and is consistent with structuralist explanations. In the contagion theory, outward orientation facilitates the flow of goods, capital, technology, and ideas. In the structuralist model, outward orientation is not a goal *per se*, but the acquisition of international technology and entry into international markets are. Thus, outward orientation is not the objective, but the result of the successful, selective promotion of certain industrial sectors.

There is ample empirical evidence that international trade did play an unusually important role in nearly all the East Asian economies (for example, World Bank 1991, chap. 5). Even allowing for their small size, Hong Kong, Malaysia, and Singapore had some of the world's highest export/GDP (gross domestic product) ratios already in the 1960s and 1970s. South Korea, Taiwan, and Thailand also moved well above international norms after switching to outward-oriented policies. These rankings are clearly the result of policy choices. Hong Kong and Singapore eliminated trade restrictions early on; Malaysia, South Korea, and Taiwan shifted to export promotion by the 1960s; and Thailand and Indonesia have made considerable progress in the last decade.

In some East Asian economies — Hong Kong, Malaysia, and Singapore — outward orientation was clearly the result of neutral policies. In others — notably South Korea and Taiwan — outward orientation was achieved by promoting exports while keeping import barriers high. In the structuralist view, these policies worked because they channelled support to targeted industries. In the neoclassical view, they worked because the combination of import barriers and broad measures of export promotion added up to essentially neutral policies — they equalized incentives between exports and domestic production.

The thrust of the evidence is that East Asian economies were more neutral — less anti-export biased — than other developing countries. South Korea, Taiwan, and Singapore all had stronger overall export incentives than the non-East Asian countries in the study. But the debate is far from settled; some structuralists have criticized the methodology of the critical South Korean study (Westphal and Kim 1982; Balassa 1982), arguing that the measurements understate the extent of distortions in the South Korean and Taiwanese incentive systems.

Also important in East Asian development has been openness towards foreign investment. Several East Asian countries offered a hospitable investment environment, at a time when other developing countries still favoured protection and nationalization. The tools used to attract investment included tax incentives (Singapore between 1968 and 1973), export processing zones (Taiwan and Malaysia), and investment promotion (Thailand). At times, the results were spectacular: foreign investment in Malaysian export processing zones (EPZs) reached 19 per cent of GDP in 1975, while much of Singapore's industry is foreign owned. Indonesia, Malaysia, and Thailand also experienced major foreign investment booms.

Foreign investment provides a case study in the virtuous interaction of policy experiments, external factors, and policy imitation. In the late 1960s and early 1970s many investing countries were searching for new investment locations due to rising costs in Japan and uncertainties over Hong Kong and Southeast Asia. Singapore, Taiwan, and other East Asian host countries met this demand by offering concessions and improving their investment regulations. The resulting investments led to further incentives for policy changes in these host countries, as well as competitive policy reactions in others wishing to participate in the boom.

While foreign investment played an important role in several East Asian countries, South Korea also achieved rapid growth while strictly limiting foreign investment. As a result, South Korea's development trajectory evolved towards firms large enough to be able to develop their own technology. These firms also tended to specialize in the large-scale production of products in the relatively stable phase of their life cycle.

Macroeconomic Discipline

Steady economic growth and low rates of inflation provide a stable framework for long-term planning, and encourage saving, investment, and efficient resource use. Steady real exchange rates, in turn, encourage the production of goods that can be exported and thus contribute to openness. Finally, prudent fiscal policies help to increase the flow of resources into productive investments, and prevent the accumulation of debt, which can frighten investors away.

East Asia has been unusually successful on most indicators of macroeconomic stability. Thomas and Wang (forthcoming) show that inflation rates were only half as high, on average, as in other lower-middle income countries (LMICs) in the 1977–90 period. Real interest rates averaged a positive 4 per cent, compared to a negative 3 per cent in other LMICs, ensuring good returns on savings and clearly indicating the cost of capital. Real exchange rates were generally competitive and less variable than exchange rates elsewhere, and less debt was accumulated.

East Asian governments kept public sector deficits well below developing country averages under a wide range of institutions (Thomas and Wang, forthcoming). In Hong Kong, Taiwan, and Singapore, conservative governments ran budget surpluses. In Thailand Parliament could reduce expenditures, but not increase them (Christensen et al., forthcoming). In Indonesia an open capital account imposed external discipline: when oil prices were high, the government limited borrowing to avoid revaluation, and when oil prices fell, it switched to austerity to prevent capital flight (Bhattacharya and Pangestu, forthcoming).

Realistic exchange rates were a hallmark of East Asian macroeconomic policy. Several of the dynamic economies began with major exchange rate reforms — devaluations, exchange rate unification, and commitment to competitive real exchange rates. Some economies even kept exchange rates undervalued (Taiwan in the 1960s and all of the NIEs in the 1980s) in order to build export market shares (Petri 1988). Although initially adopted to solve some balance of payments problem (such as the withdrawal of American aid), undervalued exchange rates were so successful in generating export growth that they became a policy objective in several countries.

Real exchange rates did become overvalued and public sector deficits did emerge from time to time (Malaysia in the mid-1970s, South Korea in the late 1970s, and Indonesia in the mid-1980s). But the periods of disequilibrium were short-lived; each triggered devaluations and decisive retrenchments in a short period of time. The unusual flexibility of East Asian economies helped to speed the resulting adjustments. Thus, while East Asian countries have macroeconomic difficulties, they have reacted more quickly and adjusted less painfully than others.

High Rates of Saving and Investment

High saving rates feature prominently in both neoclassical and structuralist interpretations of the East Asian miracles. In the neoclassical framework, high saving rates are the intervening variable between sound macroeconomic and financial policies and high rates of investment. In the structuralist framework, high rates of saving are the result of a government investment effort, which mobilizes capital from public enterprises or private investors.

East Asian saving and investment rates are exceptional by world standards, but whether they stimulate growth or are a product of it is less clear. Three countries with especially high saving rates now — Indonesia, South Korea, and Singapore — saved 10 per cent or less in the 1960s and borrowed heavily in international markets. By the 1990s, East Asian savings were significantly above world norms, but this could have been a result, rather than condition, of their success.

The countries that did achieve high savings did so in different ways. Taiwan encouraged private savings with high interest rates and a large, reliable postal savings system (Dahlman and Sananikone, forthcoming). South Korea also achieved high private savings, but with low, regulated deposit rates. Hong Kong relied on public savings, financed by the development of 'crown land'. And Singapore mobilized resources through its Central Provident Fund, which at one time imposed a 50 per cent wage contribution from employers and employees.

Effective public investments in infrastructure are cited in both structuralist and recent neoclassical theories on East Asian success. Hong Kong and Singapore established major public housing programmes and invested heavily in transportation and communications. Malaysia, Taiwan, and Singapore built industrial estates, and South Korea and Thailand developed extensive road networks (Christensen et al., forthcoming). But on the whole, most East Asian countries typically faced infrastructure constraints, suggesting that infrastructure investments at best accommodated, and not led, economic growth.

Human capital investments are prominent in all models of East Asian success. East Asian educational enrolment variables were already high compared to international norms in the 1960s (when the miracles were getting under way). East Asia's more advanced economies then rapidly increased secondary enrolment rates to nearly the Organization for Economic Co-operation and Development (OECD) levels, and developed special programmes for promoting technical skills. Singapore targets 4 per cent of earnings for training (Soon and Tan, forthcoming) and Taiwan trains more scientists and engineers per capita than Japan, Germany, or the United States (Dahlman and Sananikone, forthcoming).

But educational achievements are also high in East Asia's least successful market economy (the Philippines) as well as many Latin American and East European countries. Thomas and Wang (forthcoming) find that educational expenditures, as a percentage of GDP, are now lower in East Asia than in other LMICs. If human capital accumulation in East Asia is unique, it is not because of the current scale of the public educational effort. Rather, East Asia appears to stand out in the quality and possibly technical orientation of its educational programmes, and in its broad-based, private commitment to learning.

State Enterprises

Neoclassical analyses typically credit East Asian governments for confining their attention to infrastructure and avoiding direct production (Wolf 1988). Structuralist writing credits them with launching many new industries which private entrepreneurs were unwilling or unable to start (Wade 1990). The true picture is mixed. Thomas and Wang (forthcoming) find somewhat less intervention in East Asia than in other LMICs, and East Asian government spending rates appear to be near international norms.

State-owned enterprises (SOEs) played major roles in several East Asian countries. Singapore's government-linked companies (GLCs) accounted for 23 per cent of the assets of larger firms in 1986 (Soon and Tan, forthcoming) and Indonesia's SOEs produced 60 per cent of its manufacturing output in 1987. Thailand's industrialization began with state investments, and Malaysia's 'velvet nationalization'[6] substantially increased public ownership in the 1970s. SOEs have been also prominent in South Korea (steel, fertilizer, machinery) and Taiwan (steel, automobiles, shipbuilding, petrochemicals). Over time, the role of SOEs has been declining — in Taiwan, for example, SOEs' share of manufacturing output fell from 51 per cent in 1955 to 19 per cent in 1990 (Dahlman and Sananikone, forthcoming).

The critical point is that East Asian SOEs were unusually profitable. South Korea's POSCO and Taiwan's China Steel are among the world's most efficient steel producers, and Singapore's GLCs are nearly three times as profitable relative to assets as other firms (Soon and Tan, forthcoming). There are, of course, also unsuccessful SOEs in countries such as Indonesia and Malaysia, but the overall record is surprisingly good. It appears that SOEs have neither prevented nor most likely created the East Asian miracles.[7]

Industrial Policy

Structuralists see the selective support for new industrial activities as the signature of East Asian development strategy (Amsden 1989; Pack and Westphal 1986; Wade 1990). In this view, carefully targeted subsidies and protection enabled entrepreneurs to enter new industries by reducing costs and risks. Industrial policies became ineffective only when they became too ambitious, and tried to promote too many sectors at once (Pack and Westphal 1986).

The neoclassical view is that targeting was as likely to create losers as winners, and probably slowed the natural upgrading of industry by diverting resources into inefficient capital-intensive uses. Selective policies may have also wasted resources by encouraging rent-seeking activity (Krueger 1974). Most East Asian governments launched some industrial policy scheme: Singapore attempted a 'Second Industrial Revolution', Taiwan an 'Industrial Escalation', South Korea a 'Heavy and Chemical Industry' (HCI) drive, Hong Kong an 'Industrial Diversification' programme, Malaysia a 'Heavy Industrialization' push, and so on. South Korea's HCI drive is perhaps the most thoroughly analysed and most ambitious among these initiatives. Amsden (1989) credits South Korea HCI policies with a major role in technological upgrading. The World Bank (1987) is more neutral, noting that the drive established some dynamic industries, but also resulted in costly failures. Most retrospective analyses are critical; they argue that the HCI drive diverted capital from labour-intensive industries into inefficient capital-intensive projects (Yoo 1990). Subsidized lending to HCI projects also weakened the financial sector and increased concentration — problems that continue to haunt South Korean policy today.

Elsewhere, industrial targeting was more constrained. Taiwan provided selective support for steel, petrochemicals, automobiles, and shipbuilding; the first two succeeded, the second two failed (Dahlman and Sananikone, forthcoming). Taiwan's most dynamic sectors (apparel, electronics, and computers) had little selective support, but considerable functional support through EPZs and research institutes. In only five years Malaysia's heavy industry push created a host of low-profit enterprises in cement, steel, motor vehicles, and motor cycles (Salleh, Yeah, and Meyanathan, forthcoming). In general the region's most ambitious industrial policy initiatives (for example, in South Korea, Singapore, Malaysia, and Thailand) were scaled back or abandoned within five or ten years after they were initiated.

The unambiguously successful industrial policies were those that reinforced ongoing transformations in industrial structure. South Korea's early, general export subsidies led to a dramatic surge in trade. Taiwan's industrial estates, EPZs, and research centres helped to encourage small-scale, labour-intensive manufacturing, especially electronics. Singapore's investments in sophisticated infrastructure — including the first fibre-optic telecommunications systems outside the OECD[8] — helped to attract a new wave of advanced services.

Financial Interventions

East Asia provides an interesting test case for the structuralist position that mild financial repression (as implemented through interest rate regulations and state-owned banking) can improve the efficiency of financial intermediation (Stiglitz 1989). In the early stages of development, problems of asymmetric information may be serious due to rapid change and a lack of institutions that collect and disseminate credit data. In this setting unregulated interest rates could rise to very high levels in order to cover default risk, and credit can become unavailable for low-risk projects. Interest rate ceilings solve the problem by motivating intermediaries to ration credit and to invest in information on borrowers.

East Asia's mechanisms of financial intermediation have ranged from highly regulated, state-controlled banking systems in South Korea and Indonesia[9] to competitive, private banking in Hong Kong, Malaysia, and Thailand. In between, many countries operated dualistic systems, with regulated markets providing capital for large-scale industry, and unregulated curb markets financing smaller enterprises. On average, the region's economies were relatively monetized, and the region's ubiquitous, cohesive extended families played an important role in small-scale finance.

In South Korea an unusual two-step intermediation process emerged: credit was sold wholesale to conglomerates (at low, rationed rates) which then used internal credit markets to distribute funds to the most creditworthy subsidiaries across many industries (Lee 1992). Credit regulation may have encouraged rationing, but also invited continued government involvement in the allocation of credit. One result was that banks were required to lend to highly leveraged, risky borrowers. This systematically weakened South Korea's major banks, making the transition to a market-oriented system especially difficult.

Relatively unregulated domestic and foreign banks financed development in Malaysia, Hong Kong, Singapore, and Thailand. In Thailand private banks even assumed a role in sectoral co-ordination by reconciling conflicts over protection (Christensen et al., forthcoming). In Taiwan regulated government-owned banks coexisted with a large unregulated curb market. This market, legitimized by an unusual Negotiable Instruments Law which required issuers to honour post-dated checks, played a central role in financing Taiwan's important small-scale manufacturing sector (Dahlman and Sananikone, forthcoming).

Thus, East Asian finance is not characterized by any specific intermediation structure. The overall evidence is inconclusive: both highly regulated public and relatively open private banking systems have seen their share of financial turmoil, and yet succeeded in financing rapid growth.

Élite Bureaucracies

A key structuralist argument is that the high quality of government institutions was responsible for the East Asian success (Johnson 1982, 1987). East Asia had strong developmental states, distinguished by (1) high-level commitment to economic objectives from powerful leaders, (2) mechanisms, such as one-party states, for sheltering economic decisions from the political process, and (3) unusually powerful and capable élite bureaucracies.

Each element of this picture has varid across the East Asian experience. High-level leadership was important in South Korea, Indonesia, Singapore, and Taiwan, but the political context was more fluid elsewhere. In order to balance complex ethnic interests,

Malaysia often subordinated economic to distributional objectives (Salleh, Yeah, and Meyanathan, forthcoming) and its policy directions changed with successive prime ministers. In Thailand, with short-lived exceptions, economic policies typically took a back seat to political and military issues.

The character of bureaucracies was also variable. Small, élite agencies with authority over line ministries assumed major responsibilities in South Korea (Economic Planning Board), Taiwan (Council for Economic Planning and Development and its precursors), and Singapore (Economic Development Board). Singapore's Economic Development Board, for example, was purposefully kept small by reassigning routine functions to other agencies (Soon and Tan, forthcoming). Not only were these agencies unusually competent, but they also often had budgetary authority to impose their viewpoint on other ministries.

But there were no super ministries in Hong Kong or Indonesia, and the corresponding bodies in Malaysia (Economic Planning Unit) and Thailand (National Economic and Social Development Board) had little budgetary authority and made only broad, indicative plans. In Indonesia the top technocrats were so concerned about their limited microeconomic influence that they took pre-emptive measures — such as opening the capital account, contracting customs to a Swiss firm, and eventually liberalizing credit and trade — to limit discretion in other parts of government. While government institutions are important under government-led growth strategies, they were not a key factor in several East Asian success stories. Some countries with 'model' institutions used them in limited ways, and others pursued strategies that did not rely heavily on bureaucratic capacity.

Confucian Culture

The culturalist school attributes East Asian success to the pervasive role of Confucian traditions in much of East Asia.[10] Vogel (1991) sees Confucianism, in conjunction with other factors, as a very positive force because of its (1) legacy of meritocratic bureaucracies; (2) emphasis on learning; (3) focus on the group rather than the individual; and (4) stress on self-improvement.

Educational effort was indeed high in East Asia, and especially so in the economies with the strongest Confucian traditions (Hong Kong, South Korea, Taiwan, and Singapore). East Asian performance is especially outstanding in educational results (rather than in educational spending), suggesting a broad private commitment to education. These same four economies also developed exceptional bureaucracies, and three of them pursued relatively effective interventionist development strategies.

Despite the general Confucian emphasis on groups and authority, East Asian business–government and social relationships were varied and often contentious. Singapore came closest to the idealized relationship in its business–labour–government councils. South Korea tried to develop similar institutions in the 1980s, but its business–labour–government relations remain contentious.[11] Taiwan's government initially viewed the private sector suspiciously, but later established co-operative contacts. Social relations in Indonesia, Malaysia, and Thailand have been typical of developing countries in general, involving informal, symbiotic relationships between business and political élites (Yoshihara 1988).

The most difficult challenge facing the culturalist models is to explain why economies with traditions that are so conducive to development have only recently embarked on rapid growth. In addressing this issue, recent writings have emphasized interactions between Confucian traditions and other factors. Lim (1990) argues that "Sinic culture contains the potential for absorbing modern science and technology", but the realization of this potential requires a modernizing government and "the adoption of a free-enterprise system" (p. 50). Similarly, Chen (1988) finds that Confucian traditions are only beneficial in conjunction with a broad and high-level commitment to economic modernization.

Confucian traditions may have contributed to development in four of the seven East Asian states by encouraging education and high-quality bureaucratic control. However, other East Asian economies with weaker bureaucracies also succeeded by adopting strategies that placed more modest demands on the bureaucratic competence. Apparently, Confucian traditions played a positive role only in the context of other favourable institutions and policies. In other, earlier contexts, Weber (1951) believed that Confucianism was anti-modernizing, and Moroshima (1982) felt that only Japanese

Confucianism was conducive to development. Thus, while clearly consistent with fast growth, Confucianism appears to be neither sufficient nor necessary for it.

Imitation of the East Asian Model

East Asian countries benefited from each other's success in a variety of ways, including the imitation of their neighbours' successful policies. South Korea, Singapore, Malaysia, and several other East Asian countries were conscious and successful imitators — initially of Japan's industrial strategy, and later of each other's outward-oriented policies. For example, South Korea's general trading companies, patterned on Japan's, spearheaded the country's export drive in the 1970s and 1980s. South Korea's duty drawback and export financing schemes in turn attracted attention in several ASEAN countries and eventually throughout the world. Taiwan's and Singapore's early innovations in EPZs were also extensively replicated.

Although most countries took advantage of the experiences of neighbours, there is little evidence (with the possible exception of South Korea and Japan) of wholesale imitation. Many countries were selective in using foreign models; South Korea looked to Japan to build international-scale companies but did not always start by serving domestic markets; Malaysia focused on heavy industry but ran a relatively open trade regime; and Taiwan and Singapore encouraged knowledge-intensive industries without first undertaking an extensive heavy industry drive. Most countries were generally skeptical about the Japanese model, especially in the Southeast Asian context (Soesastro 1985).

Thus, while much copying of institutions took place, there is little evidence that countries could replicate each other's successes merely by copying policies. Institutional borrowing was not always successful; thus, while Japanese-style trading companies thrive in South Korea, they could not be replicated in Thailand.[12] The most important factor may have been the imitation of the basic commitment to an outward-oriented approach. In the details, the region's technocrats ultimately developed different and unique institutions suited to the requirements of their own economies.

Favourable External Environment

East Asia's outward-oriented strategies benefited from the expanding and increasingly open world markets of the 1960s and 1970s. Some features of this early period especially favoured structuralist approaches. In the 1970s, because their penetration of the world economy was still modest, East Asian producers were not penalized for export subsidy programmes that would be unacceptable today. They could easily license or reverse engineer critical technologies. And they could profitably enter markets for relatively standardized, capital-intensive products such as steel, something that would not be possible under today's competitive conditions.

In the 1990s new entrants into international markets are under great pressure to follow global trading rules, particularly regarding subsidies and dumping. Even if a country obeys these rules, it may face pressures to restrain exports when it penetrates deeply into a particular market. And, since firms in advanced countries are to transfer technology to potential East Asian competitors, the environment no longer favours strategies based on the independent or arm's-length acquisition of technology.

Although entering markets is more complex, East Asia remains an attractive production location. East Asian latecomers can acquire know-how from similar, nearby countries, without bearing the risks associated with pioneering investments. They can also 'plug into' marketing and sourcing networks that were established by trade contacts between developed countries and prior East Asian suppliers. Restrictions on the exports of more advanced East Asian exporters (initially Japan, but later also the NIEs) can create special opportunities for new entrants. South Korean, Taiwanese, and now Indonesian, Thai, and Chinese producers of garments, shoes, television sets, automobiles, and other products have entered American markets this way (Petri 1988).

On the whole, East Asia's external environment remains favourable: developed country markets continue to be important, and the region is well positioned in the most dynamic market of all — its own. But the implications of the environment are changing: while interventionist, outward-oriented strategies worked well during the early East Asian dynamic growth, relatively open investment and trade policies are generating the best results today. Smaller, entrepreneurial companies are better able to penetrate foreign markets than large companies that require high levels of production to break even, and foreign investments, joint ventures, and alliances are the best routes to competitive technology.

Towards a Synthesis

The range of East Asian experiences is extraordinary. South Korea and, to a lesser extent, Taiwan built their success on activist industrial policies. They controlled the financial sector, managed trade barriers strategically, and targeted industries with government investments and/or subsidies. Their success establishes the *feasibility*, if not the *necessity*, of an activist strategy. At the other extreme, Hong Kong, Singapore, and now southern coastal China opened their economies to trade, investment, and entrepreneurship from abroad. They offered stability and good access, initially, to low-cost labour, and eventually to high skills and sophisticated infrastructure. Interestingly, this same objective was achieved with *laissez-faire* policies in Hong Kong and intervention in Singapore.

Malaysia, Indonesia, and Thailand pursued strategies in between, combining a market-friendly environment with varying degrees of intervention. Well endowed with natural resources, they initially focused on raw materials. When these industries ran up against limits, they quickly switched to export-oriented manufacturing, in close co-operation with foreign merchants and investors. These economies did protect some industrial sectors, but on the whole were open to foreign trade and investment. To keep their international links intact, they maintained political and macroeconomic stability.

Each of the factors examined in the previous section offers insight into one or another of these success stories, but none fits the full diversity of regional experience. The lessons of the East Asian miracles must therefore admit multiple recipes for success. In previous 'single-factor' approaches, the region's success has been typically attributed to some single cause or cluster of determinants. In an alternative 'multi-factor' approach, success may be associated with several different policies, which can be seen as alternative ways for accomplishing some basic development objective.

Multiple Solutions to Key Functions

Underneath the enormous range of East Asian policies and institutions lie important, common aspects of economic management. For example, while South Korean development was spearheaded by private, domestic firms, and Singapore's by foreign subsidiaries and government-linked companies, both countries satisfied the common requirement for entrepreneurship in ways suited to their particular environment. The three fundamental objectives of development can be likened to the requirements for a 'track', 'steering', and an 'engine'.

Development requires a smooth track to facilitate economic growth, consisting of stable macroeconomic conditions, adequate infrastructure, and market-oriented institutions. It requires efficient steering to guide resources into economically productive industries instead of waste, speculation, and rent-seeking. Finally, it requires a powerful engine — leadership from a vital sector or entrepreneurial class that will transform economic opportunity into rapid development. East Asia's miracle economies met all three requirements, and did so with a remarkably wide range of institutions and policies.

Track

East Asia's economic environment was generally conducive to market-oriented activity. Policies favoured macroeconomic stability, competitive labour markets, relatively free entry into small-scale business, and vigorous investment in human and physical capital. To be sure, these favourable conditions did not always lead to rapid growth, and growth spurts sometimes occurred without all these in place. The correlation between the economic environment and growth is strong enough to suggest an essential linkage, but not so strong as to make the environment the single, sufficient cause of rapid growth.

The value of a market-oriented environment was enhanced in many East Asian economies by the exceptional flexibility of economic agents. Chau (forthcoming) argues that Hong Kong's entrepreneurs were not committed to any particular business or technology, but true to merchant traditions, continuously floated to niches of profitable activity. Kim and Leipziger (forthcoming) note similar tendencies in South Korea's middle-sized firms, which spanned several industries and rapidly changed their product mix to exploit trends. More fundamentally, this flexibility may be the result of history: the collapse of the traditional power structure due to war, colonialism, and shifting political and economic ties.

Market-oriented macroeconomic environments evolved in East Asia under several different government institutions and philosophies. In South Korea and Taiwan strong governments maintained stable policies; in Indonesia and Thailand stable policies resulted from self-imposed constraints on budgetary procedures and/or international financial commitments. South Korea created competitive labour markets by suppressing unions; Singapore by inviting organized labour into governmental councils. Each track provided a favourable environment for markets, but closely fitted the country's institutional framework.

Steering

East Asian economies excelled at channelling entrepreneurial and other resources into efficient activities. Because they were outward oriented, most of these economies used international competitiveness as a yardstick of economic success. Even state enterprises, though less exposed to market pressures, were often directed to become internationally competitive, and thus pursued economic rather than political goals.

International prices entered East Asia's domestic incentive systems in different ways. In Hong Kong, Singapore, and Malaysia levels of protection were low, and all firms faced international prices. In South Korea the government used export performance to determine access to subsidized credit and other privileges. In Taiwan and several other countries export-oriented firms were exempted from import duties and thus faced essentially international prices, while domestically oriented firms operated under conditions of intense competition.

State-owned enterprises were also typically accountable on economic criteria. In South Korea, Singapore, and Taiwan public companies were directed by professional managers isolated from political pressure. Public enterprises were often designed to export and had to meet international competitive standards. Over time, as their private sectors matured, East Asian economies also moved to reduce the role of public enterprises. Taiwan systematically divested its extensive industrial holdings. As more inefficiencies developed in the public sectors of Indonesia and Malaysia, these governments also embarked on privatization programmes.

Engines

The engines of growth differed widely across East Asia. Hong Kong's miracle began with a large influx of capitalists from Shanghai. Experienced in textile manufacturing, these entrepreneurs diverted machinery and intermediate goods shipments bound for China, and set up relatively large manufacturing operations. Four decades later, Hong Kong's own merchant entrepreneurs found a new niche as intermediaries between China and the world — incidentally also driving southern China's economic take-off.

South Korea's dynamism derived from a handful of large conglomerates financed by low cost, government-controlled credit. Initially selected on the basis of personal connections, the list of promoted firms was constantly pruned according to economic performance. Government policies amplified market signals: successful firms not only earned profits, but also won access to fresh capital and lucrative investment opportunities (Petri 1990). By allocating capital across a wide range of business activities, these conglomerates also helped to mitigate inefficiencies in capital markets.

Singapore relied on foreign firms. The island's initial attraction was based on low-cost labour, tax concessions, and its location along major shipping lanes. As Singapore's advantages shifted to skilled labour, foreign investment also shifted to technologically advanced industries and services. Singapore dramatically upgraded its economic base with little control over its industry and minimal sectoral intervention.

The developmental engines of Malaysia, Indonesia, and Thailand have shifted from natural resource products — rice in Indonesia and Thailand, metals and oil crops in Malaysia — to manufacturing. Flexible exchange rates and foreign direct investment played an important role in the transition.

The fit between these engines and their economic environment is remarkable. In the context of the relatively free-wheeling economic systems of Malaysia and Thailand, for example, it would have been virtually impossible to implement effectively the kind of government intervention in business investment that was practised in South Korea. In the context of South Korea's institutions, in turn, it would have been just as difficult to imagine the development of harmonious relations between the bureaucracy and foreign firms, as enjoyed in Singapore.

Fitting the Model to the Environment

A key implication of a multi-factor approach to East Asian success is that policy options must be closely fitted to a country's circumstances. Necessity often played a role in forging the right fit. South Korea and Taiwan both adopted equilibrium exchange rate policies and aggressive export promotion when their main source of foreign exchange — aid from the United States — suddenly slowed. Hong Kong and Singapore also had little choice but to emphasize trade when their historical entrepôt function was disrupted by political changes. Much later, the collapse of oil prices also pushed Indonesia towards realistic exchange rates and outward-oriented trade policies.

Other major policy choices resulted from experimentation, learning, and adjustment. East Asian policies have generally evolved through incremental adjustments, as in the trade liberalization and investment incentive measures in South Korea, Taiwan, and Thailand. East Asian economies have been also prompt in recognizing serious policy mistakes and adopting corrective measures. Important examples include the reversal of heavy industry initiatives in South Korea, Malaysia, and Singapore.

Two characteristics of East Asian governance may explain their unusual ability to adapt. One is the longevity of East Asian governments. Enjoying indefinite tenures, governments are more willing to accept short-term sacrifice for long-term benefits. Second, in many East Asian countries, bureaucracies have considerable leeway in designing and executing policy. Finally, they generally keep in close contact with the private sector, helping to generate a continuous flow of information on the consequences of policy.

Implications for Transitional Economies

This chapter argues that the commonalities in East Asian development strategy must be sought not in policies, but in functional aspects of economic management. Rapid development does not call for a specific policy recipe, but does require a set of policies that achieve fundamental goals. These include creating an environment that encourages market-oriented investment; establishing mechanisms for steering resources into efficient activities; and finding an engine of growth to generate dynamism and leadership.

How these objectives are best achieved in a particular transitional economy will depend in part of the external environment. In general, world markets today are not willing to tolerate large export subsidies, and many of the technologies required to participate aggressively in world markets cannot be acquired by reverse engineering. This argues for more import and investment liberalization than was the case with the economies that based their development on export promotion in the 1960s.

The government's capacity to manage the details of economic strategy is also important. Government-directed models of development are risky, because their performance depends critically on the quality of leaders and bureaucracies. Although some countries have succeeded under government-directed models, many have done poorly. Until the transitional economies acquire the experience needed to manage a complex market economy, it may be unnecessary and inappropriate to choose strategies that require government involvement in microeconomic choices.

The general lessons of East Asian experiences boil down to common sense rules. A stable, market-oriented environment (at least for a substantial leading sector of the economy) is essential for growth. High rates of investment in human and physical capital are also important for sustained progress. Outward orientation — which can be achieved in various ways — is an invaluable conduit for technology and a close correlate of productivity growth.

Beyond these basics, there is a need for a good steering system (for example, government or market monitoring of performance) and for an area of special growth — a leading sector. These objectives can be achieved with more or less government intervention, and with more or less private enterprise. But they must be accomplished efficiently, by the yardstick of international prices. While some countries have satisfied these requirements with effective bureaucratic initiative, both the internal and international risks of following an interventionist approach argue for simpler, more market-friendly alternatives.

Notes

1. The literature on cross-country empirical tests of the sources of growth is examined more fully in Page and Petri (1993). Sections of this chapter draw on the author's contribution to the East Asian miracle study, Peter A. Petri, "Common Foundations of East Asian Success", in *Lessons of East Asia: A Country Studies Approach*, edited by Danny M. Leipziger (Ann Arbor: University of Michigan Press, forthcoming).
2. China and the Philippines are potential candidates for inclusion in this analysis, but are excluded because their political context and hence economic policy framework have differed considerably from those of the other seven East Asian economies. Japan is also excluded because it had reached a high level of industrialization by World War II.
3. This surface diversity of institutions and policies is why the East Asian experience has proved to be so difficult to interpret, and why it is widely used to defend contradictory development strategies.
4. If market failures are systematically associated with early stages of development, it may be relatively easy to identify appropriate interventions and to choose sectoral winners.
5. The contagion hypothesis has points in common with the Japanese 'flying geese' model, which argues that latecomers follow the development patterns of economies in more advanced stages of growth (Akamatsu 1960).
6. These initiatives, developed under Malaysia's New Economic Policy in 1971, were designed to increase Malay (*bumiputra*) ownership of productive assets. In effect, state holding companies assumed the ownership of enterprises on behalf of the *bumiputra*.
7. The excellent performance of many East Asian SOEs does provide models for operating such firms elsewhere. Successful firms have been operated with professional management, at arm's length from government control and with clear incentives for profitability.
8. Soon and Tan (forthcoming).
9. These characterizations apply to conditions until the mid-1980s. Both South Korea and Thailand have now privatized major banks, and Indonesia in particular has also deregulated most of their operations.

10. Hong Kong, South Korea, Singapore, and Taiwan directly reflect these traditions, but people of Chinese ancestry also play disproportionately important roles in the economies of Indonesia, Malaysia, and Thailand.
11. Jones and Sakong (1980) provide an excellent survey of South Korean government–business relations in the early post-war period.
12. See the case of Thailand (Christensen et al., forthcoming).

References

Akamatsu, K. "A Theory of Unbalanced Growth in the World Economy". *Weltwirtschaftliches Archiv* 86, no. 2 (1960).

Amsden, Alice H. *Asia's Next Giant*. New York: Oxford University Press, 1989.

Aoki, Masahiko. "Toward an Economic Model of the Japanese Firm". *Journal of Economic Literature* 28, no. 1 (March 1990), pp. 1–27.

Balassa, Bela. *The Newly Industrializing Economies in the World Economy*. New York: Pergamon Press, 1981.

———. *Development Strategies in Semi-Industrializing Economies*. Baltimore: Johns Hopkins Press, 1982.

———. "The Lessons of East Asian Development: An Overview". *Economic Development and Cultural Change* 36, no. 3 (April 1988).

Bhattacharya, Amar and Mari Pangestu. "Indonesia: Development Transformation since 1965 and the Role of Public Policy". In *Lessons of East Asia: A Country Studies Approach*, edited by Danny M. Leipziger. Ann Arbor: University of Michigan Press, forthcoming.

Chau Leung Chuen. "An Analysis of Postwar Economic Growth in Hong Kong with Specific Reference to the Role of Government". In *Lessons of East Asia: A Country Studies Approach*, edited by Danny M. Leipziger. Ann Arbor: University of Michigan Press, forthcoming.

Chen, Edward K. *Hypergrowth in Asian Economies: A Comparative Survey of Hong Kong, Japan, Korea, Singapore and Taiwan*. London: Macmillan Press, 1979.

Chen, E. K. Y. "The Economics and Non-Economics of Asia's Four Little Dragons". University of Hong Kong, *Supplement to the Gazette* 35, no. 1 (21 March 1988).

Chenery, Hollis, Sherman Robinson, and Moshe Syrquin. *Industrialization and Growth: A Comparative Study*. New York: Oxford University Press for the World Bank, 1986.

Christensen, Scott R., David Dollar, Ammar Siamwalla, and Pakorn Vichyanond. "Institutional and Political Bases of Growth-Inducing Policies in Thailand". In *Lessons of East Asia: A Country Studies*

Approach, edited by Danny M. Leipziger. Ann Arbor: University of Michigan Press, forthcoming.

Corbo, Vittorio, Anne O. Krueger, and Fernando Ossa, eds. *Export-Oriented Development Strategies: The Success of Five Newly Industrializing Countries*. Boulder: Westview Press, 1985.

Dahlman, Carl J. and Ousa Sananikone. "Economic Policies and Institutions in the Rapid Growth of Taiwan (China)". In *Lessons of East Asia: A Country Studies Approach*, edited by Danny M. Leipziger. Ann Arbor: University of Michigan Press, forthcoming.

Fry, Maxwell J. *Money, Interest and Banking in Economic Development*. Baltimore: Johns Hopkins, 1988.

Gerschenkron, Alexander. *Economic Backwardness in Historical Perspective*. Cambridge: Harvard University Press, 1962.

Hamilton, Gary, ed. *Business Networks and Economic Development in East and Southeast Asia*. Hong Kong: Hong Kong University Press, 1991.

Johnson, Chalmers. *MITI and the Japanese Miracle*. Stanford: Stanford University Press, 1982.

– – –. "Political Institutions and Economic Performance: The Government–Business Relationship in Japan, South Korea and Taiwan". In *The Political Economy of the New Asian Industrialism*, edited by Frederic C. Deyo. Ithaca: Cornell University Press, 1987.

Jones, Leroy and Il Sakong. *Government, Business and Entrepreneurship in Economic Development: The Korean Case*. Cambridge: Harvard University Press, 1980.

Kim, Kihwan and Danny M. Leipziger. "Korea: The Case of Effective Government-Led Development". In *Lessons of East Asia: A Country Studies Approach*, edited by Danny M. Leipziger. Ann Arbor: University of Michigan Press, forthcoming.

Krueger, Anne O. "The Political Economy of Rent Seeking Society". *American Economic Review* 64, no. 3 (1974).

– – –. *Alternative Trade Strategies and Employment: Synthesis and Conclusions*. Chicago: University of Chicago Press, 1983.

– – –. "The Experience and Lessons of Asia's Super Exporters". In *Export-Oriented Development Strategies: The Success of Five Newly Industrializing Countries*, edited by Vittorio Corbo, Anne O. Krueger, and Fernando Ossa. Boulder: Westview Press, 1985.

Lee Chung H. "The Government, Financial System, and Large Private Enterprises in the Economic Development of South Korea". *World Development* 20, no. 2 (1992), pp. 187–97.

Leipziger, Danny M. and Peter A. Petri. "Korean Industrial Policies: Legacies of the Past and Directions for the Future". In *Korea's Political Economy:*

An Institutional Perspective, edited by Cho Lee-Jay and Yoon Hyung Kim. Boulder: Westview Press, 1994.

Lim Chong-Yah. "Taiwan's Economic Miracle: A Singaporean Perspective". In *Economic Development in East and Southeast Asia*, edited by Seiji Naya and Akira Takayama, pp. 38–56. Honolulu and Singapore: East-West Center and Institute of Southeast Asian Studies, 1990.

Moroshima, M. *Why Has Japan "Succeeded"? Western Technology and the Japanese Ethos*. Cambridge: Cambridge University Press, 1982.

Pack, Howard and Larry E. Westphal. "Industrial Strategy and Technological Change: Theory vs. Reality". *Journal of Development Economics* 22 (1986): 87–128.

Page, John M. and Peter A. Petri. "Productivity Change and Strategic Growth Policy in the Asian Miracle". World Bank Working Paper, Policy Research Department, January 1993.

Pangestu, Mari and Ahman D. Habir. "Trends and Prospects in Privatization and Deregulation in Indonesia". *ASEAN Economic Bulletin* 5, no. 3 (March 1989), pp. 224–41.

Petri, Peter A. "Korea's Export Niche: Origins and Prospects". *World Development* 16, no. 1 (1988).

———. "Korean Trade as Outlier: An Economic Anatomy". In *Korean Economic Development*, edited by Jene K. Kwon, pp. 53–78. New York: Greenwood Press, 1990.

———. "The East Asian Trading Bloc: An Analytical History". In *Regionalism and Rivalry: Japan and the United States in Pacific Asia*, edited by Jeffrey Frankel and Miles Kahler. Chicago: University of Chicago Press, 1993.

Salleh, Ismail, Yeah Kim Leng, and Saha Meyanathan. "Growth, Equity and Structural Transformation in Malaysia: Role of the Public Sector". In *Lessons of East Asia: A Country Studies Approach*, edited by Danny M. Leipziger. Ann Arbor: University of Michigan Press, forthcoming.

Scalapino, Robert A., Seizaburo Sato, and Jusuf Wanandi, eds. *Asian Economic Development: Present and Future*. Research Papers and Policy Studies no. 14. Berkeley: Institute of East Asian Studies, 1985.

Soesastro, Hadi. "Japan 'Teacher' — ASEAN 'Pupils': Can It Work?" In *Asian Economic Development: Present and Future*, edited by Robert A. Scalapino, Seizaburo Sato, and Jusuf Wanandi. Research Papers and Policy Studies no. 14. Berkeley: Institute of East Asian Studies, 1985.

Soon Teck-Wong and Tan C. Suan. "Public Policy and Economic Development in Singapore". In *Lessons of East Asia: A Country Studies Approach*, edited by Danny M. Leipziger. Ann Arbor: University of Michigan Press, forthcoming.

Stiglitz, J. E. "Markets, Market Failures, and Development". *American Economic Review* 79, no. 2 (May 1989), pp. 197–203.

Syrquin, Moshe and Hollis B. Chenery. *Patterns of Development — 1950–1983*. Discussion Paper no. 41. Washington: World Bank, 1989.

Thomas, Vinod and Wang Yan. "Government Policies and Poductivity Growth: Is East Asia an Exception?". In *Lessons of East Asia: A Country Studies Approach*, edited by Danny M. Leipziger. Ann Arbor: University of Michigan Press, forthcoming.

Vogel, Ezra. *The Four Little Dragons: The Spread of Industrialization in East Asia*. Cambridge: Harvard University Press, 1991.

Wade, Robert. *Governing the Market: Economic Theory and the Role of Government in East Asian Industrialization*. Princeton: Princeton University Press, 1990.

Weber, Max. "Confucianism and Taoism". In *The Religion of China*, edited by H. Gerth. Glencoe, Illinois, 1951.

Westphal, Larry and Kwang Suk Kim. "Korea". In *Development Strategies in Semi-Industrial Countries*, edited by Bela Balassa et al. Baltimore: Johns Hopkins University Press, 1982.

White, Gordon, ed. *Developmental States in East Asia*. London: Macmillan, 1988.

Wolf, Charles. *Markets or Governments: Choosing Between Imperfect Alternatives*. Cambridge: MIT Press, 1988.

World Bank. *Korea: Managing the Industrial Transition*. Washington: World Bank, 1987.

———. *World Development Report 1990*. New York: Oxford University Press, 1990.

———. *World Development Report 1991*. New York: Oxford University Press, 1991.

Yoo Jung Ho. "The Industrial Policy of the 1970s and the Evolution of the Manufacturing Sector in Korea". Working Paper no. 9017. Seoul: Korea Development Institute, 1990.

Yoshihara, Kunio. *The Rise of Ersatz Capitalism in Southeast Asia*. Oxford: Oxford University Press, 1988.

4

East Asian Transitional Economies: Economic Dynamics of Reform Process and Performance

Mohamed Ariff

Introduction

The end of the Cold War, the breakup of the Soviet empire, and the eclipse of communism have marked the beginning of a new era for the world economy in general and the former command economies in particular. To this one must add the winds of change blowing across developing market economies which have become increasingly conscious of the prowess of the market forces. Market opening and liberal economic policies have become the buzz words of the 1990s. The impressive track records of the front runners — the Northeast Asian NIEs (newly industrializing economies) and ASEAN (Association of Southeast Asian Nations) — have lent much credence to the new wave of economic reforms in the Asia-Pacific region.

The East Asian transitional economies (EATEs) have arrived at crossroads where they have to take critical decisions. As latecomers, they have certain advantages as well as disadvantages. Their main advantage is that they can learn from the market-oriented development experiences of the front runners, emulating their successes and avoiding their failures. Their main disadvantage is that they have a long way to go, after extricating themselves from the shackles of central planning, treading on unfamiliar terrains of the market-place.

A modest attempt is made in this chapter to sketch out the trends in the reform process of four EATEs, namely Myanmar, Laos, Vietnam, and Mongolia, with particular focus on progress, issues, and prospects.

Anatomy of Reforms

Vietnam

Vietnam began to undertake bold reforms under the banner of *doi moi* (renovation) in 1986, prompted partly by *perestroika* (restructuring) in the then Soviet Union and partly by the felt need to use domestic resources more efficiently. After the demise of the Soviet Union the reform process in Vietnam has gathered speed. The reforms have been quite comprehensive, encompassing macro-economic management, external trade, and foreign direct investment (FDI). New policy measures include the end of the collective system in agriculture, with individual farmers being given considerable leeway, participation of private enterprises in all economic sectors, recognition of private initiatives in corporate decisions, floatation of exchange rates, monetary measures to free interest rates so that they would reflect market conditions and inflation, budgetary measures to eliminate subsidies in production and consumption, privatization of state-owned enterprises (SOEs), establishment of export processing zones (EPZs), and liberal investment policies to encourage the inflow of FDI which include a variety of incentives such as tax holidays and 100 per cent foreign equity.

An important step towards market economy was the removal of virtually all forms of direct subsidization and price control (with very few exceptions, for example, electricity and coal) in March 1989. A series of decrees since 1990 have increased the autonomy of SOEs and exposed them to the rigour of the market.

Private ownership of land is still disallowed, but farmers are given twenty-year renewable tenure rights which can be leased, transferred, exchanged, inherited, and used as collateral for farm loans. In the financial sector policy shifts have permitted the operation of foreign banks, in addition to state commercial banks. In 1993 the first wholly private-owned Vietnamese bank was approved. Vietnamese individuals are now permitted to open accounts in dong or dollars at foreign banks. It was reported that thirteen new banking-related laws were due in 1994 and that regulations for a stock exchange were also in the pipeline.

In the realm of trade the new emphasis is on hard currency transactions, with barter trade being sidelined. Trade is no longer a state monopoly, as private sector participation is permitted. A new tariff regime was introduced in 1993, with twenty-eight different categories at tariff rates ranging from zero to 100 per cent.

Laos

The Lao PDR Government has embarked on a comprehensive programme of policy reforms, labelled as the 'New Economic Mechanism' (NEM), since 1985. The NEM is aimed at transforming the Lao economy from centrally planned to market-based. Initially the reform process was confined to improving the structure and performance of SOEs and deregulating agricultural marketing arrangements. Since 1988 the Lao Government has taken serious measures to drastically reduce direct intervention in the economy, including divestment of state enterprises.

Economic reforms in Laos have paved the way for market-determined prices, liberalization of trade, elimination of subsidies, free-market exchange rates, private sector involvement in the production and distribution of goods and services, and liberal policies towards FDI. Macroeconomic reforms include the adoption of prudent monetary and fiscal policies. The new system calls for positive real interest rates aimed at mobilizing domestic savings and efficient allocation of scarce financial resources. It is noteworthy that credit programmes with subsidized interest rates have been phased out, with the real cost of subsidies being made transparent and borne by the budget. Fiscal reforms have introduced a proper tax system, including profit tax, sales tax, land tax, etc., and terminated budgetary transfers to SOEs. Financial reforms have led to the conversion of seven branches of a single state bank into autonomous commercial banks in March 1988 and the opening of foreign banks.

The Lao Government has ended budget subsidies to SOEs and has even divested itself of some of them. Decree 17 of 1990 disallows direct government involvement in business transactions. Over 50 per cent of the SOEs have been thus disposed off. However, government disengagement thus far has taken mainly the form of joint-venture arrangements, with the state retaining major ownership.

Perhaps, the most significant step towards a full-blown market economy was the adoption of the 'one market, one price' principle which called for an end to dual prices — official and parallel prices — for goods and foreign exchange. This amounted to allowing forces of supply and demand to determine the price in the market-place. The dual exchange rates were unified during 1986–87 and a flexible exchange rate system was adopted in 1988.

Trade liberalization measures included the elimination of QRs (quantitative restrictions) on imports, reduction of import tariffs, and abolition of export taxes during 1987–88. The problem of trade distortions caused by the overvalued local currency was addressed by substantial devaluation in 1987 prior to the adoption of flexible exchange rates.

Of equal importance are the reforms in the legal framework of Laos. A National Constitution was promulgated in 1991. Already in place is a set of laws on foreign investment, contracts, penal code, inheritance and property rights, banking and insurance, labour and family law, land law, and enterprise accountability.

Mongolia

Although the reform process in Mongolia began in the mid-1980s, the transition to a market economy could not take off until after the first multi-party elections were held in July 1990. Since then Mongolia has made significant strides in the reform process, removing price controls, liberalizing foreign exchange transactions, deregulating the financial sector, and privatizing SOEs.

Government Resolution No. 20 (January 1991) represents the first major initiative aimed at reforms, slashing the number of items subject to price controls. As a result, price controls were retained in only thirty-five retail and thirty-six wholesale categories of goods and raw materials. Retail prices of most controlled items were doubled, while farm-gate prices of agricultural raw materials were raised by 132–380 per cent. Subsequently the number of commodities under price controls was further reduced and prices were adjusted upward to reflect market realities. By March 1992, there were only nine commodities subject to price controls, with all farm-gate prices being freed.

Privatization of SOEs began in July 1991 based on a voucher system which would give every citizen an equal opportunity to participate in the programme. About 70 per cent of small SOEs and 75 per cent of large SOEs have been privatized thus far.

Fiscal reforms have necessitated substantial reductions in government expenditures, reducing them by almost 20 per cent in 1991 and by over 60 per cent in 1992 in real terms as compared to 1989. Of particular significance is the fact that the shares of subsidies and transfers and that of goods and services in the budget expenditure were drastically cut. On the revenue side of the coin, income tax was introduced under the Tax Law in 1991, with rates ranging from 8 to 38 per cent. A customs duty at a uniform rate of 15 per cent was also put in place. In December 1992 the Mongolian Parliament passed a new package of tax laws (*viz.* the General Tax Law, the Personal Income Tax Law, the Company Tax Law, the Sales Tax Law, and the Excise Tax Law), introducing four new taxes which included a 10 per cent sales tax. In November 1993 the tax system was revised to broaden the tax base and to reduce tax exemptions.

Mongolia shifted from a mono-bank system to a two-tiered one in 1991, separating central banking from commercial banking. The central bank (Mongolbank) has tightened monetary and credit policies to curb inflation and ensure financial discipline. It has also instituted such banking regulations as minimum interest rates on time deposits (November 1992) and quantitative ceiling for commercial bank lending to non-banks (December 1992). Central bank bills, issued in late 1993, are seen as the principal instrument in regulating bank liquidity.

The external sector reform began with the elimination in 1989 of monopolies enjoyed by state foreign trade enterprises. The number of items subject to export licensing has been reduced to ten lately. It is noteworthy that there are no export taxes or minimum prices for exports and that all imports are subject to a uniform customs duty of 15 per cent (exemptions are applied on thirty-three categories, however). It is also of relevance to note that all foreign trade operations are now conducted using convertible currencies. A series of devaluations of the tugrik since June 1990 has brought it down from 3 tugriks=US$1 to 150 tugriks=US$1 in January 1993. After the adoption of floating exchange rates in May 1993, the tugrik has depreciated further by almost 200 per cent. In June 1993 the Foreign Investment Law was revised, liberalizing ownership provisions and simplifying bureaucratic procedures for registration and approval of new investments.

Myanmar

Economic reform in Myanmar began in 1988 in response to the rapid deterioration of the economy since 1985. The now defunct Burmese Socialist Programme Party liberalized external and internal trade before the new military regime took over power in September 1988. In March 1989 the new regime revoked the 1965 Law for the Establishment of a Socialist Economic System and introduced the open-door policy. Many rules and regulations which had impeded private sector participation in external trade were removed. In March 1989 private companies were allowed to retain 60 per cent of their export earnings and a year later they were allowed to keep 100 per cent of their export earnings. But, there are still such restrictions as export and import licensing for about twenty categories of goods, while sixteen products are subject to export ban since 1990 and ten more items, mainly of metals and minerals, were banned in 1993. Official exchange rate remains overvalued, much to the detriment of exports.

Foreign investment rules have been liberalized. The promulgation of the Union of Myanmar Foreign Investment Law in November 1988 represents a major step towards free-market mechanism. This law permits 100 per cent foreign ownership and requires a minimum of 35 per cent foreign share in joint ventures. What is more, a variety of investment incentives, including three-year tax holidays and accelerated depreciation of capital assets, is also offered, not to mention guarantee against nationalization and expropriation. But there are ambiguities which have led different ministries to interpret the investment law differently.

Disappointingly, there is no comprehensive programme to sell off the SOEs, which remain inefficient. Although the SOEs have been given greater autonomy since November 1988, the government has continued to control SOE prices (Than 1993). Privatization in Myanmar has so far taken the form of SOEs entering into joint venture arrangements with foreign or local firms. In September 1992 it was announced that fifty-five SOEs would be available for lease or joint venture and a few deals had been implemented. As a matter of fact, there were no takers, as most of the SOEs were liabilities.

Financial reforms have put an end to Myanmar's mono-bank banking system. Under the new laws, eleven domestic private commercial banks have come into existence since mid-1992 (Thein and Than 1994). But only four of them are allowed to handle foreign currency. And, there are no foreign banks operating in Myanmar, although licences have been issued to eleven foreign banks to open representative offices in the country.

Policy reforms notwithstanding, there has been no let-up in government interventions, so much so that Myanmar still has rationing and a dual-price system with government procurement price being roughly half that of open-market price (Thein and Than 1994). The existence of parallel markets for goods suggests that Myanmar has a long way to go before it can claim to be a market economy.

Policy Impact

It is encouraging to note that policy reforms in the EATEs have generally worked fairly well against many odds. An outstanding result of these bold reforms has been the growing macroeconomic stability, notably in Vietnam and Laos, although Mongolia and Myanmar pale somewhat in comparison. The average growth rate of GDP (gross domestic product) in Vietnam during the period 1986–91 was 5.2 per cent. During 1992–93, the GDP growth in Vietnam exceeded 7 per cent. Laos also posted creditable, albeit unsteady,

GDP growth rates of 14.3 per cent, 6.7 per cent, and 4.0 per cent in 1989, 1990, and 1991, respectively. However, it appears that Laos' GDP growth is being stabilized at about 7.0 per cent, judging by the performance in 1992 and 1993. In Mongolia there was a sharp decline in output in the early 1990s. Its GDP in 1991 was only 88.5 per cent of the 1989 level and it further declined in 1992 to 67.7 per cent of the 1989 benchmark. The Myanmar economy has turned around since 1989, registering positive growth rates, but GDP growth has been somewhat erratic, with high growth in 1991–92 (9.3 per cent) decelerating rapidly to 6.0 per cent in 1992–93 (Thein and Than 1994).

Vietnam and Laos have been more successful in bringing inflation under control than Mongolia or Myanmar. It is indeed remarkable that Vietnam could reduce the annual rate of inflation from 775 per cent in 1986 to 20 per cent in 1992 (Khai 1993). The monthly rate of inflation in Vietnam decelerated from 13.6 per cent in 1988 to around 2.5 per cent in the first quarter of 1994 (Doanh and McCarty 1994). Laos, too, was successful in bringing down its inflation from 76 per cent in 1989 to 10 per cent in 1991 (Pholsena 1993) and further down to about 8 per cent in 1992 (Saignasith and Lathouly 1994). By contrast, Mongolia has experienced an accelerated inflation, with monthly rates averaging 12.8 per cent before decelerating to a monthly average of 9.1 per cent in 1992, and brought it under firm control to an average of 3.7 per cent in the first half of 1994 (Lhagva and Batbayar 1994). Inflation is also a serious problem for Myanmar, where the rate of inflation averaged 25.7 per cent per annum during 1989–92.

Tax reforms, expenditure restraints, and privatization of SOEs have enforced new budgetary discipline. Commendably, budgetary deficit as a percentage of GDP in Vietnam fell from 11.4 per cent in 1989 to 2.5 per cent in 1991, although this ratio has subsequently risen to 7.2 per cent in 1992 due mainly to increased capital expenditure. In Laos government revenue almost tripled and government expenditure declined steadily during 1989–92, thereby reducing the country's budgetary deficits significantly. In Mongolia tax revenue declined by nearly 65 per cent between 1989 and 1992 and budget deficits continued to grow. Mongolia's budget deficits have been financed by increased money supply, especially in 1990 and 1991, leading to inflationary consequences. Myanmar has continued to incur large budget deficits, with the ratio of deficit to GDP rising progressively from 29 per cent in 1988–89 to 75 per cent in 1992–93.

The export performance of the EATEs, in general, has improved enormously in recent years. It is worth noting that Vietnam has emerged as the third largest exporter of rice since 1989, after Thailand and the United States. Vietnam registered for the first time a trade surplus during the first nine months of 1992 (Khai 1993). Vietnamese exports grew by 24.3 per cent in 1992. However, estimates for 1993 show that imports grew at 21 per cent, outpacing the export growth of 19 per cent (Doanh and McCarty 1994). In Laos external current account deficits declined from 18.2 per cent of GDP in 1989 to 8.8 per cent in 1992, thanks to better export performance (Saignasith and Lathouly 1994). In Mongolia, too, trade deficits declined steadily during the period 1990–92 and it is noteworthy that Mongolia registered a trade surplus for the first time in the first quarter of 1993 (Lhagva and Batbayar 1994). Myanmar has continued to register huge trade deficits during the reform period (Thein and Than 1994). A common feature in all these countries, however, is that the direction of trade has changed dramatically towards Asian neighbours.

Reference must also be made, at least in passing, to the thriving cross-border transactions in these transitional economies. This has assumed growing importance for Myanmar, Cambodia, and Laos across their borders with Thailand, and for Vietnam and Mongolia across their borders with China. Such 'informal' trade flows do play a useful role in the reform process not only because people can see for themselves how a market economy operates but also because trade flows help defuse inflationary pressures. However, a major problem associated with cross-border trade is that it allows foreign currencies to circulate so freely that it tends to blunt the efficacy of monetary policy instruments in these economies. This observation warrants not an abolition but legalization and regulation of cross-border trade.

Foreign investment has increased significantly in all these transitional economies as a result of their open-door policy. During 1988–93, Vietnam approved some 696 FDI projects amounting to US$7.5 billion. The bulk of FDI in Vietnam has gone into industry (31 per cent), oil and gas (15 per cent), and hotel and tourism (19 per cent). The major investors in 1993 in Vietnam were Taiwan (17 per cent), Hong Kong (16 per cent), South Korea (15 per cent), Malaysia (14 per cent), and Singapore (10 per cent). In Laos FDI from twenty-five countries, involving 256 projects with an aggregate value of US$448 million, was approved between 1988 and 1992 (Ariff 1993). About 35 per cent of these investments have gone into manufacturing, 19 per cent into hotel and tourism, 14 per cent into mining and petroleum, and 13 per cent into construction and transport sectors. By far the most important source of FDI in Laos is Thailand, accounting for 40 per cent of the total. Other Asian countries account for another 21 per cent. The second largest investor in Laos is the United States. FDI data for Mongolia are not available, but it appears that FDI flows into Mongolia have not thus far assumed significant proportions. Despite reforms, Myanmar has not been very successful in attracting foreign investment. Total FDI flows into Myanmar amounted to only US$909 million, which pales in comparison with Vietnam's figure of US$4 billion in 1993.

Problems and Prospects

The transition from central planning to market-based operations is by no means an easy task. The process faces many challenges and entails painful adjustments. It is a new ball-game not only for the bureaucracy, which has a lot to unlearn before it can effectively and efficiently handle the new policy environment, but also for the people, who are not used to making economic decisions. This problem is compounded by such deficiencies as infrastructural bottle-necks and shortage of skilled manpower. Legal framework is incomplete, especially with respect to property rights in the absence of which private sector initiatives cannot flourish.

Pragmatism, not ideology, appears to be the main propelling force behind the privatization drive in the transitional economies. SOEs are simply too inefficient and too costly even for socialist regimes. It is interesting to note that the term 'privatization' is still a taboo in Vietnam where it is referred to as 'equitization'. Privatization of SOEs has been slow in all the EATEs where it has taken mainly the form of leasing rather than outright sale. Most of these SOEs continue to operate as before, despite privatization, and some of them are in deep financial trouble now that government subsidies and concessional loans are no longer available. Needless to say, privatization is a lot easier in market economies where a healthy, viable private sector in already in place. Participation of foreign investors in the privatization process in the transitional economies can expedite the process.

Liberalization may not produce the expected results in the short run. More often than not, things will get worse before they can get better, a phenomenon described as the 'J-curve effect'. For example, pent-up demand could lead to a sharp increase in demand with a strong upward pressure on prices. Likewise, privatization of SOEs may result in increased unemployment. In other words, the costs of economic reforms in terms of adjustments are more visible more readily than the benefits, which will become apparent only in the long run. The danger is that this transient lag may undermine the political will to maintain the reform momentum.

Much will also depend on the pace of economic reform. Too rapid a reform may cause serious adjustment problems as it can throw the process totally out of gear. It appears that some of the difficulties encountered in Mongolia may have much to do with the rapid pace of reform. On the other hand, too slow a pace in a half-hearted fashion may also jeopardize the reform process. Myanmar seems to belong to the latter category. Interestingly, the Myanmar approach may well be described as 'swing-door' rather than as open-door policy, meaning that the doors tend to close immediately after they are pushed open. Vietnam and Laos seem to fall between these two extremes. Thus, the choice is not between 'big bang' and gradualism. For shock therapy may work under some but not all conditions.

The smoothness of the reform process also hinges on the sequence of the various reforms. While sequencing is considered important, there is no single model that is applicable to all countries or at all times. However, there is consensus that macroeconomic stabilization must precede all other reforms. For economic reforms will work well only if there is a sound macroeconomic management already in place. Countries which have paid much attention to macroeconomic stability have generally fared much better in their reform programmes than those that have not. Laxity in this regard on the part of Mongolia and Myanmar may have contributed in some measure to their bumpy ride. Lack of budgetary discipline in the early phase of the reform process in Mongolia seems to have aggravated the difficulties, forcing the regime to increase money supply with strong inflationary consequences. Likewise, lack of military expenditure restraints in Myanmar, where the Ministry of Defence calls the shots, seems to have caused problems for the reform process. By contrast, Vietnam and Laos have adopted fairly prudent monetary policy and conservative fiscal policy, paving the way for other reforms.

The future prospects of these transitional economies are bright. The single most important factor in their favour is that they are all located in the fastest growing part of the world, namely East Asia. These economies can benefit enormously from the positive spill-over effects emanating from the East Asian dynamism. Structural changes taking place in the more advanced East Asian economies tend to create opportunities for the transitional economies in the neighbourhood through relocation of industries or production processes. Factor endowments of the EATEs complement those of the more developed neighbours where wages are relatively high. FDI flows can bring with them new technology, marketing know-how, and managerial expertise, which can have a favourable demonstration impact on local enterprises. Viewed in these terms, the EATEs are likely to emerge as the next generation trailing behind the front runners in the so-called 'flying geese' pattern of development.

While the importance of FDI for the transitional economies is duly recognized, one must not lose sight of the fact that demand for FDI is outpacing its supply. Many economies in South Asia, Latin America, and Eastern Europe are opening their doors to foreign investments. This means that the EATEs will have to compete with many other countries for FDI. It is unlikely that foreign investors will rush in just because the doors are open. Most investors would opt to sit on the fence and adopt a wait-and-see attitude. There is still a strong preference among foreign investors for countries with proven track record. Competing for FDI means not just offering cheap labour and tax incentives but also providing infrastructural and institutional supports and consistent, coherent, and transparent policies with continuity.

Nationals living abroad can be an important source of FDI for the transitional economies, especially Vietnam and Laos. If the experience of China, South Korea, and Taiwan is anything to go by, overseas nationals can play a critical role in the development of the EATEs not only by repatriating their incomes to and investing their savings in their home countries but also by providing linkages for export marketing and import sourcing. In addition, they can function as a lobby wherever they are.

To be sure, economic co-operation with immediate neighbours can expedite the process. This co-operation need not necessarily be a formal one. The emergence of Growth Triangles in the border areas can lock in the reform process. Thus, Mongolia can benefit from the Tumen river delta project. Likewise Myanmar, Laos, and Vietnam can gain much by linking up with ASEAN. Economic co-operation with neighbours is particularly critical for Laos and Mongolia, which are land-locked.

It is also of relevance to note that the EATEs are resource-rich, well endowed with a variety of resources which include oil and gas, forests, and minerals. Their comparative advantage in the near and medium terms are likely to be in resource-intensive and unskilled labour-intensive activities. Land-locked Laos and Mongolia can serve as important transit points in the flow of goods across the region.

The prognosis of the reform process in the EATEs seems much better than that faced by transitional economies in Eastern Europe for another important reason, geographical location apart. Unlike the latter, the EATEs are essentially agricultural economies without being unduly burdened by ailing heavy industries and the role of the state in the EATEs was far less pervasive in terms of rigid controls on production and distribution of goods and services than was the case in Eastern Europe. As a matter of fact, market economy was never dead in some parts of the EATEs even in the heyday of communism or command system. Thus, the task of reorientating the economy from a command system to a market system is less formidable for the East Asian economies in transition than their counterparts in Eastern Europe.

Finally, it is important to underline the role that external assistance can play in the reform process. It is pertinent to point out that economic reforms in some market economies, including Indonesia and the Philippines, have been facilitated by external assistance. The World Bank, International Monetary Fund, and even direct bilateral aid flows, notably from Japan, have contributed to the successful implementation of policy reforms in these countries. The case for multilateral aid and ODA (Overseas Development Assistance) flows from developed countries is much stronger for the EATEs, which have to begin almost from scratch.

While the role of aid flows is duly recognized and endorsed, it is important not to lose sight of the fact that such external assistance is only a supplement, not a substitute, for domestic savings. This observation underscores the need for policies that would generate and mobilize domestic savings.

It is unlikely that economic reforms currently under way in the EATEs will reverse themselves. There are ratchet effects which will prevent policy backpedalling. The emergence of strong grass-root support and constituencies for the reform process in these economies augurs well. However, continued support for the reform process will depend on not only the pace of growth in these economies but also the quality of growth. For the reform process to gather momentum, it is important to ensure that benefits of reforms are passed on to all layers of social fabric through equitable distribution of income and wealth and growth without inflation. It is also important to take note of the fact that the market is capable of going to excesses and this observation calls for checks and balances.

References

Ariff, M. "The Question of Indochina Membership in ASEAN". Paper presented to the Socio-Economic Dialogue Amongst the Governments of Cambodia, Lao PDR, Thailand, and Vietnam, 23–26 August 1993, at Hua Hin, Thailand.

Doanh, L.D. and A. McCarty. "Economic Reform in Vietnam: Achievements and Prospects". Paper presented to the International Conference on Asian Transitional Economies, 29 October–2 November 1994, at Osaka, Japan.

Khai, T. "Emergence of Market Economy: Vietnam". In *Vietnam, Laos and Cambodia: The Path to Economic Development,* edited by O. Yasuda, C. Hongladarom, and Mya Than. Tokyo: The Sasakawa Peace Foundation, 1993.

Lhagva, S. and T. Batbayar. "Mongolian Economy in Transition: Present Status and Problems". Paper presented to the International Conference on Asian Transitional Economies, 29 October–2 November 1994, at Osaka, Japan.

Pholsena, K. "The Economy in Transition: Laos". In *Vietnam, Laos and Cambodia: The Path to Economic Development,* edited by O. Yasuda, C. Hongladarom, and Mya Than. Tokyo: The Sasakawa Peace Foundation, 1993.

Saignasith, C. and P. Lathouly. "Transitional Economy of the Lao PDR: Current Economic Performance, Progress, and Problems". Paper presented to the International Conference on Asian Transitional Economies. 29 October–2 November 1994, at Osaka, Japan.

Than, M. "A Brief Survey on Myanmar's Transition Economy". Paper submitted at the Researchers' Planning Meeting, 22–23 March 1993, at the Institute of Southeast Asian Studies, Singapore.

Thein, M. and M. Than. "Transitional Economy of Myanmar: Performance, Issues, and Problems". Paper presented to the International Conference on Asian Transitional Economies, 29 October–2 November 1994, at Osaka, Japan.

The Role of Foreign Direct Investment in the Development of Asian Transitional Economies

Joseph L. H. Tan

Introduction: Importance and Role of Foreign Direct Investment

Asian transitional economies (such as Vietnam, Laos, Myanmar, and Mongolia[1]), struggling as late developers, need to develop modern industrial structures as well as infrastructures (for example, systems of transport and telecommunications) and upgrade their human resources. Indeed, there is a great and urgent need for a wide spectrum of such development projects — which certainly open up vast opportunities for foreign direct investment (FDI) and multinationals to make notable contributions in areas such as modern technology, organizational and managerial know-how, international marketing, and export promotion. The basic or key proposition of this chapter is: FDI has the potential of contributing positively to the growth and development process in the transitional economies.[2] To what extent FDI can contribute to the developmental potential of transitional economies will depend on the policies of the host governments and the practices of the multinational corporations (MNCs). Given this potential, national and international policies should encourage and facilitate the flow of FDI to stimulate development in these Asian transitional economies.

There are a number of advantages FDI has over medium- and long-term borrowing (including credit from commercial banks and export credit agencies)[3]: Firstly, equity financing requires payments only when an investment earns profit, whereas debts must be repaid regardless of the economic or balance of payment situation of the country. Secondly, host countries can regulate the returns to FDI, while debt repayments, which are affected by interest rates set in international markets, are outside the control of the host governments. Thirdly, as most earnings from FDI are reinvested, only a portion of the profits are repatriated, whereas loans require repayment of capital and interest. Finally, FDI is beneficial in providing a closer match between the flow of earning from an investment and that of required payments to the capital used to finance it; thus it avoids the mismatch faced by countries borrowing short term to finance long-term investments.

External Reform: Investment Liberalization

What steps have the governments of Vietnam, the Lao PDR, and Myanmar taken to encourage or attract foreign investment? What are the opportunities open to foreign investors and entrepreneurs?

Changing FDI Regimes: Incentives and Regulations

Vietnam

One of the key elements of *doi moi*, Vietnam's renovation and reform process, is the promotion of foreign investment. Vietnam introduced a liberal new investment law in January 1988 with subsequent improvements to create a more attractive environment for foreign investors. Virtually all sectors of the economy are now open to foreign investors. However, there are priority areas which receive official promotion: import-substituting and export-oriented industries; high-technology industries, effecting technology transfer and creating skilled employment; labour-intensive industries using local inputs, including labour, raw material, and other resources; infrastructural projects; service activities, including tourism, airport and seaport services, and ship-repair. Three types of entities are permissible to FDI: business contracts between foreign and local firms; joint ventures with foreign equity participation; and 100 per cent foreign-owned enterprises.

Lao PDR

The foreign investment law, introduced in September 1988, serves various purposes of stimulating inflows of foreign technology and management capable of generating employment and improving the country's infrastructure, as well as manufacturing capability with an export orientation. This law, essentially similar to the Vietnamese one, also allows for three types of investment: wholly foreign-owned firms, joint ventures, and contract business. Significantly, the law provides: (1) guarantee or protection of foreign capital and assets against nationalization and requisition by administrative procedure; (2) security for repatriation of profits; (3) tax holidays up to four years; and (4) exemption of taxes for profits reinvested.

Myanmar

Only two months after the Lao PDR enacted its foreign investment law, the Myanmar Government introduced its The Union of Myanmar Foreign Investment Law, a significant step in its external sector liberalization to the international economy . This law has basic provisions which are broadly similar to those offered by the Lao PDR and Vietnam. (And, one would suspect that these two countries in turn must have drawn ideas from the earlier Chinese experience of foreign investment promotion and external liberalization which started almost a decade ago, in 1978.). These provisions are:

1. 100 per cent equity ownership by foreign investors;
2. joint ventures with foreign participation of at least 35 per cent of equity;
3. foreign investors can freely repatriate profits and assets with unequivocal government guarantee against nationalization and expropriation;

4. various tax incentives, including corporate income tax holiday for three years with possibility for extension; tax exemption or relief for reinvested profits; a grant of accelerated depreciation on equipment and assets; tax relief of 50 per cent for exports; customs duty exemption on capital goods and raw materials during construction period; etc.

Priorities are accorded to projects which promote exports, exploit natural resources, transfer high technology, increase employment, save energy, or contribute to regional economic development.

The investment laws of Vietnam, the Lao PDR, and Myanmar do reflect substantial and substantive similarities or overlapping legal and other provisions pertaining to the types of business organization allowed; different kinds of fiscal and other incentives; priority areas for official promotion; etc. (For more comparative details see Appendix Table 5.1.) However, there are some minor differences in provisions, depending on some notable distinctiveness of the country. Vietnam, with its relatively much larger population of over 70 million, and Myanmar, with its domestic market of over 40 million consumers, compared to the Lao population of less than 5 million, should make import-substituting industries unimportant for Laos but of considerable importance to Vietnam and Myanmar.

Results of Investment Liberalization and Promotion of FDI

The evidence, despite statistical and other limitations, seems to provide an optimistic view of favourable and fruitful FDI and MNC activities in these three Asian transitional economies. The main trends of FDI activities in these three economies are highlighted below.

Vietnam

The period 1988 to end-1994 witnessed a consistent and rapid increase of FDI to the extent that almost a thousand FDI licences had been issued, amounting to a total subscribed value of about

TABLE 5.1
Foreign Direct Investments by Country
(Committed Capital)

	Vietnam[1] US$ million	Lao PDR[2] US$ thousand	Myanmar[3] US$ million
ASEAN			
Singapore	1,055 (77)	4,689 (7)	293.35 (21)
Malaysia	582 (32)	21,877 (5)	58.45 (5)
Philippines	2 (2)	—	6.67 (1)
Thailand	227 (42)	173,364 (141)	214.74 (12)
ANIEs			
Hong Kong	1,551 (164)	15,516 (16)	59.32 (10)
South Korea	860 (92)	6,412 (6)	60.59 (9)
Taiwan	1,901 (164)	—	—
United States	223 (26)	81,852 (20)	203.19 (10)
Japan	690 (68)	2,305 (8)	101.14 (5)
Other countries	2,834 (158)	155,604 (172)	275.67 (35)
Total	10,000.7 (825)	461,619 (375)	1,273.12 (108)

Notes: 1. Figures for: Vietnam refer to the period 1988 to December 1994; Lao PDR, 1988 to June 1993; and Myanmar, as at 10 October 1993.

2. Figures in parentheses refer to number of projects.

Sources: [1] State Committee for Co-operation and Investment (reported in *Vietnam Investment Review*, 2–8 January 1995).

[2] Foreign Investment Management Committee, *Investment Opportunities in the Lao PDR*, no. 5 (June 1993), Table V, pp. 75–76. The table lists twenty-seven investing countries in the Lao PDR.

[3] Investment Commission of Myanmar (October 1994). The table lists seventeen investing countries in all.

US$10.9 billion (see Table 5.1) The lifting of the embargo by the United States in February 1994 should lead to a bigger inflow of FDI into Vietnam in the next couple of years. Presently, the largest of the cumulative stock of investment is found in industries related to tourism and hotel (20 per cent); services (13 per cent); light consumer-product industries (16 per cent); and oil and gas (12 per cent). (See Appendix Table 5.2.)

Lao PDR

From September 1988 to June 1993, the Lao PDR, like Vietnam, also experienced consistently rapid growth in FDI, though the quantum was much smaller — 365 foreign investment licences worth US$461 million were approved. The largest share, that is 33 per cent, of FDI (for 1990–92 period) went to manufacturing industries (garments, wood industries, and other manufacturing) which are more for export rather than serving the domestic market. Hotel and tourism industries took up about 20 per cent; oil exploration and mining another 15 per cent (see Appendix Table 5.3).

Myanmar

In terms of time period (end-1988–October 1994) and value of total foreign investment at almost US$1.3 billion, Myanmar did better than the Lao PDR but lagged very much behind Vietnam. The bulk of the FDI, that is about 40 per cent, went to the hotel and tourism industries; oil and gas exploration accounted for 30 per cent, while only 9 per cent was invested in the manufacturing sector (see Appendix Table 5.4).

ASEAN and Other Investments in the Asian Transitional Economies

Investments by the Association of Southeast Asian Nations (ASEAN) in Vietnam, Laos, and Myanmar have been growing yearly. As shown in Table 5.1, figures available (up to December 1994) indicate that the ASEAN countries (specifically Thailand, Singapore, and Malaysia) are the largest investors as a group — accounting for 43 per cent of the aggregate FDI in the Lao PDR ; about 35 per cent of the total foreign investment in Myanmar; much less significantly for Vietnam, at 16.6 per cent. For major developed countries like Japan and the United States, in contrast, their investments in Myanmar are rather small: 9.6 per cent and 19.2 per cent respectively; and for the Lao PDR the Japanese FDI constitutes an unexpectedly insignificant 0.5 per cent of the total compared to the American investment of 17.7 per cent. The American investment tends to be in capital-intensive ventures in the oil and mining sector. In the Lao PDR, American investment is nearly four times the average size for the other countries.

In Vietnam the Japanese investment forms 5.7 per cent of the aggregate investment; even then it is much less than that from the ASEAN countries, which amounts to almost 17 per cent. The American share is a paltry 1.7 per cent, mainly because of the official embargo, which was removed only recently. Japanese MNCs have been overly cautious; however, signs of change are discernible.[4] For instance, in September 1994 the Nomura Securities signed a joint-venture agreement, giving it a 70 per cent stake in a US$120 million export-processing zone in Haiphong, the northern port-city. Nihon Cement and Mitsubishi Material are planning a cement plant worth US$300 million. Other Japanese MNCs are arranging strategic alliances with ASEAN firms. Mitsubishi Motors and its Malaysian partner Proton will extend their joint venture to supply light utility vehicles to the Vietnamese market. Mitsubishi Electric and Kang Yong Electric from Thailand are setting up a joint-venture plant to manufacture consumer goods. The major Japanese trading firms have offices in Vietnam. Amongst them, Nissho Iwai is prominent for being in Vietnam since 1979. It is a partner in a new woodchip joint venture in Danang and also involved in an oil exploration project.

The Asian newly industrializing economies are also important investors in these four countries. Hong Kong and Taiwan are the top two investors in Vietnam, with their combined FDI amounting to US$3.46 billion, or 38 per cent of the total FDI (on approval basis). Their investment commitments in Myanmar and the Lao PDR are much less significant; this is true for South Korea as well.

Although the recent trends and pattern of FDI and MNC activities in these reforming socialist economies are favourable, there are diverse problems which need to be resolved or solved so that FDI and MNCs can possibly play an even more useful role in each of these Asian transitional economies. These problems are assessed in the next section.

Assessment and Prospects for Enhancing the Contribution of FDI: Concerns and Problems

Reforming socialist economies like Vietnam, the Lao PDR, and Myanmar may have a number of factors in their favour, such as low-cost labour, attractive natural resource endowments, and potentially important domestic market. But, the negative factors could weigh against or even outweigh these advantages, such as the high cost of doing business and serious impediments and weaknesses in the legal, financial, and industrial infrastructure. There are also bureaucratic bottle-necks in the investment approval process. As production sites for export-oriented industries, the wage costs for Vietnam are lower than Myanmar; and both are very competitive *vis-à-vis* the ASEAN-Four, except for Indonesia (see Figure 5.1). However, minimum wage costs can be misleading as the differential labour productivity and other non-wage production costs can add up to put Vietnam and Myanmar at some disadvantage. Specifically, the rental rates in Hanoi and Ho Chi Minh City are higher than those in Singapore, Bangkok and even New York and Sydney (Figure 5.2). Also in the case of Vietnam, the government supposedly established a one-stop investment centre in the State Committee for Co-operation and Investment (SCCI). (But, according to a knowledgeable analyst, it could turn out to be a one-stop centre with many doors, or at times a difficult sequence of doors! See Appendix Figure 5.1.)

Thus, in theory, the SCCI can state that investment applications can be processed within thirty days. But in practice, other ministries and local authorities also want to study the projects, resulting in a much longer gestation time of one to three years to obtain a licence. And with rent-seeking activities common in the administrative

FIGURE 5.1
Minimum Monthly Wages in Vietnam and Selected Countries

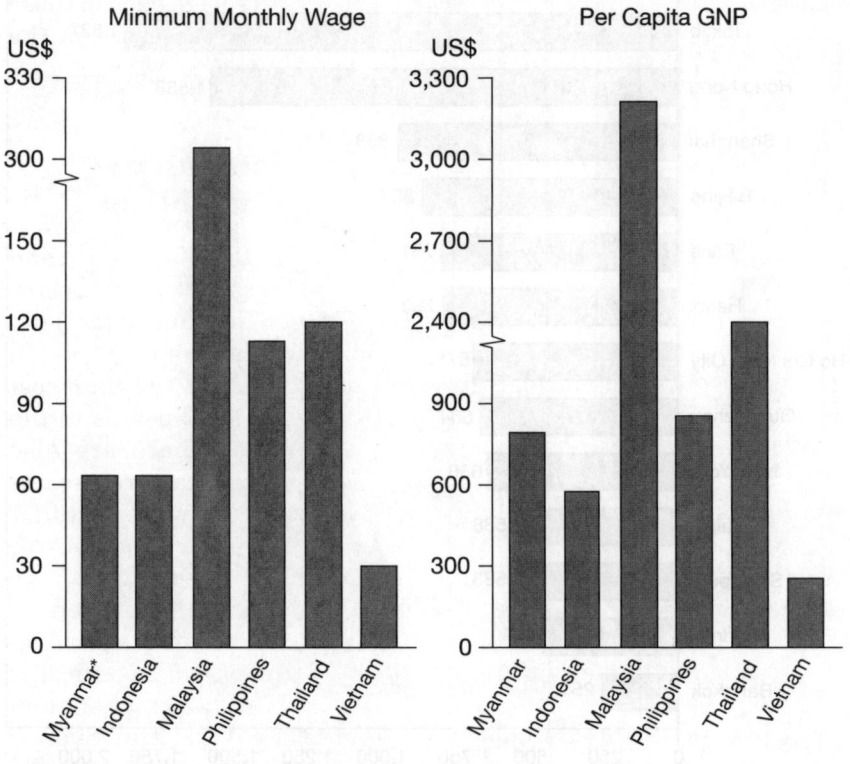

*Using official exchange rate (US$4.5 at blackmarket rate).

Source: *Far Eastern Economic Review,* 22 September 1994, p. 73.

procedures, the licence finally obtained could be costly. Recently, Deputy Premier Phan Van Khai himself cautioned his government bureaucracy with the following plea: "Procedures have been made so complicated that if we fail to readjust, they will hamper our efforts as well as the eagerness of foreign business."[5]

FIGURE 5.2
Commercial Rental Rates in Vietnam and Selected Countries

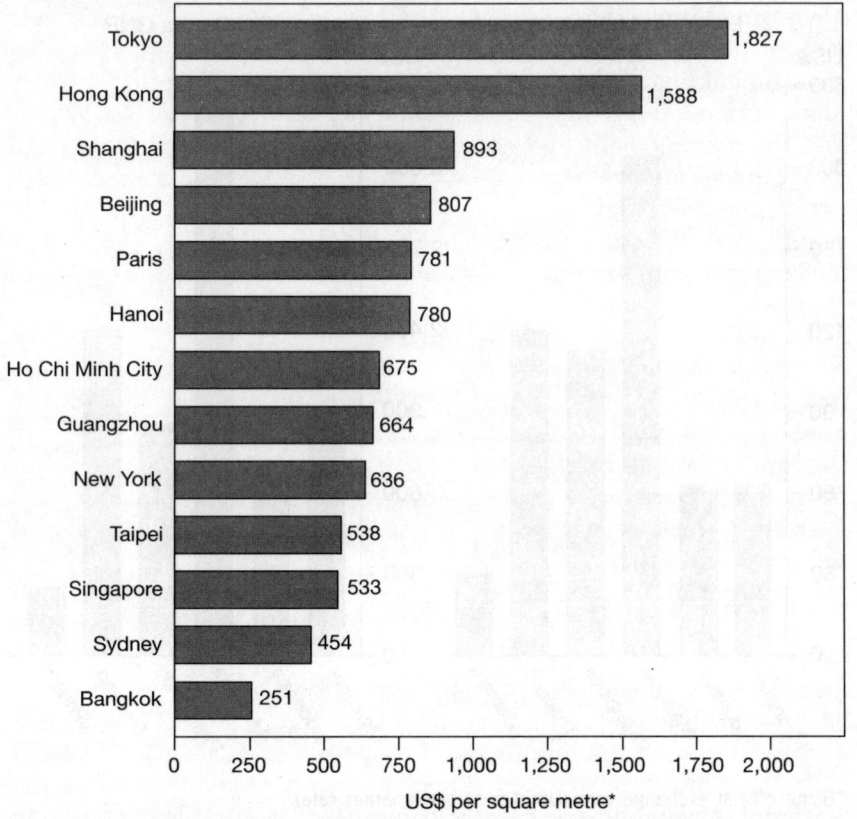

US$ per square metre*

*Includes yearly rent, service charges, and tax for prime commercial property.

Source: *Far Eastern Economic Review*, 22 September 1994, p. 73.

In the case of Myanmar, some problems have arisen from ambiguities in the law, which are open to arbitrariness and perceived as impediments to investors. For instance, some potential investors have complained that although the law provides for 100 per cent foreign ownership, in effect business is not possible without the government involvement in the (joint) venture as a necessary partner. More serious, however, are the main factors of political conditions and the management of the exchange rate. These are probably the two crucial factors which account for the markedly lacklustre performance of FDI inflow into Myanmar compared to Vietnam, roughly over the same period. Vietnam took the bold decision to float its exchange rate in mid-1989 whereas Myanmar's foreign exchange continued to be unrealistically overvalued. Political uncertainties also deterred foreign investors. The more optimistic investors had been further discouraged by a host of other impediments not uncommon in dealing with transitional economies — unpredictability of frequently changing economic policies affecting the operation of business activities; ambiguities in the legal framework; bureaucratic delays in getting production started and sustained; lack of essential infrastructure; and underdeveloped financial and other institutions.

As for the Lao PDR, red tape and inadequacy in the legal framework for business operations continue to present problems for investors. One government report advises that FDI in infrastructure (roads, ports, telecommunications, etc.) tends to have a long pay-back period and low yields. Skilled labour is scarce: "..Workers lack a sense of quality and productivity. Laos is not an attractive export processing location."[6] However, senior government officials and the National Assembly are clearly committed to further reforms to resolve these institutional limitations. Since early 1994, diverse laws have been introduced or under consideration, such as: revision to the Law on the Promotion and Management of Foreign Investment, Labour Law, Tax Law and State Budget Law, and the Law on Business Operations. The Law on Business Operations significantly allows for equality of treatment for various types of companies, including private-sector firms, which have emerged with the reform process. This is important as reforming transitional communist countries tend to favour unfairly the state sector, especially in providing bank lending. There is some evidence that such past institutional bias has been markedly reduced; for instance, credit extended to public enterprises has decreased while significant increased lending to the private sector was noted in 1993 by the Asian Development Bank.

Summary/Assessment

It is not surprising that investors from capitalist market countries consider the high political risks and uncertainties of investing in socialist countries like Vietnam, Laos, and Myanmar. However, bold early investors often complained of many operational difficulties and impediments. Some of these concerned the poor infrastructural facilities, including transport and communications as well as power and utilities. Others encompass a host of policy-induced bottle-necks common in such centrally planned or command economies, for instance complicated and restrictive access to the use of land, labour, intermediate goods, and raw materials. There are layers of bureaucratic and political impediments to overcome even before a joint venture is established and more problems in the initial stage of operation.

Nonetheless, the authorities in the host countries have been accommodating to foreign investors by offering various forms of enticements or incentives. Generally, there are two types of incentives. The first are 'genuine incentives', such as tax concessions (including reduced tax rates, tax holidays, and preferential deductions), which are the most obvious and popularly applied tax incentives, as amply discussed in the earlier section on investment laws in the three countries concerned. These incentives attempt to attract FDI into the country and channel them into priority areas of promotion instead of other economic activities. The second type of incentives are government interventions which attempt to reduce or eliminate the barriers to investment (particularly in the administrative, legal, and other institutional procedures). The latter are probably more important, particularly in the earlier phases of reform in a socialist economy (Wall and Fukasaku 1994, p. 154).

Pomfret (1994), based on his study of the notably successful

Chinese experience with FDI, distilled two main lessons for other transitional economies: firstly, that external sector liberalization of the transitional economy to the participation of FDI is a necessary but not sufficient condition to stimulate a significant or substantial inflow of FDI. Secondly, it is even more important to implement pragmatic measures to assure foreign investors of a certain level of security and predictability in the legal and administrative guarantee to protect their investments against arbitrary abuse of power; reduce and simplify bureaucratic procedure; and permit some currency convertibility. To a varying extent, these two lessons have apparently been reflected in the legal guarantees of protection of foreign investment in the investment laws of Vietnam, Laos, and Myanmar discussed earlier. However, there is still scope for improving the implementation aspects of the administrative and regulatory procedures (or type two incentives of governmental interventions to clear obstacles to the operation of MNC activities). Many would fully appreciate and agree with Pomfret's additional point: "The lessons take time to be absorbed... as officials need to overcome their suspicion of foreign capitalists and to understand foreign business practices and foreigners need to adjust to the ways..." (Pomfret 1994, p.416) of doing business in these countries.

It seems the foreign investment laws which have been introduced in Vietnam, Laos, and Myanmar are evolving legal frameworks. Presumably, the latecomer in foreign investment promotion is watching closely and learning the positive and negative lessons from the others' performance. With China's success in opening up its huge economy to large inflows of FDI into its many special economic zones and other regions, the three points raised by Pomfret have certainly been noted by the relevant government authorities in Vietnam, Laos, and Myanmar. All these three countries have progressively liberalized their investment codes and are continually attempting to improve the conditions and environment for MNCs to operate in partnership with the emerging private sector interests and government authorities.

The complaints and problems faced by foreign investors should also be balanced up with the concerns and problems faced by the government authorities and local interest groups within these three transitional economies. The Vietnamese Government is concerned about the inadequate or low levels of foreign investment being committed thus far in the industrial and infrastructural sectors. As a remedial response, the government authorities are providing support and easing conditions for BOT (build–operate–transfer) projects. For infrastructure projects such as road and port construction, irrigation and water supply facilities, and primary education, assistance is being provided since the beginning of 1994 by multilateral sources: US$286.5 million from the Asian Development Bank and US$228 million from the World Bank. On 3 February 1994 the eighteen-year-old American trade and investment embargo against Vietnam was lifted. The substantial investments from American, Japanese, and other MNCs which had withheld their investments will probably be reactivated.

Since the lifting of the U.S. embargo, the media in Vietnam have published a barrage of articles accusing foreign investors of cheating their inexperienced Vietnamese business associates and citing social problems, including traffic problems in cities like Hanoi.[7] Official circumspection with regard to foreign investors is justifiable in part because of the undesirable behaviour of some operators, particularly from Hong Kong. A good number of these early investors were small-time investors who acquired projects for speculative gain by reselling the licences issued to them. Eventually, many such licences were revoked when the projects were not implemented. The government was able to remedy this situation by hiring international accounting firms to conduct credit checks on the foreign investment applications.

In the Lao PDR the government sees a pressing necessity to expand the country's export industries. Insufficient foreign investment is being attracted to help in quickly expanding the export base and speeding up industrial development. Further reform might be needed to provide a more supportive tax system — specifically to remove any existing anti-export bias in the natural resource and sales taxes.

In Vietnam similar 'undesirable balance' in terms of the official priority for investment promotion had occurred: for instance, most investments in Hanoi were concentrated in real-estate development, which accounted for as much as 45 per cent of the total licensed investments in the first six months of 1994, compared with just 25 per cent for industry.

Concluding Remarks and Policy Implications

For the three Asian transitional economies (ATEs) of Vietnam, the Lao PDR, and Myanmar, as part of the sweeping economic reform that included the external sector (particularly foreign investment liberalization) was the dramatic change of regime — from reservations about and prohibition of FDI to its active promotion, even enticements with diverse incentives. The governments of these countries began to appreciate the proven advantages and success of hosting FDI and MNCs, as seen in the decades of rapid growth and development in the neighbouring countries of ASEAN. Foreign capital and MNCs have been harnessed to stimulate the development potentials rather than exploiting and draining the natural and human resources of the ASEAN countries. The success brought by external economic reform and investment liberalization, particularly of China's use of Special Economic Zones and coastal open cities to tap the developmental contributions of foreign equity capital, has undoubtedly given much impetus and demonstrative impact to the reform processes being pursued in Vietnam, Laos, and Myanmar. Hence, just as for China and ASEAN, these ATEs have turned positively to the promise and ability of FDI to fruitfully serve their diverse purposes, namely: solving the problem of the lack of domestic investment resources and the need for foreign exchange to finance capital and technology imports as well as access to international markets.

Some reservations need to be raised on the factors that constrain the substantial growth of FDI — both for market-oriented investment to tap the markets within these ATEs, and also for export-oriented FDI in search of lower costs of production. For the market-oriented FDI the potential or pent-up demand for modern products and services in these ATEs cannot be realized unless the household or disposable income of the population increases significantly. This means that gainful employment and labour productivity must increase as the basis for income growth. For the export-oriented type of FDI, the geographical proximity to the dynamic Asia-Pacific (ASEAN, NIEs, Japan, China) has some significant advantages for these three ATEs in mainland Southeast Asia.

What the Governments of the ATEs Can Do Further

There remains much that could be done to improve the industrial and infrastructural support systems and facilities in the ATEs. Administrative bottle-neck and other legal and political uncertainties also need to be addressed to provide greater security and assurance for foreign investments.

The primary responsibility for improving the situation lies with the host countries. To attract more FDI these ATEs need to offer a better policy environment, and closer co-ordination of economic policies. Domestic economic policies have to create credible expectations of macroeconomic stability and a better implementation of the legal and institutional business infrastructure.

For instance, the Lao PDR Government is committed to encouraging foreign investment and the local private sector. It plans to step up efforts to attract FDI of US$3 billion by the year 2000. As a domestic capital market hardly exists and the government has no commitment to borrow from the international capital markets, FDI will continue to be crucial in meeting Laos' capital needs for development. Also, the role of the private sector will be enhanced in future infrastructural development. This is significant, as the 1995–2000 government investment programme includes: US$98 million in road building and upgrading; US$41.5 million for various health care, education, and vocational training; US$56 million for irrigation; and US$40 million for rural development, particularly to encourage sedentary cash-cropping instead of slash-and-burn cultivation. The government explicitly called for overseas development assistance (ODA) under various arrangements, including bilateral and multilateral ones. Thus, not only for Laos but also for Myanmar and Vietnam, a greater role for the ATE host governments in facilitating FDI flows to their countries could also be envisaged through financial and technical assistance arranged bilaterally as well as through multilateral agencies.

Role for Japan and ASEAN

The Indochina Development Fund has been established under the initiative of the Japanese Government to facilitate economic co-operation. Japan and ASEAN also need to co-operate closely to promote peace and development in Indochina. In early 1993, during his visit to the ASEAN countries, former Japanese Prime Minister Miyazawa proposed a regional development strategy for Indochina as a whole rather than for individual countries — called the Forum for the Comprehensive Development of Indochina. The ASEAN countries are called upon to participate in this Indochina Forum. Also, specifically with regard to the mobilization of international effort to assist in the reconstruction of Cambodia, Japan, chairing the International Committee on the Reconstruction of Cambodia (ICORC), looks to ASEAN for help and co-operation. Additionally, in its leading role in the advocacy of global environmental issues, particularly on assistance to the efforts of developing countries, Japan gives priority to help ASEAN countries in their efforts to deal with environmental degradation and related problems.[8]

There is, perhaps, also a need for an international advisory group or a forum for regular consultation on FDI issues among officials and experts from Japan and other interested countries (for example, ASEAN, as in the Indochina Development Forum). The central aim should be to foster a network for the exchange of information on investment trends and policies in these ATEs and investing countries; to review obstacles to FDI; to discuss policy issues, practical measures, and instruments of investment promotion; and to promote dialogue amongst the parties concerned, including government officials, experts, and representatives from the private sector.

Role for Multilateral Development Institutions

Multilateral development finance and specialized technical agencies might review their assistance along the following lines to help improve the investment (FDI) environment. It may be necessary to review whether the mix of financial and technical assistance programmes matches the needs of the recipients; and whether there is sufficient co-ordination among the international institutions.

In terms of subregional economic development co-operation, aside from that initiated by Japan, the Asian Development Bank has also such a regional co-operation scheme with the support and involvement of six countries : the Lao PDR, Vietnam, Myanmar, Thailand, Cambodia, and the Yunnan Province of China.[9] This is a comprehensive scheme covering a range of sectors, including investment, trade, transport and communications, energy, and tourism. Economic co-operation among these six countries can provide a viable and comprehensive policy and infrastructure framework that enhances the returns on investments in general and foreign equity investment in particular. Dynamic economic development has already favourably affected parts of the subregion. Thailand and the southern regions of China are already generating double-digit growth rates. Possibly, this could stimulate similar economic performance in Vietnam, Myanmar, and the Lao PDR. And, with improving economic prospects for the subregion, growth-inducing foreign investments could be attracted to these countries which could lead to fruitful and peaceful subregional economic development co-operation, in a region previously plagued by hostilities and strife.

APPENDIX TABLE 5.1
Comparative Investment Incentives in
Indochina, Myanmar, China, and Thailand, 1992

Investment Incentives	China	Lao PDR	Vietnam	Cambodia	Myanmar	Thailand
Basic rights and guarantees						
Guarantee against expropriation	✓	✓	✓	✓	✓	✓
Guarantee against losses due to:						
(a) Nationalization	✓	✓	✓	✓	✓	✓
(b) Damage caused by war	✓		✓		✓	
(c) Inconvertibility of currency						
Remittance of foreign exchange earnings and payments	✓ ✓	✓	✓ ✓	✓ ✓	✓ ✓	
Repatriation of capital	✓ ✓		✓ ✓	✓ ✓	✓ ✓	
Exemptions from taxes and tariffs						
Capital gains tax	✓		✓	✓	✓	
Corporate income tax	✓ ✓		✓ ✓	✓ ✓	✓ ✓	✓
Taxes on imported capital goods	✓ ✓		✓ ✓	✓ ✓	✓ ✓	
Taxes on imported raw materials	✓ ✓		✓ ✓		✓ ✓	
Taxes on royalties					✓	
Withholding tax on interest on foreign loans (tax credit)					✓	
Other taxes and fees	✓		✓	✓	✓	
Extension of incentive availment period	✓	✓	✓	✓	✓	✓
Assistance to investors						
Joint-venture brokerage	✓	✓	✓	✓	✓	✓
Technical assistance	✓	✓	✓	✓	✓	✓
Processing of applications/other requirements	✓	✓	✓	✓	✓	✓

Source: Asian Development Bank (1993), Table 13 (abstract).

APPENDIX TABLE 5.2
Vietnam: Foreign Direct Investment
by Country and Sector, 1988–94

Investment by Country

Country	No. of Projects	Investment Capital US$ million	%	Legal Capital US$ million
Taiwan	164	1,901.2	19.0	917.4
Hong Kong	164	1,551.0	15.5	733.9
Singapore	77	1,054.9	10.5	525.5
South Korea	92	860.3	8.6	380.3
Japan	68	690.1	6.9	482.5
Australia	44	683.6	6.8	274.5
Malaysia	32	581.9	5.8	306.2
France	59	545.6	5.5	271.0
Switzerland	12	461.3	4.6	179.0
British Virgin Islands	10	355.5	3.5	143.9
Netherlands	16	350.4	3.5	311.3
United Kingdom	14	344.6	3.4	309.6
Thailand	42	226.6	2.3	141.3
United States	26	223.3	2.2	91.7
Bermuda	5	170.4	1.7	107.5
Total	825	10,000.7	100.0	5,175.6

Investment by Sector

Economic Sector	Percentage of Total Investment, 1988–94	Percentage of Total Investment, 1994
Hotel and tourism	20	17
Light industry	16	16
Heavy industry	14	14
Services	13	28
Oil and gas	12	2
Construction	8	11
Telecommunications and post	7	3
Agro-forestry	5	6
Banking and finance	1	<1
Aquaproducts	1	1
Culture, education, and health	<1	1
Total investment	US$10,000.7 million	US$3,704.7 million
Total number of projects	825	338

Source: State Committee for Co-operation and Investment, reported in *Vietnam Investment Review*, 2–8 January 1995.

APPENDIX TABLE 5.3
Laos: Foreign Direct Investment by Country, June 1993

	Number of Investments	Percentage	Registered Capital (US$1,000)	Percentage
ASEAN				
Thailand	141	38.6	173,364	37.6
Malaysia	5	1.4	21,877	4.7
Singapore	7	1.9	4,689	1.0
ANIEs				
Taiwan	20	5.5	44,161	9.6
Hong Kong	16	4.4	15,516	3.4
South Korea	6	1.6	6,412	1.4
Other Asian				
China	26	7.1	17,214	3.7
Macao	2	0.5	3,135	0.7
Japan	8	2.2	2,305	0.5
India	1	0.3	350	0.1
Myanmar	1	0.3	30	0.0
Vietnam	6	1.6	1,479	0.3
North America				
United States	20	5.5	81,852	17.7
Canada	8	2.2	1,195	0.3
Europe				
France	34	9.3	36,718	8.0
United Kingdom	7	1.9	11,973	2.6
Germany	3	0.8	1,250	0.3
Netherlands	3	0.8	242	0.1
Belgium	1	0.3	140	0.0
Austria	2	0.5	118	0.0
Sweden	5	1.4	456	0.1
Switzerland	1	0.3	150	0.0
Italy	3	0.8	146	0.0
Others				
Russia	13	3.6	16,834	3.6
Australia	23	6.3	19,716	4.3
New Zealand	2	0.5	93	0.0
Lebanon	1	0.3	214	0.0
Total	365	100.0	461,629	100.0

Notes: 1. The total number of investments by country of origin exceeds the total number of overall investments because some investments have multiple foreign partners.
2. The total aggregate value of investments by country is less than the total aggregate value of overall investments because the former amount excludes the proposed domestic capital of Lao investors.

Source: Foreign Investment Management Committee and Lao National Chamber of Commerce and Industry, *Investment Opportunities in the Lao People's Democratic Republic*, no. 5 (June 1993).

APPENDIX TABLE 5.4
Myanmar: Foreign Direct Investment, to October 1994

By Country

Country	Total Permitted Enterprises		Existing Enterprises	
	No.	Approved Amount (US$ million)	No.	Approved Amount (US$ million)
ASEAN				
Singapore	23	293.35	21	273.19
Thailand	19	214.74	12	60.99
Malaysia	5	58.45	5	58.45
Philippines	1	6.67	1	6.67
ANIEs				
Hong Kong	14	59.32	10	35.92
South Korea	9	60.59	9	91.19
Other Asian				
Japan	5	101.14	4	61.14
China	2	1.10	2	1.10
Macao	1	2.40	1	2.40
Bangladesh	2	2.96	1	0.10
Europe	14	220.01	11	117.35
Others				
United States	10	203.19	7	226.20
Canada	1	22.00	—	—
Australia	2	27.20	1	2.00
Total	108	1,273.12	85	936.70

APPENDIX TABLE 5.4 (continued)
By Sector
(US$ million)

Sector	Total Foreign Investment	1989–90	1990–91	1991–92	1992–93	1993–94
Agriculture	2.69				2.69	
Fisheries	90.76		77.31		5.85	7.60
Mining	163.45	54.10	55.10		33.38	20.87
Manufacturing	119.19	15.84	42.72	5.89	13.34	18.17
Oil and gas	381.09	298.05	19.04		44.50	19.50
Transport	2.00				1.00	
Hotel and tourism	513.94	81.50	86.40		3.02	311.46
Total	1,273.12	449.49	280.57	5.89	103.78	377.60

Source: Investment Commission of Myanmar (October 1994).

APPENDIX FIGURE 5.1
Vietnam: Stages of Processing Foreign Investment Applications

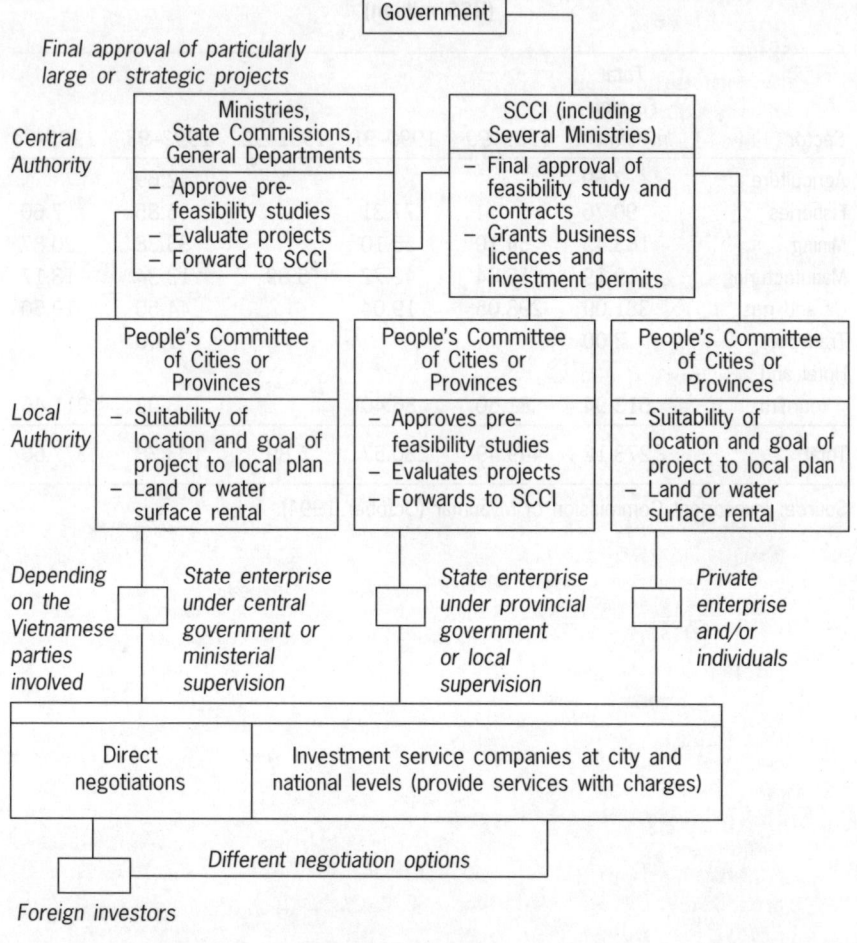

SCCI — State Committee for Co-operation and Investment.

Source: UNESCAP (United Nations Educational and Social Commission for Asia and the Pacific), *Foreign Investment Incentive Schemes — Vietnam* (New York, 1993), p. 39.

Notes

1. Mongolia is essentially left out in this overview article because of statistical and other information constraints with regard to foreign direct investment. For the same reason, the issue of the role of foreign direct investment in this geographically isolated and land-locked transitional economy is hardly (or minimally) treated in the chapter of this volume devoted to the Mongolian case-study.
2. There exists much literature on the long-standing debate of costs and benefits of foreign direct investment. This chapter does not attempt to review this extensive literature; see, for instance, Hill and Johns (1985); Meier (1989); *Asian Development Review* (1993).
3. Michalopoulos (1985).
4. *Asian Wall Street Journal*, 31 August 1994, p. 1 and p. 4.
5. Reported in *Far Eastern Economic Review*, 22 September 1994, p. 73.
6. See Singapore Trade Development Board (1992), p. 33. This report also noted, more positively, that Taiwan and Hong Kong multinationals have invested in labour-intensive industries to produce garments as Laos' exports are not subject to quota restriction in the markets of various developed countries.
7. Some observers believe the authorities periodically caution the dangers of too rapid opening up to external influence and the need to foster a restrictive political atmosphere to maintain stability whilst economic reform continues under tight control.
8. For instance, Japan provided assistance in setting up the Environmental Research and Training Centre in Thailand as well as the Environmental Management Centre in Indonesia. Japan has also jointly sponsored with the United States a feasibility study for establishing a centre in Indonesia for the preservation of biodiversity.
9. Asian Development Bank (1993). This subregional economic co-operation scheme was initiated by the bank in late 1991. Phase I of this project reviewed the serious shortage of funds against the crucial needs for various infrastructures such as transport and tele-communications, energy as well as human resource development, environment, trade, and investment. Phase II, as proposed in this 1993 study, focused on issues of consolidating subregional economic co-operation, including impediments to trade in the region; regulation and promotion of foreign investment; assessment of institutional requirements for co-operation; and joint efforts to promote tourism and environmental regulation.

References

Asian Development Bank. *Asian Development Outlook 1994*. Manila, 1994.
————. *Subregional Economic Cooperation*. Manila, 1993.
Asian Development Review 11, no. 1 (1993). Special issue on Foreign Direct Investments in the Asia–Pacific Region.
Business Times (Singapore), various issues.
Chanthavong Saignasith and Panom Lathouly. "Transitional Economy of the Lao PDR: Current Economic Performance, Progress, and Problems". In this volume.
Economist Intelligence Unit. Country Reports, various issues.
Far Eastern Economic Review, various issues.
Hill, H. and B. Johns. "The Role of Direct Foreign Investment in Developing East Asian Countries". *Weltwirtschaftliches Archiv* 121, no. 2 (1985), pp. 335–81.
Institute of Southeast Asian Studies. *Regional Economic Outlook 1994/95*. Singapore, 1994.
Jungnickel, R. "Recent Trends in Foreign Direct Investment". *Intereconomics*, May/June 1993, pp. 118–25.
Le Dang Doanh and Adam McCarty. "Economic Reform in Vietnam: Achievements and Prospects". In this volume.
Meier, Gerald M. *Leading Issues in Economic Development*. 5th ed. New York: Oxford University Press, 1989, pp. 254–67.
Michalopoulos, C. "Private Direct Investment, Finance and Development". *Asian Development Review* 3, no. 2 (1985), pp. 59–71.
Myat Thein and Mya Than. "Transitional Economy of Myanmar: Performance, Issues, and Problems". In this volume.
Pomfret, R. "Foreign Investment in a Centrally Planned Economy — Lessons from China: Comment on Kamath". *Economic Development and Cultural Change* 42, no. 2 (January 1994), pp. 413–18.
Singapore Trade Development Board. *Cambodia and Laos*. Market Information Series, in conjunction with business briefing on Cambodia and Laos, 2–3 July 1992, in Singapore.
Wall, D. and K. Fukasaku. "China's Open Economy Reforms 1978–1992". In *From Reform to Growth: China and Other Countries in Transition in Asia and Central and Eastern Europe*", edited by Lee C.H. and H. Reisen, pp. 141–82. Paris: Organization for Economic Co-operation and Development, 1994.
Yasuda, O., C. Hongladarom, and Mya Than, eds. *Vietnam, Laos and Cambodia: The Path to Economic Development*. 2 vols. Tokyo: Sasakawa Peace Foundation, 1993.

Part 2

Country Studies

6

Economic Reform in Vietnam: Achievements and Prospects

Le Dang Doanh and
Adam McCarty

Introduction

Vietnam has made substantial progress in moving from a predominantly centrally planned economic system to a relatively liberalized market economy. Indeed, by one definition, the transition to a functioning market economy was essentially achieved in 1989 when the two-price system was abolished, the exchange rate set at a reasonable level, inflation curbed with the use of interest rates, and competition in the goods market increased dramatically. The year 1989 was one of remarkable achievement, and the years since have largely seen consolidation and continued market liberalization, including, most importantly, steady progress in the difficult areas of institutional reform, such as legislation drafting, increasing tax collection and the tax base, tackling the problem of subsidized state-owned enterprises (SOEs), establishing an effective banking system, and redefining the role of government in a market economy.

This chapter surveys and evaluates the reforms which the Vietnamese have pursued over this transitional period. The pre-reform period is first examined to understand the initial conditions from which the reform began. Emphasis is given to the active and important role of parallel markets — in establishing prices and providing valuable price-responsive experiences for the SOEs. A substantive overview of the reforms, with particular reference to the 1989 stabilization programme, is then proffered, followed by an analysis of four key reform areas: SOE reform; financial sector liberalization; trade and investment; and social sector developments. For each of these four areas, a description of the reforms is accompanied by a prognosis of the impact, with ongoing policy issues highlighted. The sequencing of reforms is then reviewed in a separate section, including analyses of aspects of the political economy and the rationale underlying the reforms. The final section draws out the main conclusions of the Vietnamese experience.

The Pre-Reform Economy, 1976–88

After national unification in 1976, a five-year plan to "achieve basic socialist transition in the south" was initiated (Vo Nhan Tri 1990, p.58). All financial activity was brought under the control of the State Bank, and a drive to collectivize the villages in the region of the Mekong Delta began. The aim was also to merge the two disparate industrial regions — the predominantly light industry, import-substituting, and privately owned enterprises in the south with the northern centrally planned industrial complex biased to promote heavy-industry development.

That the plan failed in its objective to merge the two regions is hardly surprising. Infrastructural linkages were so weak that internal trade barriers strangled domestic trade. More importantly, the failure to increase agricultural output and the decline in foreign assistance after 1978 led to the plan's failure. Resistance to collectivization in the south saw output of staples fall by 9.1 per cent over 1976–78. The unqualified failure of the plan led to an economic crisis in 1979 which, in turn, precipitated a period of reforms which loosened the visibly deadening hand of central planning on the economy.

The early 1980s saw substantial increases in official prices to better reflect relative scarcities — substantial increases to plan prices were introduced in October 1981 (Tran 1989, p.91) — and to reduce the increasingly evident disparity between official and free-market prices. This adjustment precipitated a degree of 'officially sanctioned inflation' within the context of a classically 'repressed' financial system — with inflation peaking at 95.4 per cent in 1982 (see Figure 6.1). A strong supply response followed: total output of staples, which had stagnated between 1976 and 1979, increased from 14 million tons of rice equivalent in 1979 to 16.8 million tons in 1982. And the value of industrial production rose 23 per cent over 1981–83 (in constant 1982 prices).

In 1983 the price and related reforms were reversed. Attempts to strengthen planning controls aggravated demand shortages. In September 1985 the government introduced a partial reform package

FIGURE 6.1
Inflation in Vietnam, 1978–93

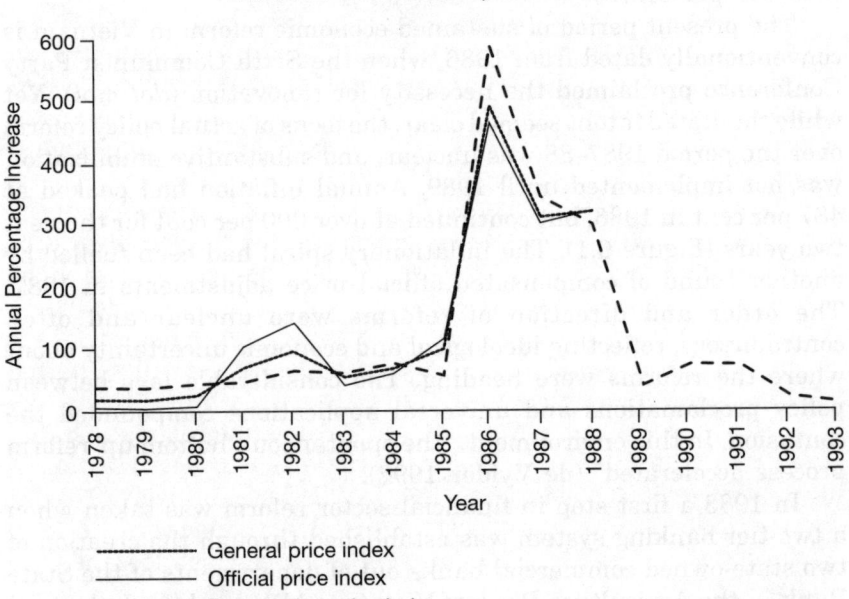

General price index
Official price index
Free-market price index

Note: With price reforms in 1989, there is no longer any distinction between official and free-market price indices.

Source: General Statistics Office (1993).

which, *inter alia*, hoped (again) to minimize the disparity between state and market prices, and in particular attempted to redress the appalling terms of trade facing the agricultural sector.[1] Also, a monetary reform was introduced whereby a new dong replaced the old on a ten-to-one basis up to limits. The main impact of this monetary reform fell upon the SOEs whose dong assets in banks diminished.[2] SOE cash shortages were then met by the government. Similarly, the price increases were accompanied by increased loans to SOEs and, importantly, wages. Money flowed into the 'household circuit' of the financial system through wage increases and from the monetarization of incomes as the ration book system was abolished. A budget collapse and spiralling inflation were inevitable. In 1984 budget revenues had covered 81 per cent of expenses, but in 1985 they covered only 55 per cent, and in 1986 the general price index rose 487 per cent.

The present period of sustained economic reform in Vietnam is conventionally dated from 1986, when the Sixth Communist Party Conference proclaimed the necessity for renovation (*doi moi*). Yet while the stated intent seemed clear, the focus of actual policy reform over the period 1987–88 was unclear, and substantive stabilization was not implemented until 1989. Annual inflation had peaked at 487 per cent in 1986, but continued at over 300 per cent for the next two years (Figure 6.1). The inflationary spiral had been fuelled by another round of compensated official price adjustments in 1987. The order and direction of reforms were unclear and often contradictory, reflecting ideological and economic uncertainty about where the reforms were heading. The considerable lags between policy proclamations and universal applications compounded the confusion. In this environment, "the spontaneous 'bottom up' reform process accelerated" (de Vylder 1992).

In 1988 a first step in financial sector reform was taken when a two-tier banking system was established through the creation of two state-owned commercial banks out of departments of the State Bank — the Agriculture Bank of Vietnam (ABV) and the Industrial and Commercial Bank of Vietnam (ICBV). However, the Vietnamese financial system in 1988 was little changed from a decade earlier, and still retained most of the dominant features of a 'classic socialist' system.[3] Two discrete monetary circuits operated: one for SOEs and one for households. The SOEs operated as protected and subsidized monopolies whose cash transactions were directed through the State Bank (substantial cash holdings were not allowed). SOE accounts at the State Bank were blocked — permissions were required to withdraw funds — and then these 'surplus funds' were appropriated by the government through high and sometimes arbitrary 'profit' taxes.[4] This "commodity inconvertibility" (McKinnon 1992, p.5) of SOE money meant that the impact of enterprise funds on the price level, under classical socialism, was contained.

In classical socialism it was through the household monetary circuit that free-market inflation could be generated (and, indirectly, official price rises as the government became increasingly unable to obtain supplies of key inputs, for example, rice, when the official price lagged behind the free-market price). Households held cash which could be spent on goods and services or deposited in banks. Predominantly, however, bank deposits were small as real interest rates were highly negative and withdrawals were sometimes difficult. Savings were mostly in substitute stores of value, such as gold, American dollars, rice, or other goods. Where the free market was weak, a degree of currency inconvertibility could apply also to households, with consequent forced savings and repression of inflationary pressures.

However, classical socialism — and associated repressed inflation — requires full control of retail prices. This was a condition never achieved in Vietnam, and consequently increased funds which flowed into the household monetary circuit led directly to inflation rather than to building up a monetary overhang. SOEs also engaged in out-of-plan activities involving cash transactions.[5] The challenge for Vietnamese planners was therefore to prevent the leakage of cash into the household monetary system, and to limit the inflationary impact of non-plan SOE activity. Strict wage and related controls were required to limit SOE money from feeding household-led inflation. The other important source for new household money was through direct fiscal expenditures. The failure to control the growth of household money, and then to maintain official price levels through a tight rationing regime, is reflected in the free-market price index of 1978–88 (Figure 6.1), which shows annual increases ranging from 39 per cent to 582 per cent for the period.

Official prices had to follow the parallel market to some degree. The need for the state to offer realistic purchase prices for agricultural production was a direct consequence of its "weakness" to implement "the logic of compulsion" in the Stalinist model.[6] Thus, in "permitting deviations, [the state] encouraged market-oriented behavior within the core institutions of the system" (Fforde 1991, p.5). Persistent inflation and the need for regular official price increases were the inevitable consequences of this soft application of central planning. In contrast, the retail price index increased about 1 per cent per year over 1980–90 (and had remained basically unchanged over 1960–80) in the Soviet Union, where strong compulsion mechanisms, and the weaker parallel market, kept inflation repressed.

Without Stalinist-style compulsion, the state was forced to adopt messy market-based procurement policies to obtain the agricultural surplus. Tran (1989, p.89) describes the prevailing policy in the 1980s:

> The State signed contracts with the producers to buy certain amounts of staple food products, effecting payment partly in materials for agricultural production at state prices and the rest in cash. Except for [these] compulsory deliveries, cooperatives and peasants had full freedom to use and market the output. The State could, however, make further purchases at negotiated prices or on a barter basis.

Crucial to this interpretation of causation is the relative strength — the leading effect — of the parallel or free market in Vietnam. Cottarelli and Blejer (1992) observe that " if parallel markets are too narrow, incomplete or inaccessible to the large majority of consumers, actual consumption would remain below its desired level, resulting in the emergence of involuntary savings with the consequent accumulation, over time, of a higher-than-desired level of wealth ['monetary overhang']" (p.51). The authors conclude that this was the case in the Soviet Union, yet this does not seem to have been so in Vietnam. De Vylder (1992) argues that in Eastern Europe "private farming and parallel markets have always played a larger role than they did in North Vietnam before the economic reforms" (p.4), but available price data do not support this conclusion after 1979.

The General Price Index of Figure 6.1 is a weighted average of the Official and Free-Market indexes up to 1988. The weightings given to these two indexes changed markedly each year and are, presumably, reflections of their relative importance and shares in aggregate economic activity.[7] Figure 6.2 shows the relative shares of these two indexes. The free market has always had a significant share of the aggregate index (in contrast, the Chinese equivalent

FIGURE 6.2
Proportionate Shares of the Official and Free-Market Price Indexes in the General Price Index of Vietnam

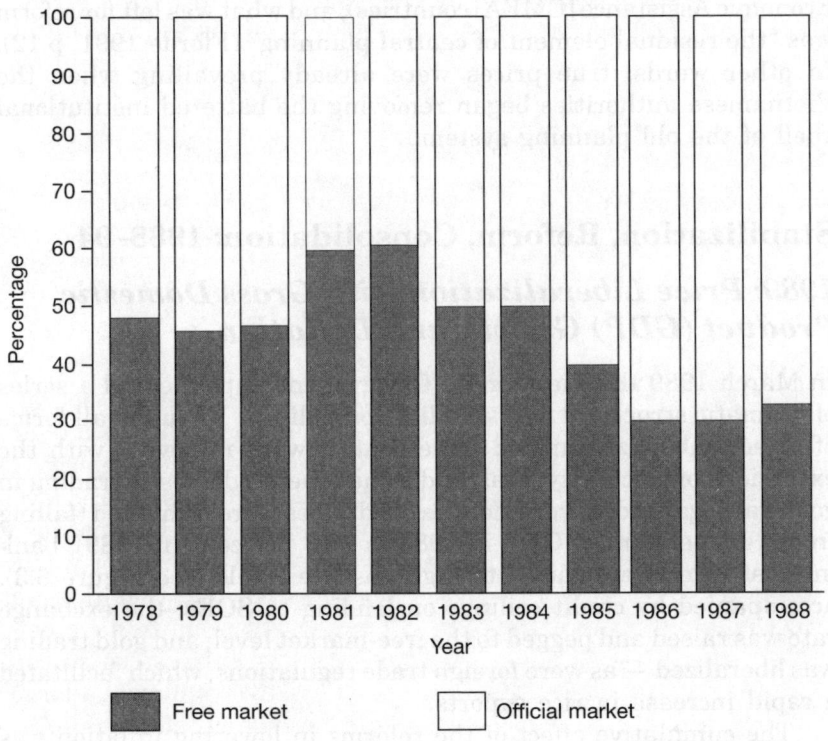

Source: General Statistics Office (1993).

share was around 12-15 per cent in the 1980s).[8] Over 1978–80, the free-market share ranged from 44 to 48 per cent of the aggregate index; it then rose to its peak at 61 per cent in 1982, before progressively falling to 24 per cent in 1987.

Paradoxically, the failure to maintain a classical socialist financial and pricing system put the Vietnamese economy in a strong position to undertake its price shock therapy of 1989. Repressed inflation associated with monetary overhang had been eliminated by free-market exchanges and annual inflation of over 300 per cent in the preceding three years. Free-market prices had come to dominate much economic activity (with the notable exception of key industrial sector inputs, where low prices could be maintained through the subsidized trading and aid relationship with Council of Mutual Economic Assistance [CMEA] countries), and what was left for reform was "the residual element of central planning" (Fforde 1991, p.12). In other words, true prices were already prevailing when the Vietnamese authorities began removing the battered institutional shell of the old planning system.

Stabilization, Reform, Consolidation: 1988–94

1989: Price Liberalization with Gross Domestic Product (GDP) Growth and Deflation

In March 1989 the Vietnamese Government implemented a series of dramatic structural and stabilization policies. Virtually all forms of direct subsidization and price control were removed (with the exceptions of electricity, coal, and some others); domestic trading in gold was legalized; government expenditures were tightened (falling from 14.1 per cent of GDP in 1988 to 12.3 per cent in 1989); bank interest rates were raised to high positive levels (see Figure 6.3), accompanied by credit ceilings on lending to SOEs; the exchange rate was raised and pegged to the free-market level; and gold trading was liberalized — as were foreign trade regulations, which facilitated a rapid increase in rice exports.

The cumulative effect of the reforms in lowering inflation was impressive. The inflation rate, which exhibited monthly increases of 13.6 per cent in 1988, rose by 9.2 per cent in February 1989, but then progressively fell and was even negative from May to July 1989 (Figure 6.3). As a result of excessive credit to the budget in the second half of 1989, monthly inflation rose to around 2.5 per cent and maintained that level into mid-1990.

Early 1989 witnessed a relative revival of faith in the domestic currency after years of near hyperinflation, with a consequent monetarization of the economy and of household saving portfolios. In a once-off event, households shifted into monetary assets which increased money demand as a percentage of GDP, and saw inflation rise only 34.7 per cent for the year despite an increase in M2 of 170 per cent.

FIGURE 6.3
Vietnam: Relationship between Consumer Price Index and Interest Rate for Savings, January 1988–June 1995

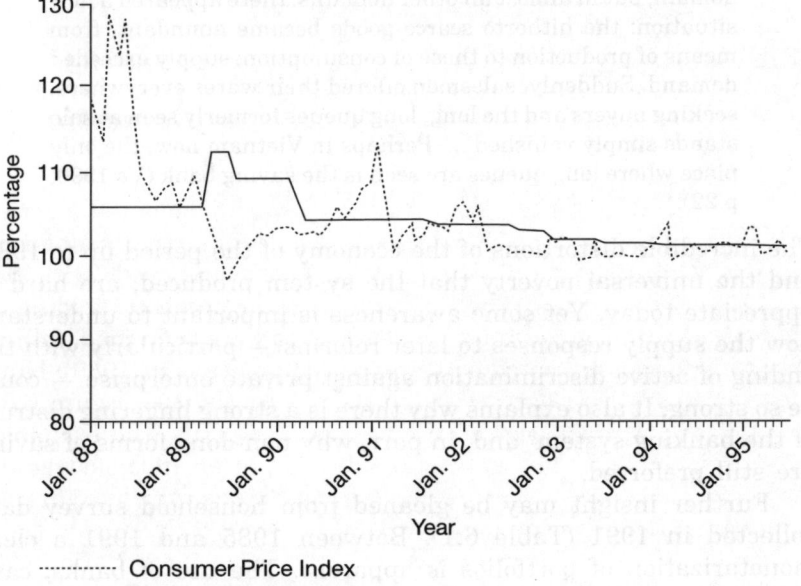

A variety of indicators provide evidence of this household monetarization. The real purchasing power of gold and dollars fell about 25 per cent over three months to May 1989, as households shifted into dong — much of which went into bank deposits (Dollar 1993). Over ten months from March 1989, household deposits in the commercial banks increased 630 per cent to 1.51 trillion dong (World Bank 1991); from 0.8 per cent of GDP at end-1988 to 3.8 per cent at end-1989 (Lipworth and Spitaller 1993).

Another aspect of the changing household portfolios was that hoarding of goods, particularly rice, stopped. Vietnamese commentators give this phenomenon particular importance:

> ...some people believe that thanks to a bumper harvest, the food problem in 1988 was satisfactorily settled. But it is not exactly so. In 1989, the average food output was 320 kgs per head, the same as in 1982. But the food problem in 1982 was extremely tense, while 1989 saw not only an adequate food supply for the people, but also an export of 1.4 million tons and an unprecedented food reserve. And not only in the food domain, but in almost all other domains, there appeared a new situation: the hitherto scarce goods became abundant, from means of production to those of consumption; supply exceeded demand. Suddenly, salesmen offered their wares everywhere, seeking buyers and the long, long queues formerly seen at sale stands simply vanished .... Perhaps in Vietnam now, the only place where long queues are seen is the saving bank (Vo 1990, p.22).

The incredible distortions of the economy of the period up to 1986, and the universal poverty that the system produced, are hard to appreciate today. Yet some awareness is important to understand how the supply responses to later reforms — particularly with the ending of active discrimination against private enterprise — could be so strong. It also explains why there is a strong lingering distrust of the banking system[9] and, in part, why non-dong forms of saving are still preferred.

Further insight may be gleaned from household survey data collected in 1991 (Table 6.1). Between 1985 and 1991 a clear monetarization of portfolios is apparent. The use of banks, cash holdings, and informal lending increased, while the number of households saving in gold, rice, and other goods decreased. However, in 1991 holdings of gold, rice, and other goods were still registered as the most important components of saving portfolios.

The once-off increased monetarization of the economy in 1989 helped to limit dramatically the inflationary impact of sweeping price reforms and continued strong monetary growth. That this occurred in a context of 8 per cent GDP growth for the year is even more extraordinary. This outcome was the result of lagged supply responses in the services and agricultural sectors to institutional changes introduced in 1988 (Figure 6.4). In 1988 the co-operative method of agricultural production was abandoned in favour of households (Decree 10 of April), and encouragement of small private enterprises became official policy (Resolution 27/HDBT of March and Decision 16/NQTU of July). The consequence was high growth

TABLE 6.1
Changing Saving Portfolios of Hanoi Households, 1985–91

Form of Saving	Households out of 1,000 Sampled		% Change 1985–91	1991 Importance Ranking*
	1985	1991		
Gold	177	114	–35.59	1.56
Dollars	46	62	34.78	1.86
Dong cash	97	110	13.40	2.17
Rice	85	67	–21.18	1.48
Other goods	436	305	–30.05	1.57
Banks	271	292	7.75	1.80
Informal lending	25	28	12.00	2.07
Credit co-operatives	59	35	–40.68	1.91

*Household heads were asked to rank each form of saving in 1991, with '1' being 'most important'. This index is the mean of all respondents, and hence a low score indicates importance.

Source: Survey of 1,000 Hanoi households conducted by Adam McCarty in 1991, with the assistance of the Vietnamese Institute for World Economy.

in these areas in 1989, which more than compensated for declining industrial production (which fell 2.8 per cent).[10]

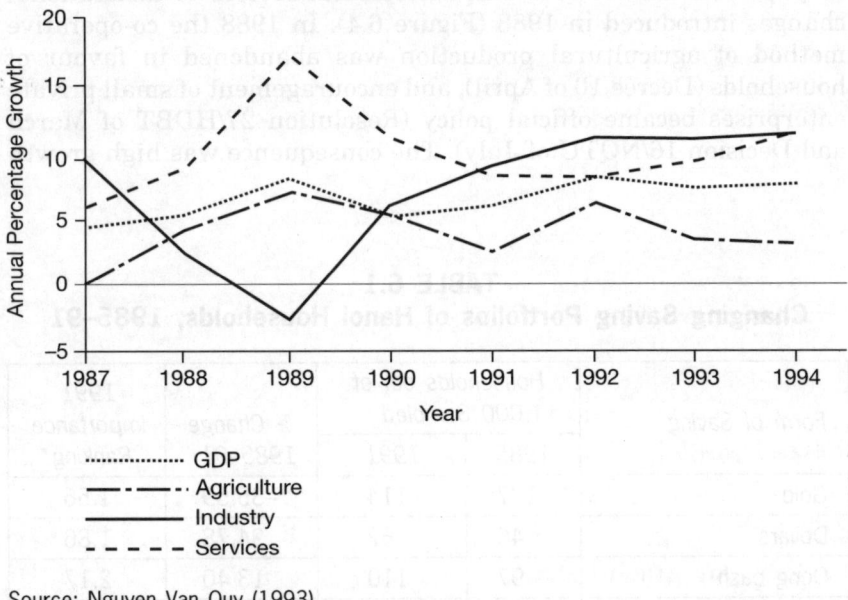

FIGURE 6.4
GDP and Sectoral Growth Rates in Vietnam, 1987–94

Source: Nguyen Van Quy (1993).

Macroeconomic Stability after 1989

Fiscal expansion in late 1989 continued into 1990. Inflation returned at significant monthly rates and the real interest rate became negative again in August 1990 (Figure 6.3). Increases in budget revenues, particularly from oil exports in 1990, helped to contain inflation below three digits annually (Figure 6.1), but the fundamental causes — money-financed budget deficits and SOE subsidization — remained.

FIGURE 6.5
Vietnamese Budget Items as Percentage of GDP

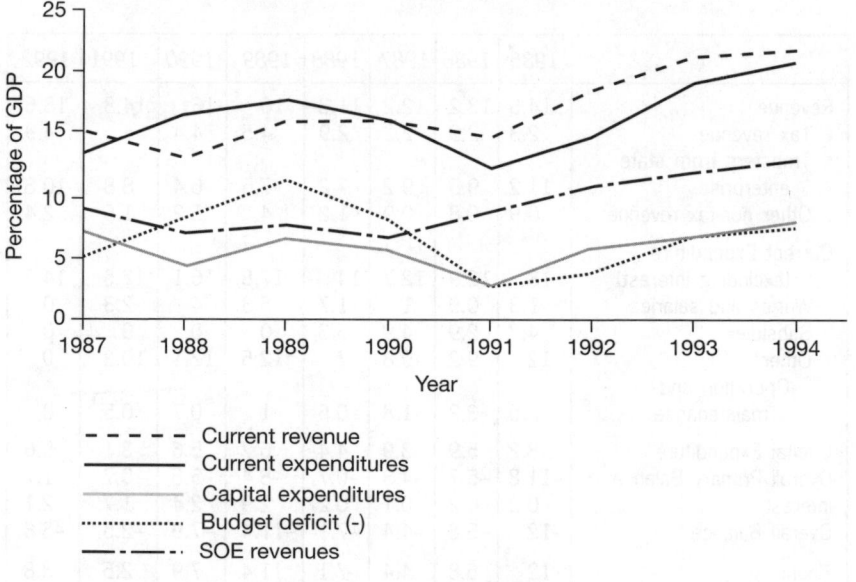

Sources: Nguyen Van Quy (1993) and World Bank (1993).

In 1991 significant cuts in government current and capital expenditures pushed the budget deficit down to 2.5 per cent of GDP (see Figure 6.5).

At a Central Committee meeting of the Communist Party in December 1991, macroeconomic stability and control of inflation were declared the priority policy objectives to 1995. This announcement preceded an anti-inflationary drive, characterized by large-scale selling of dollar and gold reserves to draw dong from circulation, which pushed the inflation rate down to 17.4 per cent for 1992. The momentum has been maintained and inflation for 1993 was about 7 per cent. Stability in the exchange rate, and in gold buying and selling, has also been maintained since 1991. Meanwhile, the State Bank has progressively lowered interest rates, the monthly

TABLE 6.2
Summary of Budget Operations in Vietnam, 1985–92
(In percentages of GDP)

	1985	1986	1987	1988	1989	1990	1991	1992
Revenue	14.5	13.2	12.2	11.3	16	16	14.8	18.6
Tax revenue	2.3	2.9	2.2	2.9	4.5	4.4	4	4.9
Transfers from state								
enterprises	11.2	9.5	9.2	7.2	7.5	6.4	8.8	10.8
Other non-tax revenue	0.9	0.8	0.9	1.2	4	5.2	1.5	2.4
Current Expenditure								
(excluding Interest)	18	12.9	12.7	14	17.8	16.1	12.5	14.7
Wages and salaries	1.3	0.9	1	1.7	5.3	4	2.3	0
Subsidies	4.7	2.9	4.9	5.3	0	0	0	0
Other	12	9.2	6.8	7	12.5	12.1	10.2	0
Operation and								
maintenance	2.5	3.2	1.8	0.5	1	0.7	0.5	0
Capital Expenditure	8.2	5.9	3.9	4.4	6.7	5.6	3.1	5.6
Overall Primary Balance	–11.8	–5.7	–4.3	–0.7	–8.4	–5.6	–0.7	–1.7
Interest	0.2	0.2	0.1	0.2	2.9	2.4	1.7	2.1
Overall Balance	–12	–5.8	–4.4	–7.1	–11.4	–7.9	–2.5	–3.8
Financing	12	5.8	4.4	-7.1	11.4	7.9	2.5	3.8
Foreign grants and								
loans (net)	4.9	2.2	1.4	2.4	4.4	4.9	1.9	2.8
Domestic loans	7.1	3.6	3	3	8.1	3.1	0.6	1
State Bank (net)	7.1	3.6	2.9	2.9	8.1	3.1	—	—
Government securities								
(net)	0	0	0.1	0.1	—	—	—	—
Arrears	—	—	—	1.7	–1.1	—	—	—

Notes: 1. — Data not available.
2. Due to wage/price reform measures undertaken during the year, 1985 data may not be entirely consistent with data of other years.
3. For 1985–88, figures include amortization.
4. Figures for 1992 are preliminary.

Source: World Bank (1993).

rate for three-month deposits falling from 2 per cent to 1.4 per cent in 1994 (Figure 6.3).

Government revenues from SOEs have remained surprisingly buoyant over the reform period (Figure 6.5 and Table 6.2). This is surprising because the substantial restructuring of the SOEs since 1989, including a 'hardening' of their budget constraints, is typically associated with declining revenue contributions to the government. It would seem that the strong supply response to the reforms has also been evident in the SOEs (in aggregate), and this has given the government some time to diversify its tax system.

Control of the fundamental causes of monetary and inflationary growth is increasing. Indirect subsidies to SOEs lowered significantly in 1992. In 1993 current budget revenues increased 13 per cent, in part because prices have increased for petrol, postal services, and electricity, as the government moves to broaden the tax base (although these areas are still lightly taxed by international standards). However, pressures to increase government expenditures (including salary increases for public servants) and a continuing rise in the capital expenditure budget, up from 3.1 per cent of GDP in 1991 to 6.8 per cent in 1993, pushed the budget deficit up to 7.2 per cent of GDP for the year (Figure 6.5). On the other hand, more diversified means of deficit financing, including experimental bond floats, have reduced the deficit impact on money supply growth (estimated at 16 per cent [M2] for 1993, down significantly from 33 per cent in 1992 and 79 per cent in 1991). Non-inflationary financing of the budget deficit began in 1992 (Le Dang Doanh 1994) and planned to continue into 1994, with consequent annual inflation forecast at only 8-9 per cent.

Figure 6.5 also illustrates the impressive record of budget control over the transition period in Vietnam. In 1989 the deficit had risen to 11.4 per cent of GDP, but controls on current expenditure and maintained revenue flows saw it fall to 2.47 per cent of GDP in 1991. Since 1991, the increase in revenues has facilitated maintenance of the deficit at about a manageable 7 per cent of GDP. Pressures to increase current expenditures remain, and the need to rapidly increase capital expenditures will soon be evident. Deficits of up to 10 per cent of GDP may develop in the next few years. This is not necessarily undesirable, especially if the additional spending is going into the capital budget or to health and education, but a return to double-digit inflation would then be likely.

Despite recent increases, the present level of government capital expenditure is inadequate and will have to rise significantly to meet the counterpart commitments of donor projects in the future. Much of the 1993 expenditure increase went to funding the 500KV north-south power line. This project, for which work began in 1992, has exceeded the initial cost estimate of US$300 million by about 60 per cent. Also, work began before completion of the feasibility study, the tendering procedures were sloppy, and instances of corruption have been revealed. This project experience indicates the weak institutional capacity of the Vietnamese agencies to implement large infrastructure projects to international standards. Consequently the absorptive capacity of the economy — the ability to turn aid commitments into disbursements — will be a key issue for the rest of the decade.

In 1993 the Vietnamese Government announced that it required US$40 billion in capital investments to meet its development goals to the year 2000. This is an optimistic target, yet in mid-1994 the target was raised to US$50 billion (Reuters, 18 May 1994). The government planned to raise half of the capital from domestic sources. Domestic savings have risen steadily since 1989, but are still low at 8.7 per cent of GDP in 1993 (about US$1 billion). Foreign direct investment is targeted to produce about US$13 billion of the desired capital (foreign direct investment capital commitments over 1988–93 totalled US$7.5 billion). The final US$7 billion is projected to come from aid donors. With the US$1.86 billion of aid commitments secured for 1994, it seems that commitments, if not actual disbursements, should meet the target.

Taken together then, what can we conclude about Vietnamese macroeconomic policy over recent years? Firstly, that the stated priority of the leadership is indeed reflected in actual events and policies: the commitment to macroeconomic stability is sincere. Secondly, that there exists an understanding of the fundamentals of macroeconomic management and a willingness to take some tough decisions. The abolition of the two-price system in 1989 came as a surprise to many Vietnam observers, as did the dramatic credit squeeze; the control of budget expenditures in 1991; and the progressive renovation of SOEs and reduction of their subsidies in recent years. Indeed, Vietnam has won acclaim from *Euromoney* and *Asiamoney* as the "best-managed economy for 1993".

The third conclusion is that a record of stability is beginning to generate *expectations* of continued stability. Expectations of macroeconomic stability facilitate the development of long-term lending by the financial sector — medium- and long-term credits by the banks increased by 63.5 per cent in 1993; short-term by 18 per cent (Nguyen Van Quy 1993, p.10) — and increase the degree of monetarization of economic activity.

However, many problems remain which could threaten continued long-term stability: pressures to increase the government deficit; a worrying speculative boom in real estate; poor terms of trade for the rural sector; continuing ideological ambiguity from the Vietnamese leadership about the desired direction of reforms; and continuing high unemployment and growing social problems. However macroeconomic stability seems assured for the immediate future.

Factor Markets

While a stable macroeconomy is a prerequisite to sustained growth, liberalization of the factor markets — goods, capital, and labour — will determine the pace and nature of that growth, and hence the structure of demand for labour. The following sections review the policies which have liberalized these markets in recent years and assess the specific key areas of reform.

The Goods Market

Prices for goods and services in Vietnam are now predominantly determined by market supply and demand, as the government continues to move from direct involvement in resource allocation and production to indicative planning and regulatory responsibilities. The goods and services market operates more freely than the others mainly because it is the most difficult to control, especially trading. Smuggling has led to an influx of overseas goods, and poor tax collection has meant low effective tax rates on importing and trading. Consequently, since 1989 the number and variety of consumption goods available in Vietnam have increased dramatically and domestic products are becoming increasingly competitive with imports.

The Capital Market

The Vietnamese capital market remains extremely underdeveloped. For example, 78 per cent of bank loans still go to SOEs (down from over 90 per cent in previous years). Interest rates are still set by planners, and the State Bank lacks adequate independence from the government in setting monetary policy. Informal credit markets exist for small-scale activity, but the bulk of private sector activity is self-funded. A people's credit system is being tried out again. Progress is being made, but a fundamental hurdle is a lack of skills in conducting banking businesses in the competitive market environment. Seven foreign banks have been licensed to operate, and much can be learnt from them, but it will take some years before Vietnamese banks would be able to compete on equal terms.

An ineffective capital market limits the expansion of private sector ventures; props up weak SOEs; hinders the mobilization of domestic capital resources; and facilitates the channelling of existing private savings into less productive activities like real estate speculation. In short, it preserves the status quo and reduces the rate of economic change and growth.

The Labour Market

A labour market exists in Vietnam, but in a highly distorted form. Private sector activity is small-scale and employment is conducted informally. Unskilled agricultural labour is becoming increasingly mobile, and many labourers work seasonally on urban construction sites as the construction boom continues. However, skilled workers and state employees still operate in highly regulated labour markets. The requirement to obtain the permission of employers to leave a job is still common in many occupations. Wages and other remunerations are still highly regulated for state employees, and labour mobility — to move from one city to another — remains restricted.

FIGURE 6.6
Agricultural Production in Vietnam, 1976–93

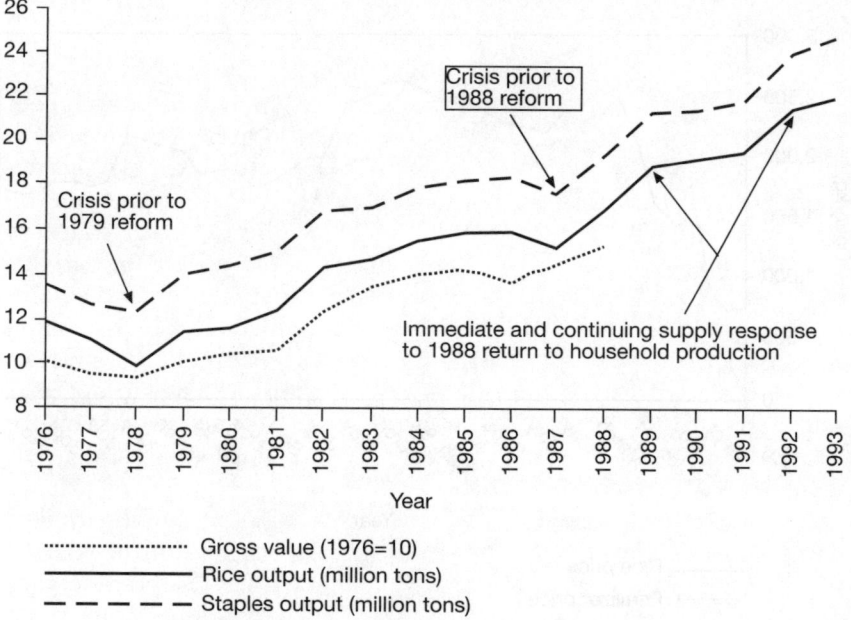

Gross value (1976=10)
Rice output (million tons)
Staples output (million tons)

Notes: 1. Gross value of agricultural production is an index at 1982 prices.
2. Total staples output is in millions of tons of rice equivalent.

Sources: Le Thanh Nghiep (1993) and Le Dang Doanh (1994).

Without an efficient labour market the development of new industries and employment opportunities is retarded. Empowering employees to move on to new occupations in different companies, and in different cities, and to negotiate for wages which reflect the real need for their services, facilitates the rate of increase of employment in the various growth areas of the economy.

FIGURE 6.7
Rice and Fertilizer Price Movements in Hanoi,
July 1990 to December 1993

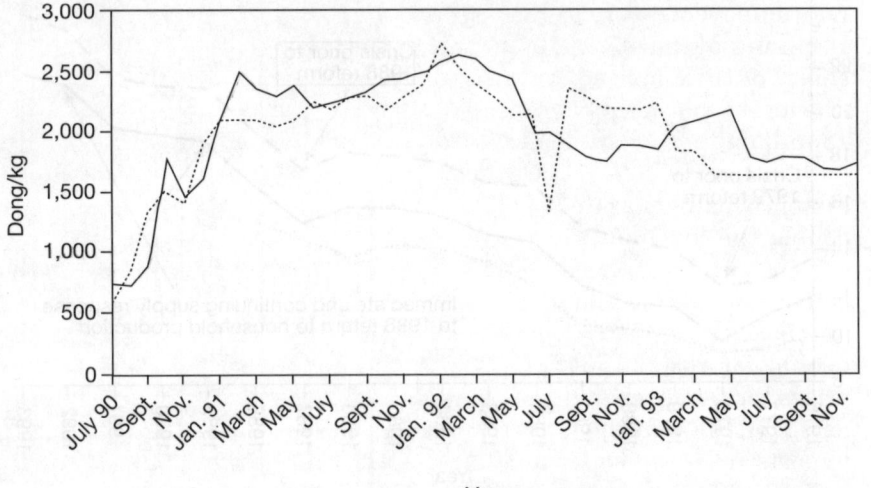

Source: Le Dang Doanh (1994).

Key Reform Areas

Agriculture

Employing 77 per cent of the Vietnamese labour force, and producing 40 per cent of GDP, the agricultural sector constitutes the backbone of the productive economy in Vietnam. While it is typically a declining sector over the development process, agricultural production will remain an important component of aggregate production (and determinant of domestic demand) in Vietnam well into the next century. Indeed, the issue of food sufficiency still remains relevant to Vietnam, and due consideration of a balanced growth development strategy is necessary.

Figure 6.6 shows the unsteady rise in agricultural production since 1976. It also shows how the agricultural sector has driven the reform movements over that period — reforms have been crisis-led. Declining output over 1978-79 had precipitated the liberalization efforts of 1979 and the contract system introduced in the early 1980s (the messy marketization described above). From an output of around 13 million tons of staples prior to 1979, production rose to about 16 million tons, where it stagnated until the co-operative production system was dismantled in 1988. Total output is now approaching double the level of 1978.

The output changes are also responses to relative price changes, both for rice output and for key inputs. Fertilizer is the most important purchased input for rice production, and its price is highly correlated to that for rice output (Figure 6.7). There was a rapid rise in the prices for fertilizer and rice in 1990, when the supply of subsidized fertilizer through the CMEA trading relationship ended. Fertilizer imports from the convertible area rose from 406,000 tons in 1989 to 1,161,000 tons in 1990, and then doubled again in 1991. Since 1990 both rice and fertilizer prices have fallen in relation to the prevailing inflation rate. Thus, the purchasing power of farmers has been declining relative to urban areas in recent years, even when increases in output are accounted for.

The agricultural sector highlight for 1993 came on 14 July when the National Assembly approved a new land law. Annual crop farmers were given twenty-year renewable tenure rights to their land, which was to be a maximum of three hectares. The new code allows citizens to transfer, exchange, lease, and inherit rights to use farmland. They can also use land as collateral for farm loans.

The consequences of this new law are unclear. Certainly security of tenure and freedom of choices are commendable, but in conditions of poverty and without an effective formal banking system, lending activity is often conducted at usurious rates. An unjustly landless peasantry could emerge over the years to come.

Crisis in agricultural production has been a driving force for liberalization in Vietnam. Other crises, such as the collapse of the Soviet Union (and its communist parties), with the subsequent loss of aid and subsidized CMEA trade flows, and civil disorder in Myanmar and China have contributed to the forces compelling change. With the crises overcome, the embargo lifted, and multilateral aid flows resumed, one may now wonder about the strength of commitment by a fundamentally unchanged and conservative leadership to continue with radical restructuring and its concomitant loss of economic control.

Financial Sector Restructuring and Legal Framework

Establishing, on paper, the two-tier banking system in 1988 had little immediate impact on the financial system. It was not until the monetarization of 1989 that the formal Vietnamese banking system "came of age" — when deposit growth caused "a transformation of the degree of penetration of the banking system in the economy" (World Bank 1991, p.76). In 1989 deposits grew from 0.8 per cent of GDP to 3.8 per cent (still low by international standards, and constituting "a major constraint to economic growth" [Asian Development Bank 1991, p.10]), and M2 as a share of GDP had increased from around 11 per cent in 1988 to 24 per cent in 1989 (World Bank 1993, p.65).[11]

The increase in monetary depth in 1989 was followed by important institutional reform in 1990. On 1 October 1990 the Law for the Vietnamese State Bank and the National Law on Banks, Co-operative Credit Institutions, and Financial Institutions became effective. The State Bank was specifically prohibited from commercial banking activities, but was empowered with the formal legal powers of a central bank, including: authority to set and enforce reserve requirements, to engage in open market operations, to manage official exchange reserves, and to establish an effective system of bank supervision (Asian Development Bank 1991, p.11). The second decree gave the state commercial banks greater autonomy and permitted them to compete with each other and to seek capital from sources other than the state.

However, in 1990 the actual functioning of the financial system remained much the same as it had before. SOE money was still channelled into the commercial banks and most of their lending went straight back to SOEs. Indeed, the relationship between the commercial banks and the SOEs, and the gradual weaning of the latter by imposing harder budget constraints[12] is a central aspect of the financial and economic liberalization of transitional economies.

M2 as a share of GDP fell back to slightly over 18 per cent in 1990 and 1991, while the growth in deposits lagged behind inflation, as real interest rates became negative again and banks had little incentive to mobilize deposits anyway (as the interest rate regime made financial intermediation unprofitable).

The proportion of lending to non-state enterprises (NSEs) has been increasing rapidly since 1991, albeit from a low base. In June 1992 credits granted to the non-state sector represented 15 per cent of total commercial bank lending, and by June 1993 these had grown to 22 per cent (Economist Intelligence Unit 4th Qtr 1993, p.34).[13] Strong forces are pushing this trend. As we have seen, the budget constraints facing SOEs are being progressively hardened; the institutional environment (laws and property rights) is improving and reducing the risks associated with NSE lending; and bank autonomy and experience are increasing.

The Agricultural Bank of Vietnam (ABV) was prompt in adapting to changed circumstances. Authorization for lending to farm households was given in July 1991 (Directive 202/HDBT), and within six months the bank had lent 405 billion dong (about US$36 million) to 558,680 households (about US$65 per household). Initial repayment rates were excellent, and "to free itself for its new private sector market, ABV cut credit delivery to 3,048 state enterprises and 12,397 agricultural production cooperatives" (Pham 1992, p.14). ABV lending in 1991 was for three months at four monthly interest rates ranging from 1.8–6 per cent, depending on the geographic region of the borrower.[14] The average lending rate of about 3.5 per cent was equal to the deposit rate paid on three-month deposits, with consequent bank losses on financial intermediation.

The legal and property rights framework to support bank lending is also gradually being strengthened. It is important to appreciate that this process involves a devolution of economic and legal autonomy from the state to individuals, and that prior to the recent reforms, "law was in reality Party policy, either dressed in the formality of legislation or exercised through administrative fiat" (Gillespie 1992, p.3). Legal codes under central planning are rudimentary and, without precise rules, "individuals will tend to look for guidance outside of the law, and in these circumstances State ideology will assume a quasi legal status" (Gillespie 1992, p.9). The task of developing a commercial rights-based legal system is therefore formidable, both technically and politically.

A variety of commercial laws have been passed since 1986. These include the Land Law (1987), which established private use of allotted land in agriculture, and a series of ordinances which have begun to codify contractual procedures.[15] The Law on Private Enterprises and Law on Companies were introduced in 1990. Changes to the Constitution in 1992 allowed individuals to exercise property rights over both income-producing assets and personal property (Khng 1993). A bankruptcy law was introduced in 1993, as was a new land law that clarified property rights and allowed mortgages on land. At least fourteen new ordinances and laws were expected to be passed in 1994. These included a commercial law, a domestic investment law, an insurance law, and a mortgage law (Mehta 1994).

Enforcement of these new laws presents a different set of institutional constraints. The legacy of the Party-dominated legal system is that "courts have yet to develop a high level of commercial expertise or a robust form of independence" (Gillespie 1992, p.9). Yet codification, and clarity of rights on paper, is an important first step to developing an effective legal and property rights framework for a market-based economy. The strengthening of that framework has a direct impact on financial sector development, by lowering the risks in lending to the non-state sector, through improved collateral arrangements, contracts, and, of course, property rights. As the World Bank (1991, p.7) observed : "Recent growth in output [and bank lending] has in fact been concentrated in those areas where property rights have been strengthened."

A notable feature of financial sector reform since 1988 has been the early encouragement of a wide range of non-state financial intermediaries. Many of these already existed when the National

Law on Banks, Co-operative Credit Institutions, and Financial Institutions became effective in 1990. These included shareholding and housing banks, as well as rural and urban credit co-operatives. However, while numerous and diverse, the aggregate size of the non-state intermediaries remains quite small. In June 1993 total loans made by the eight branches of foreign banks, the three joint-venture banks, and the twenty-two joint-stock commercial banks represented only 11 per cent of those made by the state commercial banks (Economist Intelligence Unit 1993/94, p.24). These banks will remain a minor though dynamic part of the financial sector for some time.

Substantive and innovative reforms are continuing in the Vietnamese financial sector. In 1993 the first fully private Vietnamese bank was approved; Vietnamese individuals were permitted to open accounts (in dong or dollars) at foreign banks; interbank trading and the payments system have improved markedly; and, importantly, the Vietnamese commercial banks have been given permission to seek foreign shareholdings of up to 30 per cent in their businesses. Thirteen new laws were due in 1994, as well as regulations for a stock exchange due that year or in 1995 (Beaulieu 1994).

Progress has been made in turning the Vietnamese financial sector into its market-oriented equivalent. The prudential de-regulation of the past five years has achieved much. However, the inevitable conclusion must be that the Vietnamese financial system remains ineffective at mobilizing resources and channelling them to productive investments. Improved financial resource mobilization relates, in part, to the question of credibility — in banks, in the reform process, and in the government. Only continued reform, macroeconomic stability, and improved bank services will foster the necessary confidence in future expectations to draw development money into the banking system. A better interest rate regime would also help, particularly one that gives an incentive for banks to mobilize deposits. Finally, continued institutional reforms and improved supervision of financial institutions will generate efficiency gains, reduce lending risks, and help to establish the formal financial sector as the focus of resource mobilization that it should be.

TABLE 6.3
Incremental Capital-Output Ratios for Vietnam, 1988–92

	1988	1989	1990	1991	1992
ICOR	2.14	1.56	1.15	2.06	1.58

Source: Le Dang Doanh (1994).

State-Owned Enterprise Reform: Hardening Budget Constraints

A significant degree of operational autonomy was first given to the SOEs in the early 1980s, when official sanctioning of (already widespread) out-of-plan production activities was given (Fforde and de Vylder 1988). SOE non-plan activity was, in theory, only a supplement to plan commitments, but it became increasingly important over time and gave enterprise directors valuable experience at price-responsive production (free-market prices).[16] In 1985 the system of enterprise accounting was improved,[17] and in 1987 SOE directors were given increased autonomy over their production activities, including the formulation of plans, the purchase and sale of assets, the setting of some prices, labour recruitment, and in finance (they could choose which bank they wanted to hold accounts with).[18] However, control of the SOE financial circuit remained tight, and a May 1988 International Monetary Fund (IMF) report notes that: "To ensure the proper control on state enterprise activities, there is a limit on cash holdings by enterprises and they are also discouraged from engaging in cash transactions with the state sector agencies (e.g., other enterprises and cooperatives)" (p.26). Further, "there is a limit on...withdrawal of deposits by enterprises and enterprises cannot lend to each other" (p.30).

The 1989 price shock therapy included the removal of the two-price system and an ending of direct budget subsidies to SOEs. Enterprises found that the markets had transformed from supply-led structures focused on rationed inputs to ones led by consumer demand. Credit limits on bank lending were enforced. The net result was a dramatic shakeup in the SOE sector, and a hardening of budget constraints. In 1989 industrial output fell by 2.8 per cent (Figure 6.4), and industrial employment in the state sector fell by 14 per cent (767,300 persons). A 1991 survey of twenty-seven industrial enterprises in Hanoi (McCarty 1993) found that employment in these enterprises was only 62 per cent of its 1986 level, and that eleven (41 per cent) of the twenty-seven directors had been newly appointed over 1989–91.[19]

The impressive supply response of the SOE sector to the 1989 shakeup — industrial output increased by 6 per cent in 1990 — contributed to the revival of the SOE contribution to government revenues (Figure 6.5) and to their ability to repay bank loans. Explanation for the strong output response lies in part with appreciating that the in-plan production of the SOEs had been a naturally declining part of overall production for some years.[20] SOEs had continued to participate in the 'game' of plan production so long as subsidized inputs continued to be supplied through the two-price system, and so long as tight financial and other controls forced them to. The removal of physical planning and rationing in 1989 removed much of their incentive to produce for the plan. However, the government still controlled access to finance, hired and fired the managers, and continued to provide cheap inputs through imports from the CMEA trading relationship.

Some SOEs, particularly those producing consumer and building industry products, benefited directly from the 1989 reforms and the associated rise in consumer demand. Other reasons for increased industrial output included a once-off releasing of hoarded stocks by enterprises (de Vylder 1992, p.18), and an increase in the utilization of existing capital stocks.[21] Improved utilization of existing capacity is reflected in the extremely low Incremental Capital-Output Ratio (ICOR) over 1989–90[22] (Table 6.3).

A variety of forces were supporting the increase of bank credit to SOEs in late 1989. Banks were faced with an on-lending problem after the rapid buildup of deposits in 1989. For SOEs, bank lending now became the main mechanism for continuing soft budget constraints, and for government authorities facilitating bank credits became important for maintaining control over the SOEs and ensuring continued revenues from them.[23] Therefore, despite credit controls and higher interest rates earlier in the year (Figure 6.3), domestic credit to non-financial state enterprises increased 74 per cent in 1989 (World Bank 1993, p.282), which was slightly more than double the rate of inflation. Increasing levels of subsidized credit (real lending rates were mostly negative from February 1990 to March 1991 [Figure 6.3]), combined with inflationary financing of the government deficit, helped to push inflation up to 67 per cent annually over 1990–91.

In 1991 the collapse of the CMEA trading relationship removed another prop of SOE subsidization. The ability of the government to provide cheap material inputs was now limited to a few key commodities like land and electricity. Further, a series of decrees since 1990 have increased SOE managerial autonomy and continued to harden the budget constraints SOEs have been facing. Decree 332 (October 1991) established the right of SOEs to manage their assets, while Decree 388 of the same year "provided for the first time legal rules for the process of state enterprise formation and the objectives for their operation" (World Bank 1993, p.58).

Also, Decree 315 (1990) had initiated a review of existing SOEs to evaluate the extent of debt and SOE liquidation requirements. A Debt Resolution Committee was established in March 1991, and as "of July 15, 1992, some 1,259 enterprises had been liquidated, out of around 4,000 that have ceased operation. For other loss-making enterprises, the guiding principle seems to be to avoid liquidation through mergers with profitable enterprises" (World Bank 1993, p.73).[24]

In 1992 "subsidised credit from the banking system was virtually stopped" (World Bank 1993, p.51), and real lending rates became positive again. The lending rates for state and non-state enterprises were almost unified by the end of 1993 (Economist Intelligence Unit 1993/94). More recent pronouncements[25] have clarified the commitment to continued restructuring of SOEs and of SOE management, including experiments with boards of directors and privatization. Regulations for boards of directors and a comprehensive state enterprise law are being prepared.

It has been noted above that financial and production control of the Vietnamese SOEs was never as comprehensive as in many centrally planned economies. One consequence of this was that SOE money leaked into the household financial circuit and fed free-market inflation. Another consequence was that SOEs devoted increasing shares of resources to out-of-plan activity (Fforde and de Vylder 1988), which provided valuable experience in operating under market conditions where relative and absolute prices mattered (de Vylder 1992). These features of the SOE sector in Vietnam play an important role in explaining the success of the 1989 stabilization, and in the quick recovery of industrial production shortly thereafter (see Figure 6.4).

In other aspects, control of SOEs in Vietnam seems to have been tighter than in other transitional economies. Vietnam has not allowed the development of 'wildcat' SOE-owned banks which has plagued the financial liberalization of Russia. Also, in some transitional economies it has been noted that SOE "wages and employment are subject to a joint maximization. Workers will not be constrained directly by the labor demand curve but by the firm's profit level" (Commander 1992, p.9). In the context of soft enterprise budgets, increases in wages can therefore get out of control when union interest groups are strong. However, "the greater link between firm performance and wages in Viet Nam, compared with other transitional economies, has probably contributed to a healthier SOE sector" (World Bank 1993, p.72), and SOE wage-push inflation has not been a problem.

An explanation for the relative control of SOE wages in Vietnam lies in understanding that there has always been a large free market — money could matter — and that leakages from the SOE financial circuit, monetary and otherwise, have always been significant. Consequently, unable to repress inflation, the authorities have always had to fix SOE wage levels and set increases to output performances.[26] That is, wage-push inflation has always been an issue in Vietnam, whereas in many of the more rigorously controlled former centrally planned economies the rationing system so dominated that money holdings became irrelevant. With liberalization efforts, these strongly rationed economies found themselves with substantial monetary overhangs and new problems when, at last, money mattered to wage earners in the SOEs.

The extent of interfirm and bank debts in Vietnam is "on a far smaller scale than in other transitional economies" (World Bank 1993, p.72). Indeed, net interfirm credits and bad debts in the

Vietnamese banking system total less than 5 per cent of GDP, while in Romania and Russia net interfirm arrears alone constitute over 25 per cent of GDP (World Bank 1993, p.14). In 1991 the total debt of the main 10,000 Vietnamese SOEs was about 9 trillion dong (9 per cent of GDP), of which about a third were bad debts (one trillion dong of bad debts being owed to the banks). The bank debt was limited because much of SOE financial assistance, until about 1990, had come from direct budgetary transfers.

The Vietnamese SOE sector is also different from its Chinese and East European counterparts in a number of other ways. Vietnam has not been burdened with a large heavy industry complex. Most of Vietnam's SOEs are involved in light industries (World Bank 1993, p.56). The share of the industrial SOE sector in the economy was also smaller; in 1989 it produced 10.5 per cent of GDP, while in China the figure was 57 per cent, and in Poland (1985) 40 per cent (World Bank, 1992).

However, the industrial SOEs still constitute a significant proportion of the non-agricultural economy of Vietnam, and they continue to be the main source of government revenues (from a trough of 40 per cent of total budget revenue in 1990, the SOE contribution to the budget rose to 61 per cent in 1991 and has fallen only marginally since then [see Figure 6.5]). The SOEs also remain the main customers of the commercial banks. In 1991 only 10 per cent of new credit went to the non-state sector, although this increased to 35 per cent in 1992 (World Bank 1993, p.68).

Commentators frequently remark that, in Vietnam and other transitional economies, there seems to be a continuing "bureaucratic bias towards feeding SOE 'investment hunger' through state loans" (Gates and Truong 1992, p.12).[27] In fact, continued SOE lending by the banks has a commercial logic aside from reasons of seemingly irrational bias or preference. Banks lend to SOEs with an expectation of being bailed out should any enterprise fail. This is an inevitable consequence of the continuing soft-budget constraints facing SOEs. The expectation of being bailed out for poor lending to SOEs is based on past experience and can be viewed as probability estimate to be included in loan risk assessment. Kornai (1993) notes that in such circumstances, each "party, counting on the other to continue to behave in the habitual way, itself abides by the unwritten terms of the contract" (p.318).[28]

FIGURE 6.8
Vietnam's Changing Trading Partners, 1985–93

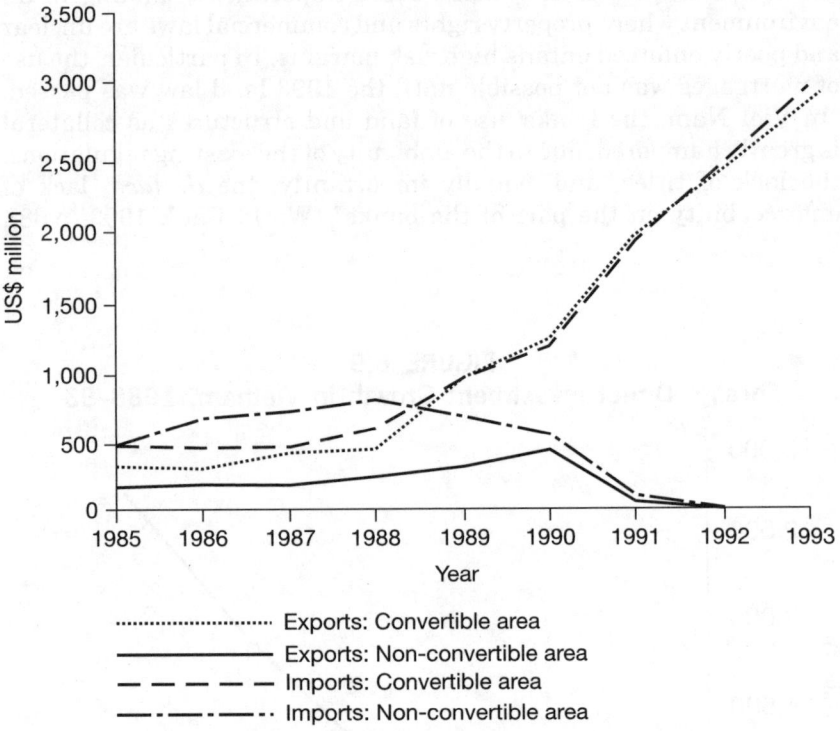

Note: 2.55 transferable rubles per dollar over 1985–87; 2.4 per dollar thereafter.
Source: Le Dang Doanh (1994).

Consequently, the perceived degree of commitment by the government to hardening the budget constraints facing SOEs — the question of reform credibility — becomes central to the success of the reform process itself.[29] Expectations of bail outs induce high and non-economic bank lending, which in turn puts pressure on the government to support failing SOEs, increase the budget deficit, and fuel inflation. The point to note, however, is that the lending decisions of the banks in this context are not irrational, unnecessarily biased, or inexplicably bureaucratic.

The obverse of the explanation for continued strong lending to SOEs is that lending to NSEs remains highly risky. NSEs do not get bailed out when in trouble. More importantly, lending in an environment where property rights and commercial laws are unclear and poorly enforced entails high risk margins. In particular, the use of mortgages was not possible until the 1993 land law was passed. "In Viet Nam, the banks' use of land and structures as collateral is greatly hampered, due to the ambiguity of the existing regulations, the lack of titles, and, equally importantly, the *de facto* lack of enforceability on the part of the banks" (World Bank 1993, p.68).

FIGURE 6.9
Foreign Direct Investment Growth in Vietnam, 1988–93

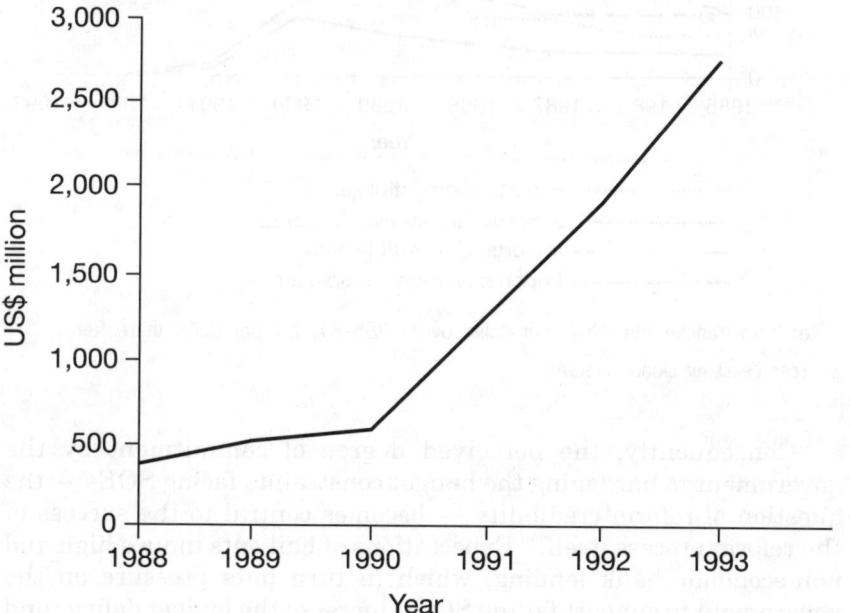

Note: Commitments including counterpart contributions; actual disbursements much less.
Source: Le Dang Doanh (1994).

Thus, although lending rates to NSEs were set at higher levels (lending interest rates were almost unified by 1993), the SOEs remained the main customers of the commercial banks.

Reform of SOEs has been substantial since 1989. A significant hardening of their budgets has been accompanied by institutional reforms to enable them to operate effectively in a market economy. Official privatization has been minimal and liquidations confined mostly to the smaller enterprises, yet because they have been weaned from their main sources of subsidization — budget allocations and subsidized bank lending — the restructuring must be regarded as a success. This is especially so as this weaning has been accompanied

TABLE 6.4
Total Foreign Direct Investment in Vietnam by Sector, 1988–93

Sector	Number of Projects	Total Capital (US$ million)	Legal Capital (US$ million)
Heavy industry	115	1,326	581
Oil and gas	25	1,186	1,132
Light industry	165	1,075	468
Agriculture and forestry	101	314	159
Aquaculture	35	1,020	653
Hotel and tourism	95	1,437	860
Transport and communications	45	500	287
Construction	50	451	197
Services	34	263	109
Finance and banking	15	152	151
Others	13	18	12
TOTAL	693	7,742	4,609

Source: Le Dang Doanh (1994).

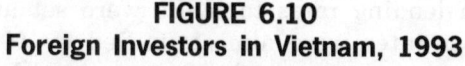

FIGURE 6.10
Foreign Investors in Vietnam, 1993

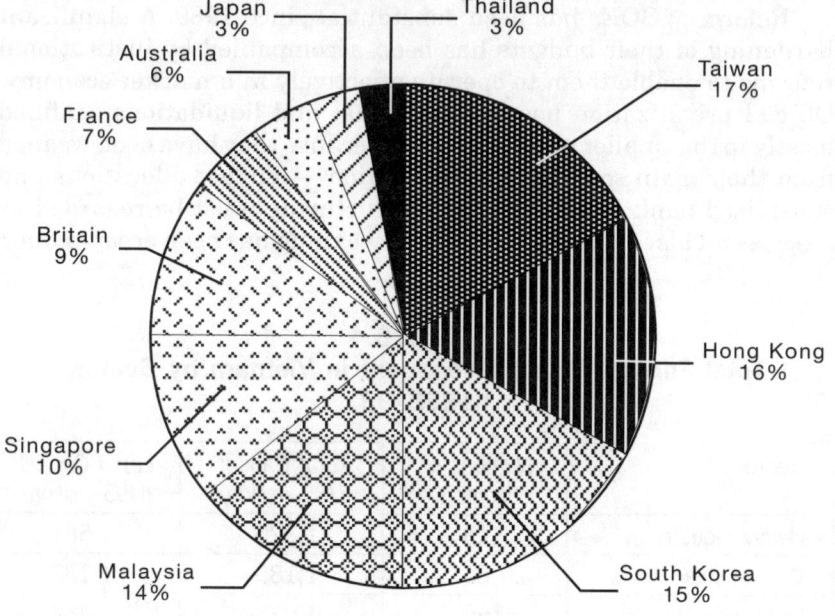

Shares of US$2.8 billion of commitments in 1993

Source: Le Dang Doanh (1994).

by rising output, maintained government revenue flows, and increased competitiveness from the SOEs.

Trade

The value of total Vietnamese exports was anticipated to have risen about 19 per cent in 1993, down from the impressive 24.3 per cent growth of 1992. Oil exports had remained high (3,823 million tons in the first eight months of 1993), although the quantity and value of rice exports had declined. Total imports for 1993 were forecast to have increased some 21 per cent for the year, yet initial figures for the first eight months reported a 36 per cent increase over the same period in 1992. This is in part a lagged demand response to attempts to restrict import growth in 1992, when the value of total imports grew only 6.3 per cent. Motor cycle imports, for example, which fell from 49,530 units in 1991 to 28,619 in 1992, then totalled 49,479 for only the first six months of 1993. Smuggling, estimated at from 15 per cent to 30 per cent of official trade levels, increased in 1993 in response to the government's attempts to implement a new tariff regime and better collection of customs duties. The new tariff code was introduced in January 1993. It has twenty-eight different categories with rates ranging from zero to 100 per cent and is, typically, too complex to administer effectively.

The buoyant trade performance is one of the remarkable achievements of Vietnam's transition from central planning. The value of total trade increased steadily from 1988, with only a slight levelling out in 1991 when the CMEA-area trade collapsed. The switch to hard currency exporting was achieved largely because Vietnam's main exports were primary products which found a ready world market. They had few unwanted industrial export activities, as the 1993 World Bank report notes: "Unlike Eastern Europe, and even China, Viet Nam has few of the large, inefficient industrial plants that plague these other socialist economies". They therefore did not have the problem of switching from producing products totally unwanted by the world market (Lada cars, most machinery, etc.) to those which were.

The share of CMEA trade had been falling steadily since 1988, but the collapse came in 1991. In 1990 CMEA imports formed 32 per cent of total commodity imports (at 2.4 transferable rubles to the dollar); however in 1991 this fell to only 5.7 per cent. Major convertible area imports in 1992 were refined petroleum (US$570 million) and fertilizers (US$235 million), out of a total of US$2,535 million of imports. Major exports were crude petroleum (US$790 million) and rice (US$420 million), out of a total of US$2,475 million of exports to the convertible area.

Foreign Investment

From 1988 to end-1993, some 696 foreign direct investment (FDI) licences had been issued in Vietnam, with a total subscribed value of US$7.5 billion. The level of foreign investment has been increasing rapidly (Figure 6.9) and the ending of the embargo should give additional impetus over 1994-96. However, of that US$7.5 billion in commitments, only about US$2 billion has been disbursed, and much of that to the oil sector and into hotel construction (see Table 6.4). The 1993 World Bank report concluded:

> Important changes in the framework for foreign investment will be required before Viet Nam is likely to see large amounts of non-oil investment. Recommended changes include eliminating the provision that gives minority partners veto power in a joint venture; reducing the number of agencies that must approve foreign investment projects; and abolishing the list of promoted sectors [picking winners].

The main foreign investors are the neighbouring newly industrializing economies. Taiwan, Hong Kong, South Korea, and Singapore were four of the largest five investors in 1993 (Figure 6.10). Japan, which has less interest in low-technology, low-skill productive activities, was only the ninth largest investor. Countries like Australia, France, and Britain were competing to establish a presence in areas such as telecommunications before the American embargo was lifted.

An interesting trend is the increased foreign investment in northern Vietnam. From 1988 to 1991 only 25 per cent of the subscribed value of all FDI went north, but in 1992 the portion rose to 40 per cent, and in the first quarter of 1993 it was 80 per cent. Major northern projects include a Taiwanese cement factory (US$228 million), a Daewoo television factory (US$140 million), and a US$150 million joint venture to build an export processing zone in Haiphong.

Opportunities for foreign investors increased markedly in 1993. The Vietnamese authorities are concerned about the low levels of FDI going into the industrial and infrastructure sectors, and the official support and easing of conditions for build-operate-transfer projects is one response. Other opportunities will flow from the resumption of multilateral project activity. The Asian Development Bank has already committed US$286.5 million, and the World Bank US$228 million, to projects beginning in 1994. They include road building, port rehabilitation, primary education, irrigation, and water supply activities.

TABLE 6.5
Social Sector Indicators in Vietnam and Other Countries

	Vietnam	Indonesia	Thailand	China
Human development index (HDI)	0.498	0.499	0.713	0.614
GDP per capita at PPP*, 1989	1,000	2,034	3,569	2,656
Life expectancy at birth, 1990	62.7	61.5	66.1	70.1
Average calorie supply, 1986 (per day)	2,300	2,580	2,330	2,630
Population per doctor, 1984	1,000	9,460	6,290	1,000
Adult literacy rate, 1985 (%)	84.4	71.8	90.7	68.2
Years of schooling, 1980 (average)	3.2	3.1	3.5	4.8
Enrolment rates (primary and secondary), 1986–88 (%)	69	84	58	83
Primary drop-out rate, 1985-87 (%)	50	20	36	32
Educational attainment index	57.3	48.9	61.6	47.1
HDI rank (out of 160 countries)	99	98	66	82
GDP rank (out of 160 countries)	142	117	73	133

* PPP refers to a Purchasing Power Parity index which attempts to measure the real purchasing power of nominal incomes across countries. The 1989 PPP per capita for Myanmar, Bangladesh, and India were US$595, US$820, and US$910 respectively.

Sources: Hainsworth (1993), pp. 165–78. PPP data from United Nations Development Programme Human Development Report, 1991.

Lifting of Embargo

On 27 January 1994 the United States Senate voted 62-38 in favour of lifting the eighteen-year-old trade and investment embargo against Vietnam. With such endorsement, President Clinton promptly lifted the embargo on 3 February 1994. The impact of the ending of the embargo continues to be a subject of much speculation. The Asian Development Bank pushed its 1994 GDP growth forecast for Vietnam up to 9 per cent (from 8.2 per cent) after the announcement, and predicted double-digit growth in 1995. Generally, Vietnamese commentators are even more optimistic about the consequences, while other observers — including us — are more cautious.

There are good reasons for caution. Major American companies had already established representation in Hanoi before the embargo was lifted: General Electric, IBM, Caterpillar Co., Baker & McKenzie, Citibank, and Bank of America already had offices in Vietnam. Coca-Cola was being produced at a plant run by a Singapore subsidiary. Mobil Corporation had recently secured an exploration lease, and Philip Morris had announced its plans to produce Marlboro cigarettes and milk products in Vietnam. Other American companies had already been effectively operating in Vietnam for some years through subsidiary operations in countries like Australia and Hong Kong.

Therefore, the level of genuinely new American direct investment that follows the lifting of embargo may be quite low. On the other hand, substantial investments from American, Japanese, and other companies have certainly been delayed pending the lifting and these projects will now be revitalized. Tourism and hotel construction, for example, can expect a rush of developments.

Social Sector Concerns

A reported literacy rate of 85 per cent puts Vietnam on a par with Thailand and above most neighbouring countries. Health indicators are also, overall, better than for countries like Bangladesh, India, and Indonesia. Certainly, a healthy and educated population is a stimulus to long-term growth. According to the World Bank, "Investing in people, if done right, provides the firmest foundation for lasting development" (World Bank Development Report 1991, p.4). In the modern world this is becoming increasingly so: economic development can no longer be viewed primarily as a function of given factor endowments — an allocative efficiency problem. In the modern world the most important factor of production is human capital and, to a large extent, this is a factor that is 'made' through education and training strategies. Thus, with the rising relative importance of human capital inputs, issues relating to the appropriate mix and depth of that human capital stock — the making of that productive input — become as important as allocative issues in maximizing development.

The perceived decline in health and education services over the transitional period in Vietnam is therefore a matter for concern. The number of pupils undertaking primary education, for example, has declined by 10 per cent since 1988 as parents withdraw them to work on the land or in household production activities. In both sectors real levels of government expenditure have fallen and state sector wages have continued to lag behind inflation. (State sector wages halved in real terms between 1989 and 1991; a doctor now receives the equivalent of US$18 per month.) In the 1991-92 academic year, 20 per cent of teachers quit their jobs or retired (*Vietnam Investment Review*, 13 September 1992). Without external funding assistance the government will be hard pressed to halt the decline in these sectors over the short term.

Table 6.5 shows that human development in Vietnam has been roughly on par with developing countries in the region, even though it has fallen behind in terms of GDP. Maintaining this position over the transition and restructuring the existing health and education systems will be formidable challenges for the Vietnamese Government. Allowing a deterioration of the social sectors may have only a marginal impact on development in the short run, but for long-term development there is no better investment.

Permitting official salaries to fall to meagre levels has led to the institutionalization of a variety of quasi-legal and inefficient work practices throughout the public sector. Routine permissions and information must be purchased, doctors sell their medicines, teachers use school time to undertake second jobs, everybody moonlights. The meagre salaries are generally regarded as retainers, with much actual work undertaken requiring negotiated payments (for example, to attend meetings or lectures, conduct research, work on a project). The high transaction costs and efficiency losses of this low salaries phenomenon are substantial and complex. (It is also a phenomenon common to many developing countries, and yet the institutional consequences are given little attention in research.)

For the vast majority of the rural population, the reforms since 1988 — notably, the abolition of the state purchasing networks, the dismantling of the co-operative structures, and the introduction of long-term land leases — have led to substantial increases in their standards of living. Rural discontent is therefore quite limited, although it may increase. The most significant problems have been land ownership disputes in the south as families try to regain land taken from them in previous collectivization drives. The more private nature of land ownership relations in the south is also beginning to generate a landless class (according to Fforde [1991] "around 25% of the [southern] rural population are becoming indebted, borrowing at rates of up to 15-20% per month"), increasing rural–urban drift, and associated problems. Rural–urban migration, however, is still greatly restricted and significant squatter settlements have yet to develop.

Incomes in Ho Chi Minh City are approximately double the equivalents in Hanoi. This discrepancy should remain for some time as Ho Chi Minh City continues to grow faster and labour mobility is restricted. The north–south antagonism that the 'rise of Saigon' will generate is difficult to gauge. It seems likely that Ho Chi Minh City and its government will be a key force for continued reform, but any expectations of broad cultural or ideological conflict seem misguided.

Income distributions within urban centres are also becoming increasingly skewed as commercial middle and upper classes develop. A continued deterioration of income distribution must be expected. Consequences of this will include increasing resentment and agitation from those whose incomes remain relatively stagnant — particularly in Ho Chi Minh City where the economic resurgence of the Chinese community is warily accepted. State employees, including doctors and teachers as well as many public officials and Party cadre, are the persons being left behind as most of the new money is being made from trading and small-scale production and service activities. In such an environment, rent-seeking and corruption may be expected to increase.

However, the most important immediate social problem is the large-scale unemployment and under-employment. Total state sector employment has fallen by about 250,000 persons each year since 1989. Something like 500,000 soldiers have also been demobilized over the same period. Returning worker migrants have added to this supply. The demographic profile aggravates the situation by increasing the number of persons of working age by 3.7 per cent per year (39.2 per cent of the Vietnamese population was under 15 years of age in 1990). The rapid growth in the private sector has soaked up some of this labour force growth, but unemployment is still estimated at between 1.9 to 6 million persons, depending on one's definition. It is a serious problem, and one which will generate severe social pressures if the present rapid rates of private sector employment growth seriously falter.

The Sequencing of Reforms

The appropriate sequencing of reforms in transitional economies continues to be a subject where generalizations abound but convincing arguments are scarce. A consensus is discernible which views macroeconomic stability as a prerequisite for structural adjustment reform (James 1994), although Rana (1993) argues for an "Asian approach ... wherein the implementation of most aspects of microeconomic reform ... is earlier than macroeconomic reforms" (p.10). However, given that macroeconomic stability is desirable with or without microeconomic distortions, its place as an early reform objective may be accepted.

An explicit *general rule of sequencing* should be that market-oriented reforms be undertaken immediately unless there are strong institutionally based reasons for delays. The dead-weight losses of retaining distortions over time demand explanation.

Much of the literature about sequencing gets confused over semantic issues. The meaning of 'liberalization', or interpretations of 'gradual' versus 'rapid' reform, for example, differs between authors. Differences in chronologies (when reforms began) and differences in quantifying comparisons (how to measure the degree of liberalization in trade, property rights, trade, etc.), highlight the lack of a common methodology for analysing institutional change in transitional economies. Familiar economic indicators are used for comparison: Are interest and exchange rates still state-determined? What is the budget deficit and money growth? However, the transition of economies from planning to markets is largely one of institutional reform, and agreed measures of appropriate institutional indicators are lacking: What is the degree of continuing SOE subsidization? How autonomous is the State Bank? How pervasive are non-tariff barriers? How secure are property rights? To what degree is the economy still rationed? Obviously, developing indexes for institutional indicators is a highly subjective exercise. However, sensibly done, it could provide more consistent grounds for international comparisons and help to substantiate or refute the wide variety of opinions about the desirable pace and nature of sequencing.

Nevertheless, with or without additional indicators, arguments for prudential sequencing need to specify the necessary constraints required to answer that general rule of sequencing: Why not do it now? The securities–bank dichotomy is therefore an artificial one, as reform in each does not necessarily constrain the other. Both can be pursued, as they are doing in Vietnam. In this context, those who would cite China as "the leading example of a successful gradualist approach to liberalization" (Rana 1993, p.9) need to demonstrate more than the fact that the gradual reform process produced positive results; they need also to show that it was economically preferable in many respects to a rapid process. That gradual reforms can work is of interest, but of more interest — and importance — is to show in what peculiar institutional conditions they are preferable. In the case of Vietnam, and typical of transitional economies, the institutional constraints have primarily been soft budgets — and their accompanying institutional arrangements — and the need to codify, monitor, and enforce appropriate rules of the game.

For the Vietnamese example, the definitional problems begin with deciding the starting year of reforms. Le Dang Doanh (1994) notes that 1979 saw the beginning of market-focused reforms, which although subsequently reversed, laid the foundation for the more comprehensive reforms almost a decade later. In 1985 a radical programme of price adjustments was initiated. It was hoped to 'crowd out' the parallel market through official market price increases. The 1985 policies pushed inflation up to over 300 per cent for the next three years, and because they did not aim to remove the rationing system they can be dismissed as a starting date. In December 1986 the Sixth Communist Party Congress declared the beginning of the renovation period, so this is the year most commentators choose, yet 1987 may therefore be a more appropriate first year. However, the fact is that substantive institutional reform and removal of the rationing system did not occur until 1988-89. The return to household production in agriculture in 1988 is a valid choice for starting year, or even the removal of the two-price system in 1989. Overall, 1986 remains our choice, as it is already the generally accepted starting year by commentators, and because it is the year that a firm political commitment to market-based reform was declared — if not put into practice. However, on economic criteria alone, 1988 seems a more appropriate starting year.

Vietnam's economic reform has been gradual; whether by design or default is open to debate. Partial marketization in 1979 saw an increase in the market share of economic activity, which was only partly reversed with the return of conservative policies in the mid-1980s. The residual planning system was then highlighted for reform in 1986. Over 1987-88 a variety of institutional reforms were introduced: the Foreign Investment Law; dismantling of the co-operative system; and the removal of active discrimination against the private sector. These institutional reforms produced a supply response which overwhelmed the negative growth impact of removing the two-price system in 1989 — a year which also saw substantial trade liberalization, a depreciation of the exchange rate in line with the parallel rate, and a substantial hardening of the budget constraints faced by the SOEs.

Therefore, the lesson for other transitional economies is that the supply responses of institutional changes should be planned for (in size and timing). Appropriate sequencing of positive-growth changes can help alleviate, and generate support for, the subsequent negative short-run impact of other policy changes (such as removing subsidy mechanisms). The impressive monetarization of 1989 is a case in point, and we would add the positive consequences of prior institutional reforms to Dollar's (1993) conclusion: "It was not simply the result of higher interest rates. In my view, it was the coordinated price reforms, plus trade liberalization, that restored confidence in the currency" (p.214). In other words, reform stability can be enhanced by an appropriate sequencing of positive-growth and negative-growth institutional and policy changes.

A final note about political economy issues. It was argued above that much of the impetus for the impressive economic reforms in Vietnam has come from crises — primarily in agriculture, and secondarily from changes in the international environment. When the crisis passed, conservative forces regained strength and market-based policies were either reversed (mid-1980s), or considerably slowed (as happened prior to the 1992 Seventh Party Congress). Since 1989, the move to a market-based economy became irreversible, but the pace and boldness of reforms could be considerably slowed in times of relative prosperity. Those times are now, with an ending of the embargo and a resumption of multilateral lending.

Note the role of multilateral lending in alleviating crisis situations. The link is rarely made in political economy literature. Haggard and Webb (1993) note that in "countries disposed against reform ... additional finance creates perverse incentives, allowing governments to postpone adjustment" (p.157). We would argue that no government, developed or otherwise, embraces reforms; there is a considerable bias for the status quo in any government. The question then becomes one of degree: How disposed against (decentralizing market-oriented) reform is any particular government? Governments with a strong bias for the status quo only initiate reforms when a crisis makes them unavoidable. In such circumstances, multilateral lending provides international legitimacy to a regime, as well as — direct or indirect — budgetary support, which may facilitate the delaying of politically unattractive economic reforms.[30] This negative crisis-alleviating consequence of multilateral lending needs to be weighed against the positive pressures of conditionality and the role of such lending in bankrolling reform programmes.

The Vietnamese Transitional Experience

Impressive reforms are continuing in Vietnam. The highlight of the Vietnamese economy since 1992 has been the consolidation and subsequent maintenance of macroeconomic stability. The annual inflation rate was brought down to about 7 per cent in 1993. The exchange rate, gold trading, and interest rates have also stabilized. This has been in a context of sustained growth, with GDP forecast at 7.5 per cent growth for 1993, an approximate 19 per cent increase in exports, and a marginal rise in food production despite declining relative prices. Another highlight is the return of major international lenders to Vietnam, with US$1.86 billion of commitments for 1994 coming out of a recent donor conference. It was not all roses: the American embargo lingered on until February 1994; Vietnamese bungling and corruption concerning a large infrastructure project (the north-south powerline) have heightened concerns about aid absorptive capacity; and the mid-term Communist Party Conference, scheduled for late-1993, was postponed several times to early 1994 as members debated how to deal with the increasingly vocal criticisms and the desirable pace of economic reform.

In general, we are optimistic about the Vietnamese Government's capacity for reform. The commitment to macroeconomic stability is sincere, and the ability to take tough decisions to achieve this end has been proven. The numerous institutional reforms required will take time but are occurring, including the reform of the SOEs. The task of creating efficient factor markets will also take time, and will probably progress slowly as it involves the removal of entrenched rent-seeking networks and the disruption of various interest groups and monopolies.[31]

However, even given the above concerns, the prospects for development and rapid growth in Vietnam are considerable. The present reform process is irreversible, although as we noted above, the pace of reform may slacken as the impetus from various internal and external crises fades. Certainly though, the direction of reforms is clear. The demonstration effect of its Asian neighbours is unstoppable. To the year 2000, Vietnam will continue to introduce outward-oriented policies, and become a dynamic and competitive member of a region in which its poor economic performance has made it an exception since unification.

Notes

1. The official-price food-grain component of the General Price Index (inflation measure) had been lower than the aggregate index for the entire 1978-84 period. Indeed, the official purchase price for rice remained at 0.4 dong/kg throughout 1985 and until March 1986, while the free-market price rose steadily to 12 dong/kg. The increasing disparity between official and market prices discouraged the production of surpluses and made it difficult to collect any that did exist.

2. In "classically socialist repressed financial systems" (McKinnon 1992), SOEs do not have control of their bank deposits; deposits are mandatory and withdrawals require permissions. Hence, even forewarned, the SOEs were unable to react to the new dong policy and their deposits in excess of quota limits were simply appropriated by the state.

3. 'Classical socialism' is a term used by McKinnon (1992). It refers to the "strong rationing" Soviet/Stalinist-style planning model which was imposed upon the countries of Eastern Europe and which the Vietnamese authorities tried, but with only limited success, to copy for Vietnam.

4. The lack of importance of money as an incentive device needs to be noted here. "As long as all decisions for allocating resources are actually made by the central planning agency, seizing enterprise profits *ex post facto* need not be particularly damaging to managerial incentives." (McKinnon 1992, p.4.) Put another way, allocations of inputs (or permissions to purchase inputs) were the binding constraints on economic activity. These constraints determined the "commodity convertibility" of the bank deposits, and even if these had just been appropriated, then credit at nominal interest rates was readily available.

5. Classical socialism entailed strict control of enterprise money, which was not the case in Vietnam. Out-of-plan activities had grown since 1979, and over 1987-88 SOEs were given increased autonomy in financial matters, including the setting of wages (Fforde and de Vylder 1988).

6. "Failure in 1978-79 to force the needed rice out of the Mekong showed once more that this intrinsic element of the Stalinist model [compulsory procurement] was being softened in Vietnam" (Fforde 1991, p.6).

7. If X=Free-Market share and Y=Official-Market share, then the weights for 1988, for example, are calculated by solving the two equations: $X+Y=1$ and $313.2X + 294.8Y = 308.2$

8. "The weight of free market prices in the overall retail price index", from a 1990 World Bank report cited in Peebles (1992, p.25).

9. The Economist Intelligence Unit (1992-93) quotes a national survey

which reported that only 6 per cent of the Vietnamese population use banks at all.

10.   A 1991 survey of 1,000 non-state enterprises found that 48 per cent had established their operations since 1987, with 17 per cent having begun in 1989 alone (Ronnas 1993, p.5).

11.   Again low by international comparison. The *World Development Report 1989* cites average M2/GDP figures of 43, 31, and 32 per cent for high-growing, medium-growing and low-growing economies respectively (Roman 1993, p.14). Vietnam is also a largely cash economy, with currency in circulation constituting about one-third of total liquidity.

12.   'Bail out' refers to the notion that SOEs will be financially supported by the government should they incur losses. The degree of SOE subsidization and the extent to which operational losses are met by the government relates to the softness of the budget constraint facing the enterprise: subsidized and frequently bailed out SOEs face soft budget constraints.

13.   Beaulieu (1994, p.5) quotes shares for NSE lending of 7 per cent in 1991, 15 per cent in 1992, and 28 per cent in 1993.

14.   "The average of loan to State Enterprises is 2.4%/month and loans to this sector account for 30% of the total capital of [ABV], while loans to farm households at 4-5%/month account for only 10%." (Pham 1992, p.17).

15.   Ordinance on Economic Contracts, 1989; Ordinance on Economic Arbitration, 1990; Ordinance on Civil Contracts, 1991 (Gillespie 1992, p.5).

16.   This experience may be a partial explanation for the prompt SOE supply response to the more substantive reforms of 1989. Indeed, Wood (1989, p.567) remarks that "...in general the speed with which they [SOE directors] seemed to be starting and thinking like businessmen rather than bureaucrats was remarkable". However, it would seem that many of them had been doing this for some time, and many were never slothful bureaucrats anyway. It may even be argued that the demands of running a state enterprise in an ill-functioning centrally planned system are just as demanding as directing an enterprise in a competitive market with clear rules of the game.

17.   Directive 156/HDBT of November 1985.

18.   Decree 217 of November 1987.

19.   Eight of the eleven new directors came from within the enterprises, and five (26 per cent) of the directors in 1991 were women (McCarty 1993).

20.   Fforde and de Vylder (1988) cite "an informed Vietnamese commentator" who reported that for most SOEs producing consumer products, between

50 and 100 per cent of total production inputs were obtained commercially from the parallel market by 1988 (p.103).

21.   The increase in electricity output was only 30 per cent of capacity gain over 1981-85 (Fforde and de Vylder 1988, p.101). In 1987, the United Nations Industrial Development Organization (UNIDO) calculated actual utilization rates of installed capacity for twenty industries involved in agricultural processing. The rates ranged from 20 to 85 per cent (UNIDO 1991).

22.   A low ICOR is desirable, as it indicates that less new capital investment is required to produce an additional unit of output. "ICORs are typically in the range of 3-4" (World Bank 1993, p.7).

23.   Tax collection in Vietnam is 'bottom-up', a sort of unhealthy "fiscal federalism" (McKinnon 1992). Consequently there is unproductive competition between and within levels of government to support and maintain control of SOEs as direct sources of revenue.

24.   Le Dang Doanh (1994) reports that the number of SOEs had fallen from 12,000 in 1990 to 7,050 by June 1993 (about 2,000 mergers and 3,000 closures, but mostly of small local government operations). A survey of Hanoi SOEs in 1991 found that none of the larger ones had been liquidated and that two had been merged (McCarty 1993).

25.   Decree 462 (February 1992) and a Directive of March 1993.

26.   While monetary benefits have been fixed, non-monetary benefits have proliferated. Workers might be given shares of output (packets of cigarettes) or inputs (steel bars). Provision of housing is the most important benefit for many SOE workers. SOEs which have benefited from reforms of recent years (mostly consumer goods producers) have often undertaken massive housing construction for their workers. If these non-monetary remunerations are included into wage calculations, then the World Bank conclusion may be disputed. However, in purely *monetary* terms, control of wages is impressive.

27.   In a similar vein, the Economist Intelligence Unit (1992-93) remarks that in 1990, the Vietnamese "banks reverted to their traditional role of providers of cheap credit to hard-pressed state enterprises rather than acting as neutral financial intermediaries" (p.49).

28.   Kornai also argues that "custom and habitual behavior induce the parties to observe the terms of the [unwritten] contract" (1993, p.317) and cites Becker (1992) to support his claim. We find this an inadequate explanation for the forces which make informal contracts work. Without an enforceable legal framework, contracts can only work if the benefits of participation to *each* agent outweigh the cost of breaking the contract. In such circumstances, links and backing from senior persons or organizations — a form of insurance — become important; as do

expectations of benefits from future contracts. The game theory of incomplete contracts is a useful approach for analysing this issue (see Hart 1989).

29. Similarly, Commander (1992) notes that: "If a stabilization program does not enjoy full credibility, the contraction that high interest rates are supposed to induce may not result." That is, SOEs will continue to want loans, and banks to give them, if bail outs are expected to continue.

30. Politically unattractive from the point of view of the ruling regime, not the country. Those who posit a welfare-maximizing government are incorrectly applying the competitive paradigm conclusions of standard economic theory (for example, profit maximization by firms). Countries and their 'managers' are not competitive in this sense. Welfare or growth maximization is, all other things being equal, a desirable but not necessary condition for regime survival.

31. Indeed, an important aspect of future SOE reform will be the removal of regional monopolies of production and distribution. This is partly a legacy of the old system, but also due to the continuing patronage of political institutions (local governments, ministries) to whom the SOEs still directly contribute revenues.

References

Asian Development Bank (ADB). *Economic Review and Bank Operations: Socialist Republic of Vietnam*. Manila, July 1991.

Bartlett, A. and A. McCarty. "Ideas for the Organisational Reform of the Vietnamese State Planning Committee". Working paper. Hanoi, September 1993.

Beaulieu, C. "Dong, Dollar or Gold? Savings Accounts, Bonds or Stocks? What to do with Your Money in Socialist Vietnam". Institute of Current World Affairs, Discussion paper, January 1994.

Becker, G.S. "Habits, Addictions, and Traditions". *Kyklos*, 45 (1992): 327–46.

Beresford, M. *Vietnam: Politics, Economy and Society*. London: Pinter, 1988.

Blommenstein and Spencer. "The Role of Financial Institutions in the Transition to a Market Economy". International Monetary Fund, Working paper WP/93/75, October 1993.

Bofinger, P. "The Transition to Convertibility in Eastern Europe: A Monetary View". In *Currency Convertibility in Eastern Europe*, edited by J.

Williamson, pp. 116–38. Institute for International Economics publication. Washington: Johns Hopkins Press, 1991.

Boi Cao Cu . "Adjustment in ABV towards a Market-Oriented Agricultural and Rural Banking System". In *Workshop on Transition towards a Market-Oriented Rural Banking System*. Hanoi: Vietnam Bank for Agriculture, May 1992.

— — —. *Survey in Rural Credit in Vietnam*. Hanoi: Faculty of Banking and Finance, Hanoi Economics University. 1992.

Bowles and White. "Contradictions in China's Financial Reforms: The Relationship between Banks and Enterprises". *Cambridge Journal of Economics* 13 (1989): 481–95.

Cho Yoon Je. "McKinnon-Shaw versus the Neostructuralists on Financial Liberalization: A Conceptual Note". *World Development* 18, no. 3 (1990), pp. 477–80.

Commander, S. "Inflation and Transition to a Market Economy: An Overview". *The World Bank Economic Review* 6, no. 1 (1992), pp. 3–12.

Cooper, R. "Comment on Seminar Papers". In *Currency Convertibility in Eastern Europe*, edited by J. Williamson, pp. 310–14. Institute for International Economics publication. Washington: Johns Hopkins Press, 1991.

Cottarelli, C. and M. Blejer. "Forced Savings and the Monetary Overhang in the Soviet Union". In *Trials of Transition: Economic Reform in the Former Communist Bloc*, edited by Keren and Ofer, pp. 50–81. Boulder: Westview Press, 1992.

Dang Duc Dam and Le Hong Nhat. "Macroeconomic Stability: Obstacles and Solutions". *Economic Problems*, June 1992, pp. 3–9.

Dapice, D. "Vietnam at the Starting Point: Just Another Successful Asian Economy?". In *The Challenge of Reform in Indochina*, edited by B. Ljunggren. Cambridge, Mass.: Harvard Institute for International Development, January 1993.

Dollar, D. "Vietnam: Successes and Failures in Macroeconomic Stabilization". In *The Challenge of Reform in Indochina*, edited by B. Ljunggren. Cambridge, Mass.: Harvard Institute for International Development, January 1993.

de Vylder, Stephan. *Towards a Market Economy? The Current State of Economic Reform in Vietnam*. Stockholm School of Economics, Reprint Series no. 91, 1992.

Dornbush, R. and A. Reynoso. "Financial Factors in Economic Development". *American Economic Review*, May 1989, pp. 204–9.

Economist Intelligence Unit. *Indochina: Vietnam, Laos, Cambodia*. Country reports, 1991 to 1st Quarter 1994.

— — —. *Indochina: Vietnam, Laos, Cambodia*. Country profiles, 1991–92, 1992–93, 1993–94.

Fforde, A. "The Political Economy of 'Reform' in Vietnam — Some Reflections". Working paper, 1991.

Fforde, A. and S. de Vylder. *Vietnam — An Economy in Transition*. Stockholm: Swedish International Development Authority, 1988.

Floro and Yotopuolos. "Income Distribution, Transaction Costs and Market Fragmentation in Informal Credit Markets". *Cambridge Journal of Economics* 16 (1992): 303–26.

Gates, C.L. and Truong D. "Reform of a Centrally Managed Developing Economy: The Vietnamese Perspective". Nordic Institute of Asian Studies (NIAS), Report no. 9, 1992.

Gelb, A. and P. Honohan. "Financial Sector Reforms in Adjustment Programs". World Bank, Working paper 169, March 1989.

Genberg, H. "On the Sequencing of Reforms in Eastern Europe". International Monetary Fund, Working paper WP/91/13, February 1991.

General Statistics Office. *Statistical Data of the Socialist Republic of Vietnam, 1976–1990*. Hanoi: Statistical Publishing House, 1991.

— — —. *Vietnam Economy, 1986–1991: Based on the System of National Accounts*. Hanoi: Statistical Publishing House, 1992.

— — —. *Economy of Vietnam: Reviews and Statistics*. Hanoi: Statistical Publishing House, 1992.

— — —. *Vietnam: The Blazing Flame of Reforms*. Hanoi: Statistical Publishing House, 1993.

Gillespie, J. "The Development of Commercial Legal Rights in Vietnam". Paper presented at Vietnam Update Conference, November 1992, at Australian National University.

Haggard, S. and S. Webb. "What Do We Know about the Political Economy of Economic Policy Reform?". *The World Bank Research Observer* 8, no. 2 (July 1993), pp. 143–68.

Hainsworth, G. "Human Resource Development in Vietnam". In *Vietnam's Dilemmas and Options: The Challenge of Economic Transition in the 1990s*, edited by M. Than and J. Tan L.H. Singapore: Institute of Southeast Asian Studies, 1993.

Hart, O. "Incomplete Contracts". In *The New Palgrave: Allocation, Information and Markets*, edited by John Eatwell et al., pp. 163–79. London: Macmillan, 1989.

Heng, H.K., Russell. "Vietnam 1992: Economic Growth and Political Caution". In *Southeast Asian Affairs*. Singapore: Institute of Southeast Asian Studies, 1993.

Hiebert, Murray. "Red Capitalists: Private Entrepreneurs Flourish Despite Hurdles". *Far Eastern Economic Review*, 20 February 1992, pp. 51–52.

Hilbers, P. "Monetary Instruments and Their Use during the Transition from a Centrally Planned to a Market Economy". International Monetary Fund, Working paper WP/93/87, November 1993.

International Monetary Fund. *Vietnam — Recent Economic Developments*. May 1988.

— — —. *Vietnam — Staff Report*. September 1990.

James, W.E. "Policy Reform Sequencing in Indonesia, Sri Lanka, and India". Conference paper presented at annual meeting of International Centre for Economic Growth, May 1994, in Jakarta.

Kornai, J. "The Evolution of Financial Discipline under the Post Socialist System". *Kyklos* 46 (1993): 315–34.

Kotowitz, Y. "Moral Hazard". In *The New Palgrave: Allocation, Information and Markets*, edited by John Eatwell et al., pp. 207–13. London: Macmillan, 1989.

Lai Quang Thuc. "Some Main Features of Vietnam's Banking System and Finance Market". *Vietnam Economic Review* 23, no. 1 (March 1994), pp. 29–35.

Le Dang Doanh. "Economic Reform and Development in Vietnam". National Centre for Development Studies, Australian National University, Working paper no. 92/5, 1992.

— — —. "Economic Reform in Vietnam: Achievements and Prospects". Paper presented at International Centre for Economic Growth (ICEG) Asian Transitional Economies Workshop. April 1994, in Jakarta.

Le Thanh Nghiep. "Agricultural Development: Issues and Proposals for Reform". In *Vietnam's Dilemmas and Options: The Challenge of Economic Transition in the 1990s*, edited by M. Than and J. Tan L.H. Singapore: Institute of Southeast Asian Studies, 1993.

Lipworth, G. and E. Spitaller. "Viet Nam — Reform and Stabilization, 1986–92". International Monetary Fund, Working paper WP/93/46, May 1993.

McCarty, A. "Development and the Conditions for Success in Vietnam". Paper presented at the Indochina Roundtable Conference hosted by the Institute of Southeast Asian Studies, October 1992, in Singapore.

— — —. "Economic Growth Scenarios for Vietnam". Paper presented at Vietnam Vocational and Technical Education Planning Workshop, 15 November 1993, in Hanoi.

— — —. "Enterprise Reform in Vietnam, 1986–91". In *Vietnam's Dilemmas and Options: The Challenge of Economic Transition in the 1990s*, edited by M. Than and J. Tan L.H. Singapore: Institute of Southeast Asian Studies, 1993.

McCarty, A. et al. *Vietnam Data Bank 1976–91*. National Centre for Development Studies, Australian National University, November 1992.

McKinnon, R. *Money and Capital in Economic Development*. Washington: Brookings Institution, 1973.

———. "Financial Liberalization in Retrospect: Interest Rate Policies in LDCs". Paper presented at a conference, 1986, at Yale University.

———. *The Order of Economic Liberalization: Financial Control in the Transition to a Market Economy*. Baltimore: Johns Hopkins University Press, 1991.

———. "Macroeconomic Control in Liberalizing Socialist Economies: Asian and European Parallels". Centre for Pacific Basin Monetary and Economic Studies, Working paper 92–05, March 1992.

McMillan, J. and B. Naughton. "How to Reform a Planned Economy: Lessons from China". *Oxford Review of Economic Policy* 8, no. 1 (Spring 1992).

Mehta, H. Article in *Reuter News Service*, 19 May 1994.

Mirakhor and Delano. "Interest Rate Policies, Stabilization, and Bank Supervision in Developing Countries: Strategies for Financial Reforms". International Monetary Fund, Working paper WP/90/8, 1990.

Nguyen Thi Ngoc Hien. "Socio-Economic Conditions in Hanoi, 1981–1986". Interview by Le Dang Doanh. April 1994.

Nguyen Van Quy. "The Economic Outlook for Vietnam, 1993–1995". Paper presented at 6th Workshop on Asian Economic Outlook hosted by the Asian Development Bank, October 1993, in Manila.

Nguyen Xuan Oanh. "Some Reflections on Economic Development and Transitional Economies — with Special Reference to Vietnam". Working paper, September 1992.

North, D.C. *Institutions, Institutional Change and Economic Performance*. Cambridge: Cambridge University Press, 1990.

Peebles, G. "Why the Quantity Theory of Money Is Not Applicable to China, Together with a Tested Theory That Is". *Cambridge Journal of Economics* 16 (1992): 23–42.

Pham Ngoc Phong. "Monetary and Financial Policy and Its Impact on Agriculture and Rural Area". In *ABV-APRACA Workshop on Transition towards a Market-Oriented Rural Banking System*. Hanoi, May 1992.

Pleskovic, B. "Financial Policies in Socialist Countries in Transition". World Bank, Policy research working paper 1242, January 1994.

Rana, P.B. "Reforms in the Transitional Economies of Asia". Asian Development Bank, Staff paper, December 1993.

Riedel, J. "Vietnam: On the Trail of the Tigers". *The World Economy*, no. 4 (1993), pp. 401–22.

Roman, L. "Financial Institutions in Transition — the Case of Vietnam". Stockholm School of Economics, Working paper, 1993.

Ronnas, P. "Private Entrepreneurship in the Nascent Market Economy of Vietnam — Markets and Linkages". Paper prepared for the European Vietnam Studies Conference hosted by the Nordic Institute of Asian Studies, August 1993, in Copenhagen.

Scheuer, D. "Consultancy Report on Monetary Statistics at the State Bank of Vietnam". International Monetary Fund report, 20 June 1991.

Seibel, H.D. "The Making of a Market Economy: Monetary Reform, Economic Transformation and Rural Finance in Vietnam". Edited conference papers, 1992.

Shaw, E. *Financial Deepening in Economic Development*. New York: Oxford University Press, 1973.

Solimano, A. "Inflation and Growth in the Transition from Socialism: The Case of Bulgaria". World Bank, Working paper 659, April 1991.

Tran Ngoc Vinh. "Renewal of Financial and Monetary Policies, and the Circulation of Material Goods at Home and Foreign Trade". In *Doi Moi: Economic Reforms and Development Policies in Vietnam*, edited by P. Ronnas and O. Sjoberg, pp. 83–107. Stockholm: Swedish International Development Authority, 1989.

United Nations Development Programme–World Bank Trade Expansion Programme. "Viet Nam: Economic Policy for Transition to an Open Economy". Country report, May 1993.

United Nations Industrial Development Organization (UNIDO). *Vietnam — Industrial Policy Reform and International Cooperation*. Industrial Development Review Series. 1991.

Vietnam Bank for Agriculture. "Workshop on Transition towards a Market-Oriented Rural Banking System". Collected papers. Hanoi, May 1992.

Vietnam Investment Review, 2–8 May 1994.

Vo Dai Luoc. "Fighting Inflation in Vietnam: Achievements and Problems". *Economic Problems*, June 1990, pp. 18–32.

Vo Nhan Tri. *Vietnam's Economic Policy Since 1975*. Sydney: Allen & Unwin, 1990.

Vo Nhan Tri and A. Booth. "Recent Economic Developments in Vietnam". *Asia-Pacific Economic Literature* 6, no.1 (May 1992), pp. 16–40.

Vu Quoc Huy. "Socio-Economic Conditions in Hanoi, 1981–1986". Interview by Le Dang Doanh, April 1994.

Wei Hui. "Bank Intermediation and Monetary Growth in China". Paper presented at a seminar, 13 May 1994, at the Australian National University.

Williamson, J., ed. *Currency Convertibility in Eastern Europe.* Institute for International Economics publication. Washington: Johns Hopkins Press, 1991.

Wood, A. "Deceleration of Inflation with Acceleration of Price Reform: Vietnam's Remarkable Recent Experience". *Cambridge Journal of Economics* 13 (1989): 563–71.

World Bank. *Transforming a State Owned Financial System: A Financial Sector Study of Viet Nam.* April 1991.

– – –. *Vietnam: Restructuring Public Finance and Public Enterprises. An Economic Report.* April 1992.

– – –. *Vietnam: Transition to the Market. An Economic Report.* July 1993.

7

Transitional Economy of the Lao PDR: Current Economic Performance, Progress, and Problems

Chanthavong Saignasith
and Panom Lathouly

Socialist Transformation during 1975–85

The Lao PDR's current economic structure, which is primarily agrarian, rural, and typified by low-level technology, is the product of centuries of isolation and economic domination by its neighbours. Since the fourteenth century, the country has experienced long periods of warfare, which resulted in the waste or expropriation of any surplus that the economy could generate. Colonial rule between the end of the nineteenth century and 1954, when the country became independent, provided peace and political stability, but little economic growth and limited investment in infrastructure and social services. Between 1954 and 1975, the country again suffered from a period of war, which divided the country and produced not only physical destruction but also immense structural distortions to the predominantly agricultural economy. The warfare drove hundreds of thousands of people off the land, mainly into Vientiane, whose artificially inflated economy was sustained by military and military-related expenditures. The creation of the Lao People's Democratic Republic in December 1975 represented the establishment of the first unified central government since the country's independence, and presented the opportunity for a cohesive attempt to set in train the long-term development of the country. However, the immediate priority of the government was to establish political and administrative control and make emergency arrangements for feeding and resettling the population, rather than attempt to deal with the long-term obstacles to development. It was not until 1977 that long-term development could become the central concern of the government.

To address these problems, the first task of the government was to establish control over the economy. To effect that, a planning structure was gradually put in place, while socialist institutions were created. It was during the Interim Three-Year Development Plan (1978–80) and the First Five-Year Plan (1981–85) that a system of centralized physical planning was adopted. Its main characteristics were that farm output, material allocation, employment, investment, exports, and imports were determined by the central government, and the principal plan targets were established in physical term independently of the system of incentives provided by prices, wages, and exchange rates.

Economic Performance during 1978–80

Since the beginning of the Interim Three-Year Development Plan, the Lao PDR economy has experienced substantial growth, from the artificially low base of 1977. Table 7.1 provides a statistical summary of the economic performance for the period, and indicates the country's internal and external performance. Gross domestic product (GDP) is estimated to have grown by approximately 7 per cent per annum between 1978 and 1980, led by the agricultural sector and in particular by about 11 per cent per annum increase in rice production. Forestry, industry, internal trade, and transport also appear to have increased activity levels substantially. However, the improvements in domestic activity were not generally translated into improvement on the external account, and while imports rose over the period, exports stagnated after 1979, and a large current account deficit had to be financed by external assistance. The running down of the country's current account over the 1978–80 period stemmed primarily from poor growth of exports, which was due to a number of factors. One

TABLE 7.1
Lao PDR: Summary Indicators of Economic Performance, 1977–80

	1977	1978	1979	1980
GDP growth (%)	−2	2	10	10
Rice production ('000 tons)	693	724	867	1,010
Consumer prices (% increase)	90	72	867	1,010
Exports of goods (US$ million)	9.0	11.8	35.2	30.5
Imports of goods (US$ million)	64.0	89.7	116.0	130.2
Current account balance (US$ million)	−73.2	−101.1	−105.3	−119.4

Sources: International Monetary Fund, *Recent Economic Developments*, 22 July 1980 and 21 September 1981; State Planning Committee, Lao PDR; and State Bank of Laos.

factor was the closure of the Lao–Thai border which prevented official exports during 1980 and 1981; other factors were the decline in domestic production, especially tin production, and the inability of Societè de Commerce Lao (the sole export-import company for the Lao PDR) to carry out its responsibilities.

The recovery of domestic economic activity between 1978 and 1980 can be attributed to three factors. First, by the end of 1977, the worst consequences of the war had been mitigated by resettlement schemes and the establishment of central and provincial government administrations, and the economy, severely damaged by the 1977 drought, had bottomed out. As a result, it was a natural consequence of a more stable environment that economic activity would recover from the very low level of 1977. Second, the weather improved, particularly in 1979 and 1980, so that harvest of rice and other crops increased rapidly. And third, the government introduced significant and wide-ranging policy reforms between 1978 and 1980 which were designed to stimulate agricultural and industrial production and trade, to raise domestic budgetary revenues, and to improve the budgetary and monetary situation. The measures included reforms to the exchange rate and procurement prices and the removal of some restrictions on the internal movement of agricultural goods.

In May 1978 the government agreed to a one-year programme with the International Monetary Fund (IMF), and qualified for a first credit trade purchase and a trust fund loan of SDR 6.8 million. Under the programme the kip was devalued from KL 200 to KL 400 per dollar in May 1978 so as to narrow the gap between official and parallel market foreign exchange rates. There were increases in some official procurement prices, notably of agricultural goods.

The improvement in the economic performance, however, was not matched by the fiscal performance of the government. The government was running a large budget deficit in 1978, 1979, and 1980, with revenue covering only 40 per cent of overall expenditures and only 68 per cent of recurrent expenditures. Therefore, the budget depended on foreign assistance to cover all development expenditures and a portion of recurrent expenditures (Table 7.2).

TABLE 7.2
Laotian Government Budget, 1978–80
(In millions of kips)

	1978	1979	1980
Revenue	105.7	232.0	748.2
Transfers from state enterprises	32.7	148.2	567.8
Taxes of private sector	55.2	48.4	98.3
Other revenue	17.8	35.4	82.1
Expenditures	572.5	636.0	1,776.9
Current expenditures	384.0	393.9	1,028.0
Wages and salaries	104.9	113.9	269.6
Materials and supplies	87.3	95.5	667.8
Subsidies	168.3	165.3	68.0
Public debt service	23.5	19.2	22.6
Capital investment	189.5	242.1	784.9
Deficit	–466.8	–404.0	–1,028.7
Financing	466.8	368.1	1,024.7
External resource	431.0	354.5	1,028.7
Banking sector	35.8	13.6	–4.0

At the end of the Interim Three-Year Plan in December 1980, the government conducted its own assessment of the economy's performance and recognized that, while there had been a substantial recovery in economic activity and rice self-sufficiency was reached in 1980, achievements remained limited in a number of areas. Its assessment:

1.   Economic management remained weak, particularly in the manufacturing sector and in the agricultural co-operative sector;
2.   Despite doubling of the dollar value of exports in 1978–80, exports amounted to only 21 per cent of imports so that the country remained heavily dependent on external assistance;
3.   There were unfinished projects in many sectors due to shortage of skilled workers and domestic budgetary resources; and
4.   Border problems between the Lao PDR and Thailand aggravated the already severe transport constraints of the country.

TABLE 7.3
Lao PDR: Evolution of GDP, 1980–85
(In millions of kips, at 1982 prices)

	1980	1981	1982	1983	1984	1985
NMP (Net Material Products)	9,625	10,227	10,430	10,211	11,695	12,533
Depreciation	578	614	626	613	702	752
Government and other services	1,800	1,913	1,951	1,910	2,188	2,345
GDP	12,003	12,754	13,007	12,734	14,585	15,630
Growth rate (%)		6	2	–2	15	7
GDP deflator	42.8	59.8	100	158.9	202.0	313.0
GDP at current prices	5,137	7,627	13,007	20,231	29,462	48,922

Source: World Bank economic mission to the Lao PDR, *Report 1986*.

Achievement of the Five-Year Plan (1981–85)

Overall, the major achievement of the Five-Year Plan during the 1981–85 period was the increase in agricultural output, which grew by about 4.7 per cent per annum, mainly because of the increase in rice output (Table 7.4). Food self-sufficiency, the major objective of the Interim Three-Year Plan (1978–80) as well as of the Five-Year Plan (1981–85), was reached in 1985. However, despite the rapid growth of agricultural output during 1981–85, there was little evidence that public investment in the sector contributed much to it. Despite large investment in the industrial sector, industrial output, instead of being the most dynamic as forecast, declined by about 12 per cent from 1985. The main reason for the poor performance was the fall in manufacturing output by 10 per cent and slow growth of electricity and mining output. In the forestry sector, the exploitation of logs by state enterprises remained far below potential output, so that sawmills and plywood factories were running below capacity, and exports of logs amounted to less that one-third of the projected amount.

The transport sector expanded at about half the rate initially planned while the shortfall in the trade sector was even greater. Of

TABLE 7.4
Sectoral Output Growth in Lao PDR, 1981–85
(Annual growth rate in percentage)

Agriculture	4.7
Industry	–2.6
Electricity	1.3
Mining	5.8
Manufacturing	–7.5
Construction	2.3
Transport and communications	7.2
Commerce	4.4
Housing	3.5
GMP (Gross Material Products)	5.0

Source: State Planning Committee, Lao PDR.

the public investment 62 per cent was concentrated in the transport, agriculture, and industry sectors, which were considered to be crucial to economic growth.

As indicated in Table 7.5 the main budgetary revenues were non-fiscal revenues generated by public enterprises (66 per cent of total government revenue), which means that state-owned enterprises played a major role in economic activities. Import taxes accounted for only 2.8 per cent of the value of imports, amounting to only 10 per cent of fiscal revenues due to tariff exemptions for imports from former socialist countries.

Financing of the budget deficit mostly came from former socialist countries in the form of commodity and capital assistance.

Forces Motivating Reforms

At the end of the First Five-Year Plan (1981–85), major imbalances in the economy had emerged. Inflation was rising, an overvalued

TABLE 7.5
Laotian Government Budget, 1981–85
(In millions of kips)

	1981	1982	1983	1984	1985
Revenue	989	2,755	3,496	4,948	6,143
Non-tax revenue	593	1,980	2,440	3,279	4,238
Transfers					
from public enterprises	521	1,895	2,113	2,962	3,831
Tax revenue	396	775	1,056	1,669	1,905
Current expenditure	1,028	2,259	2,945	4,126	5,439
Current surplus	−39	496	551	822	704
Capital expenditure	928	3,216	3,750	4,258	5,035
Overall deficit	−967	−2,720	−3,199	−3,436	−4,331
Financing	967	2,720	3,199	3,436	4,331
External resource	967	2,720	3,199	3,436	4,331

Source: Ministry of Finance, Lao PDR.

multiple exchange rate was constraining export development, the trade deficit was increasing, and the country remained dependent on external sources to finance almost all investment expenditures due to the low level of domestic saving and poor resource mobilization. It was against this background that the government initiated a far-reaching programme of structural reforms in 1986 known as the New Economic Mechanism (NEM).

Macroeconomic Imbalances

During the implementation of the First Five-Year Plan (1981–85), the Lao PDR achieved some progress in economic development. However, viewed from the standpoint of most aggregate macroeconomic indicators, the achievement of growth was costly. This indicated that the key elements required for sustained economic growth remained weak.

Public Finance

Since the creation of the Lao PDR, a major constraint to more rapid and sustainable economic development has been the poor fiscal performance and consequent negative implication for domestic resource mobilization. Public savings have been negative. These were reflected in the central government budget, which became the main instrument for centralizing state resources and allocating national income between consumption and investment. Most of the government revenue was transferred from the savings of public enterprises in the form of profits and depreciation.

As seen in Table 7.6, revenue declined from 14.4 per cent of GDP in 1981 to 12.5 per cent in 1985, and in the evolution of the budget the overall deficit was reduced from 20 per cent of GDP in 1981 to 8.9 per cent in 1985, but this apparent improvement was mainly due to the undervaluation of budgetary investment expenditures by using official exchange rate. Investment would amount to 24.9 per cent of GDP in 1985 and overall budget deficit would reach 23.5 per cent of GDP, a higher ratio than in 1981, if the market exchange rate was used.

TABLE 7.6
Laotian Central Government Budget, 1981–85
(Percentage of GDP at current prices)

	1981	1982	1983	1984	1985
Revenue	14.4	21.2	17.3	16.8	12.5
Non-tax	8.7	15.2	12.1	11.1	8.6
Tax revenue	5.7	6.0	5.2	5.7	3.9
Current expenditure	20.0	17.4	14.6	14.0	11.1
Current surplus	−5.5	3.8	2.7	2.8	1.4
Capital expenditure	14.5	24.7	18.5	14.4	10.3
Overall deficit	−20.0	−20.9	−15.8	−11.6	−8.9
External financing	20.0	20.9	15.8	11.6	8.9

Sources: Ministry of Finance, Lao PDR; World Bank, *Country Economic Memorandum 1986.*

Balance of Payments

The poor performance of the export sector was a reflection of the lack of the development of comparative advantage, with the exception of the electricity sector. Forestry products were the main source of export earnings during the 1981–85 period. There was substantial state involvement in the sector through the creation and operation of nine state forestry enterprises. The main forestry export to the convertible currency area, however, declined during 1981–85. The main factors accounting for this were low official procurement prices for logs relative to parallel market prices, transportation bottle-necks, rigid management of state enterprises by technical ministries, and the government's decision to ban the private sector from production and trade in timber.

The slower growth of exports compared to that of imports during 1981–85 contributed to the negative balance of payments and widened the current account deficit from US$69.2 million in 1981 to US$95.3 million in 1985 (see Table 7.7). Increased imports, particularly from the non-convertible area, created more foreign debt-service payment. As indicated in the table, net capital inflows increased steadily during the 1981–85 period, from US$51.4 million in 1981 to US$99

TABLE 7.7
Lao PDR: Balance of Payments, 1981–85
(In US$ million)

	1981	1982	1983	1984	1985
Exports	23.1	40.0	40.8	45.1	47.6
Imports	–109.5	–132.2	–149.4	–153.9	–163.3
Trade balance	–86.4	–92.2	–108.6	–108.8	–115.7
Service (net)	–6.3	–7.1	–12.5	–5.5	–7.6
Transfers	23.5	31.0	25.4	28.9	28.0
Current account	–69.2	–68.3	–95.7	–85.4	–95.3
Capital account	51.4	60.2	76.5	89.6	99.0
Non-convertible area (net)	46.7	48.8	62.8	77.2	95.8
Convertible area	4.7	11.4	13.7	12.4	3.2
Errors and omissions	13.2	3.8	31.1	–7.0	—
Change in reserves	4.6	4.3	–11.9	2.8	–3.7

Source: State Bank of the Lao PDR.

million in 1985. This changed composition of capital inflows had accumulated foreign debt to the non-convertible area as well.

Investment Inefficiencies

One of the major impacts on the reforms in the Lao PDR results from investment inefficiencies. During the period of command economy, the effort to bring about economic growth had been based on a programme of substantial investments reflected in a high rate of investment — about 25 per cent of GDP. Since domestic savings amounted to less than 3 per cent of the GDP, the country had to resort to external financing for investment. However, both the natural resources and assets created through investments had not been utilized to their full potential. As a result, some of the benefits expected from high investment rates had failed to materialize.

From 1977 to 1985 investment increased from about 19.1 per cent of GDP to about 25 per cent of GDP, yet the average real growth rate of GDP declined from 7 per cent per annum in 1977–80 to 5 per cent per annum in 1980–85. This implies an increase in the amount of capital per unit of output, which suggests that the overall efficiency of investment was low, and only about one-third of the land was nominally developed during the dry season. A similar situation existed in the transport sector, where the utilization of state resource was low.

The Management of the Public Sector

During 1981–85 the government of the Lao PDR regarded the ownership of the means of production and distribution as a key element for economic management. To effect that, a planning structure was put in place. Public enterprises were created largely through nationalization. To ensure output expansion, public enterprises were almost completely managed by supervising ministries, with only routine decisions being taken at the enterprise level. In agriculture, the government contemplated the collectivization of production through state farms and co-operatives. In the other sectors (construction, transport, and trade) the policies of the government were to be implemented by:

1. direct control of credit distribution through a single bank, the State Bank of Lao PDR;
2. regulation of private sector activities; and
3. price control on commodities and services and subsidies.

The main characteristic of the planning process was that the public enterprises' output, employment, and investment decisions were determined by the central ministries, with the main targets of the development plans established in physical terms independently of prices, wages, and exchange rates. In such a system, the allocation of resources was seen to be under the direct control of the government so that financial incentives appeared irrelevant as far as the implementation of the plans was concerned.

Although the expansion of the state sector was consistently pursued, the lack of financial and human resources prevented it from growing sufficiently and rapidly to replace the private sector entirely. As a result, the government's policy towards the private sector shifted between strict administrative control and limited regulation of activities.

As a result, public sector management was grossly inadequate, as reflected in the poor financial performances and macroeconomic imbalances. It was against this background that the government reappraised its development strategies and embarked on a series of reform processes aimed at improving the use of the country's resources and restraining further increases in external borrowing.

The New Economic Mechanism

Objectives

The government of the Lao PDR has formally undertaken economic reform since November 1986 to move from a centrally planned to market-oriented economy. This reform package is called the New Economic Mechanism (NEM), which consists of a wide array of reforms affecting the economic system, including measures aimed to deregulate, stabilize, and improve the performance of the economy. These reforms were necessitated by the fact that the central planning system had created deficiencies in the functioning of the country's administration and the performance of its economy, as discussed earlier.

Initial reforms during 1986–88 were largely limited to improving the structure and performance of state enterprises and selected deregulation of agricultural marketing arrangements. Subsequently, the reforms were broadened to incorporate the establishment of a market-based economy and transformation of the economic structure and incentive system and the role of the state.

From 1988, a key reform was the modification of the state's role away from direct intervention in the productive sectors of the economy towards a regulatory and service role to ensure efficient operation of the market economy. This included the divestment of state enterprises and the development of a legal and institutional framework for economic and commercial activities. Additional reforms included price deregulation and elimination of consumer subsidies, alignment of the official exchange rate with market rates, and the promulgation of a foreign investment law.

Macroeconomic Reforms to Enhance Economic Stability

Since 1988, the government has taken major steps to improve the process of macroeconomic management. A key element has been fiscal policy, money supply, and exchange rate management. Priorities have been to reorganize the finance and banking system to support the expansion of trade, and to reduce exposure to bad debts from state enterprises. Another priority has been to maintain a stable exchange rate programme in support of the process of restructuring, expansion of the economic base, and increased export earnings.

Monetary Reforms

The maintenance of a tight fiscal and monetary regime is essential to reduce inflation and thereby maintain economic competitiveness. A key component is the use of credit control procedures that form part of the restructuring of the financial sector. Hence, interest rate policy is one of the most important instruments for financial management. In the past the government mobilized external financial assistance for two major users: the state enterprises and the agricultural sector, to which credit was given on subsidized terms. During the implementation of the NEM, the interest rate policy required that deposits should earn positive real rates with the objective of mobilizing domestic resources. Credit programmes with subsidized interest rates were phased out, with the real cost of subsidies made transparent and borne by the budget. The Central Bank has been playing a key role in these areas.

Fiscal Reforms

The government went through two major tax reforms in 1988 and 1989 to adapt its revenue system to the requirements of a decentralized market-oriented system. Before March 1988 the main source of budgetary revenues came from the transfer of the operating surpluses of state enterprises to the budget. The reform of March 1988 introduced a proper tax system, including profit tax, sales taxes, import duties, and agricultural production taxes. (Later in March 1993 the agricultural production taxes were abolished, but a land tax was introduced to complement the land-ownership decree in 1922.) These decrees reduce the role of non-tax transfers. A second tax reform was enacted in June 1989 to tackle some of the flaws of the previous reform, in particular the multiplicity of profit tax rates and the limited coverage of indirect taxes, and to introduce new levies, such as a personal income tax, and expand the natural resource tax.

In early 1988 wages were gradually adjusted accordingly and their payment in kind was eliminated in September 1989. Consistent with the new policy, budgetary transfers to state enterprises, as either investment funds (with the exception of public utilities) or subsidies covering operating losses, were terminated. In the same spirit, the government's borrowing from the Central Bank was well controlled. Finally, a major reduction in civil service employment was undertaken in 1988, which affected 20–25 per cent of all government employees.

Exchange Rate and Price Reforms

The most far-reaching step taken by the government has been the adoption of the one-market, one-price principle, which calls for the elimination of the dual-price system (official and parallel prices) for goods and foreign exchange and all prices of goods and services have been determined by the market, except a few commodities such as electricity. Pursuant to this policy, the official exchange rate is maintained at the market level. Market pricing according to market supply and demand conditions has been introduced to create incentives for the agricultural sector. The prevalence of a market exchange rate signals a major policy adjustment towards the development of an export-oriented monetized economy. The government recognizes that the maintenance of a stable official exchange rate is crucial to expand export earnings, increase private investment, and reduce the deficit. In order to stabilize and maintain the competitiveness of the exchange rate, the primary responsibility is to maintain positive interest rates, reduce inflation to a level comparable with major trading partners, and maintain the official exchange rate within 10 per cent of the market rate.

Trade Reform

The domestic trade sector was reformed in 1987 with a view to facilitating the inter-regional flow of goods and drawing more heavily on the resources of the private and co-operative sectors. Before the reforms, the market system was complex and inefficient and featured extensive administrative interference in the direction and volume of domestic trade flows. In particular, farmers were not allowed to move rice across provincial borders. The movement of goods between provinces was generally limited to state companies. This policy aggravated the impact of natural barriers and poor infrastructure which hamper national economic integration. These restrictions were abolished in 1987. Domestic trade has been opened to private and co-operative traders and administrative and regulating authorities have been instructed not to interfere in trade. At the same time, the various state trading companies were restructured to enhance their operational efficiency. Others were dismantled, such as the government rice procurement companies, as a result of the abolition of payment of wages in kind and potable water. All procurement and distribution activities involving state companies must be based on contracts, with prices and other contract terms freely negotiated between the parties. This liberalization, which permitted the market economy to function, has led to a substantial increase in internal trade.

Similarly, Laos has taken important steps in market reform to liberalize the foreign-trade sector, which used to be almost completely monopolized by the state. All economic agents, private or public, now have access to imported goods through licensed traders. The licensed traders include state bodies as well as a large number of mixed and private import-export companies. No restriction applies to the range of goods they are entitled to import, and imports are still subject to import licences. A new import tariff was introduced in March 1988 in the context of an overall tax reform. Tariffs were streamlined and coverage was extended. In the past, the import tax played an insignificant economic or revenue role as imports were:

1. monopolized by the state;
2. evaluated for tax purposes at a grossly undervalued exchange rate; and
3. exempted from tariffs if they were from former socialist countries.

Under the tax reform, the tariff-rate range has been narrowed from 0–200 per cent to 0–100 per cent with eleven tariff bands, the zero rate applying to project imports and those financed by grants; and the higher rates (above 30 per cent) to luxury goods. Imports are now evaluated at the market exchange rate for tax purpose and tariff exemptions for imports from former socialist countries have been removed.

Financial Reforms

The Lao PDR Government has initiated a complete restructuring of the financial sector as well as the reform of monetary and credit policies. With regard to the financial sector, the government decided in March 1988 to separate central and commercial banking functions of the existing mono-bank system. This process was formally introduced by the law on the creation of seven branches of the State Bank, which have already been transformed into autonomous commercial banks. Three branches are located in the capital, including the Bank for External Trade. Similarly, four provincial branches have been converted into commercial banks serving all provinces. One state-private joint-venture bank, The Joint Development Bank, was opened in October 1989, which would stimulate competition. Since December 1992, Thai banks have opened branches in Vientiane. They include Siam Commercial Bank, Thai Farmers Bank, Thai Military Bank, Krung Thai Bank, Bangkok Bank, and Bank of Ayoudhya. The Central Bank is supposed to conduct monetary policy guided by broad macroeconomic objectives through the use of a combination of quantitative controls, reserve requirements, and interest rate regulations. The credit policy includes provision of credit privileges to private and public enterprises on equal footing. At present, financial reforms are developing towards indirect monetary control instruments and allowing interest rates to be freely determined by market forces.

Improving the Efficiency and Performance of the Public Sector

A central element of the ongoing economic reform process is the improvement in the efficiency of the public sector in order to increase the effectiveness of support services. Three related activities that have been the focus of efforts to date are:

1. To restructure the role and functions of government;
2. To continue the divestment of state enterprises, including the closure of non-viable enterprises, and improving the efficiency and performance of retained state enterprises; and
3. To complete the legal and regulatory framework necessary to facilitate the operations of an efficient market economy.

Role of Government

In the transition to a market economy, the government's primary role will be to provide an economic environment that encourages both the mobilization of resources into productive areas and the efficient use of these resources. This will require the government to allocate resources to those areas where significant favourable spread-effects exist. Such public services include the provision of public infrastructure, social facilities and services, and support services (such as training). Where the government is now supplanting rather than facilitating market operations, it will have to withdraw from these activities. In agriculture, for example, it will phase out its input supply and crop procurement activities which can largely be undertaken by the private sector, and will provide only the necessary policies and investments to give market incentives to both the users and potential suppliers of these inputs.

The reduction in the direct involvement of government in production will allow substantial reduction of employment in the civil service, except in those areas responsible for the delivery of key social services. At the same time, the efficiency of the civil service will be increased by improving pay condition and by providing extensive training to upgrade staff qualifications. Substantial staff retraining will also be needed, particularly in planning, so that they can carry out their functions effectively in a market economy.

Divestment of State Enterprises

During the Second Five-Year Plan (1986–90) the government made a major attempt to reduce the responsibility of public sector financing of state enterprise operations by granting autonomy to state enterprises, ending direct budget subsidies to them, and divesting itself of some state enterprises. In March 1990 Decree 17, dealing with the conversion of state enterprises to other forms of economic entities, was promulgated to define the changed role of the state in the market economy. As stated in the decree, no government administration can be directly involved in business transactions, which are to be dealt with by the various economic agents on the basis of rational economic profit.

Despite a clearly defined commitment to full divestment of state enterprises except the strategic ones, most disengagements have been through lease contracts. Where joint-venture arrangements were made, the private sector retained major share ownership. The government recognized that without full privatization of assets, the manager will have little incentive to maintain and improve the asset base.

For enterprises retained by the state, the objective will be to improve their production efficiency and financial performance as well as to improve the quality of management and labour. The remaining state enterprises will be required to adopt a standard accounting system which is consistent with current international standards.

Legal and Regulatory Framework

A central element of the ongoing process of adjustment to a market economy is the establishment of a legal infrastructure which will:

1. provide the basis for commercial transactions and investment decisions; and
2. incorporate the necessary property and ownership rights to allow free trade and commercial transactions.

Development of such a regulatory framework has already been addressed with the promulgation of laws on foreign investment, contracts, the penal code, inheritance and property rights, banking and insurance, labour and family law, accounting law, business law, customs law, budget law, banking law, arbitration decree, land law, and guarantee law. A National Constitution was promulgated in 1991. In addition, to complete the legal framework for commercial activity, the Lao Legal Working Group formed pursuant to the Harvard/United Nations Development Programme/World Bank Lao Project has completed a study on business/commercial legislation in the following areas: enterprises, sureties, arbitration, bankruptcy, cheques, promissory notes, and others. The results and recommendations are being submitted to the Lao Government for consideration.

Pace and Sequencing of the Reform Programmes

In early 1987 the first national conference on NEM was held. One important point that was acknowledged and approved at the conference was that the economy would not be able to achieve the objectives of the Lao economic reform unless there was also a reform in the financial sector, particularly the banking sector. In early 1988 the government held many meetings to discuss the drafts of many decrees that were to support NEM in the following stages of economic reforms. Those decrees were finally adopted in March 1988. They were:

1. Decree No. 9 on state tax system. This decree was the starting point of the fiscal reform.

2. Decree No. 10 changed the role of economic planning from central planning to indicative planning.
3. Decree No. 11 on the conversion of the banking system into a commercial one to create a two-tier banking system which separated the central bank from commercial bank. This decree was the starting point of the banking sector reform.
4. Decree No. 12 on the directions and measures to increase the circulation of commodities and currencies.
5. Decree No. 13 on state monopoly of import-export management abolished state monopoly on imports and exports.
6. Decree No. 14 on state price policy. With this decree the government made a very bold step to liberalize the prices of goods and the rate of foreign exchange, where previously they were fixed by the state.
7. Decree No. 15 on the organization of trade business system from the centre down to the localities and grass roots in the private sector.
8. Decree No. 16 on the policies towards the individuals and private economic sectors and Decree No. 17 on the participation of the private sector in the economy. These two decrees encouraged the participation of the private sector in the economy.

Recent Economic Performance

The government of the Lao PDR has made substantial progress since 1986 in transforming its economy from a centrally planned into a market-oriented system. The emphasis placed since 1989 on credit, monetary, and fiscal reforms led to financial stabilization, as evident by falling inflation, a significant improvement in fiscal performance, and the improvement in the balance of payments (Table 7.8). The exchange rate has been relatively steady since 1990 and the country has been consolidating its foreign reserves position. These economic reform processes and developments have been supported by concessional loans from various international institutions, notably the World Bank, the International Monetary Fund, and the Asian Development Bank. Such loans and technical assistance have substantially helped lessen the unfavourable budgetary and balance-

TABLE 7.8
Lao PDR: Key Economic Objectives and Indicators, 1989–93[1]

	1989	1990	1991	1992	1993
	(Percentage changes)				
Real GDP growth	13.5	6.6	4.0	7.0	6.5
Consumer prices (end of period)	75.9	19.6	10.4	8.0	7.0
Liquidity [2]	89.3	14.0	15.7	37.2	64.6
Growth in credit to					
non-governmental sector	73.0	11.2	15.7	23.6	51.7
Interest rate (one-year deposit)					
(in percentage; end of period)	36.0	36.0	18.0	18.2	12.0
Export (value) [3]	9.5	24.2	22.9	37.3	57.9
Import (value) [3]	10.2	–3.5	14.3	7.3	16.8
	(In percentage of GDP)				
Government revenue	8.2	9.9	10.3	10.7	12.0
Government expenditure	24.7	23.4	20.9	20.6	18.2
Current	9.3	11.4	11.3	10.9	11.2
Capital	15.4	12.0	9.6	9.7	7.0
Government current account balance [4]	–1.1	–1.5	–1.0	–0.2	0.6
Overall fiscal balance (cash basis)					
With grants	–12.5	–10.7	–6.8	–5.2	–4.4
Without grants	–16.4	–14.4	–11.3	–9.9	–7.8
Domestic financing	–3.4	0.8	2.7	0.6	1.5
Foreign financing	15.9	9.9	4.1	4.6	2.9
External current account balance					
With official transfers	–9.6	–6.9	–4.3	–3.5	–0.9
Without official transfers	–11.5	–9.6	–11.0	–8.8	–8.4
Debt-service ratio [5]	15.9	10.3	11.2	6.5	4.7
Gross external reserves [6]					
In millions of U.S. dollars	60.8	64.8	57.2	85.5	150.9
In months of total imports	3.8	4.2	3.2	3.9	4.8
of which:					
Gross official reserves	—	—	1.7	2.0	2.3

Notes: [1] Up to 1992, the fiscal year coincided with the calendar year. In 1992, the fiscal year was changed to an October/September basis. Data in this table for 1993 continue to refer to calendar year basis for all variables except the fiscal data, which are on a fiscal year basis.
[2] Broad money supply, including foreign currency deposits.
[3] In terms of U.S. dollars.
[4] Excludes grants.
[5] As a ratio of exports of goods and services.
[6] Including commercial banks' reserves.

Source: Data provided by the Lao authorities. Reproduced from Chi Do Pham (1994), Table 1, p. 16.

of-payment impacts consequent upon the wide-ranging reforms undertaken by the government.

Economic Growth and Sectoral Performance

The economic performance of the Lao PDR during the 1986–90 period has yielded mixed results. Following growth of about 5 per cent in 1986, output stagnated in 1987 and 1988 because of drought-induced reduction in agricultural output and hydro-power production. Because of the strong interlinkage with the agriculture sector, the manufacturing and services sectors were also depressed. The GDP fell by about 6 per cent in 1987 and continued to fall in 1988. The situation improved remarkably in 1989 and 1990, as the GDP grew about 14.3 per cent in 1989 and 6.7 per cent in 1990 due to good weather and strong growth in the industry and services sectors, and continued to grow in 1991 and 1992.

Rice production recovered and increased from 1.0 million tons in 1988 to about 1.4 million tons in 1989 and 1.5 million tons in 1990, but fell in 1991 to about 1.3 million tons because of poor weather and flood in the southern provinces, the locations for the major rice-growing areas. Rice production increased again in 1992 to about 1.5 million tons due to good weather. There was strong growth in cash crops such as corn, soy bean, tobacco, and cardamom in 1990, 1991, and 1992 (Table 7.9). The high growth rates in the production of electricity, tin, wood products, food products, and tobacco also contributed to the growth rates of 1991 and 1992. At the same time, the construction and manufacturing sectors witnessed strong growth as domestic and foreign investors responded to the new opportunities presented by the reforms. Overall, real GDP rose by an average of 7 per cent annually during 1989–92 (Figure 7.1). The impact of the reforms on the services sector has been more pronounced. During the years 1990, 1991, and 1992, there had been remarkable increases in the number of small private commercial enterprises operating in Vientiane and major cities such as Savannakhet, Pakse, and Luang Prabang. In particular, a number of new enterprises have been established which are capable of supplying vehicles, machinery, computer equipment, spare parts, and consumer goods that previously had to be ordered from Thailand. A number of private enterprises

TABLE 7.9
Lao PDR: GDP by Industrial Origin, 1988–93
(At 1990 constant market prices, in billions of kips)

	1988	1989	1990	1991	1992	1993
Agriculture	308.90	342.20	371.83	365.35	395.54	402.23
Crops	164.56	206.41	224.97	195.63	221.17	196.73
Livestock and fishery	116.07	119.90	127.36	145.69	158.85	165.47
Forestry	28.27	15.89	19.50	24.03	15.52	40.03
Industry	56.18	75.84	88.10	105.64	113.59	125.26
Mining and quarrying	0.82	0.98	0.89	0.83	0.93	1.27
Manufacturing	37.53	52.34	60.46	78.40	85.78	92.36
Construction	12.17	15.09	17.91	17.74	19.06	22.13
Electricity, gas, and water	5.66	7.43	8.84	8.67	7.82	9.50
Services	129.26	148.05	147.37	156.98	163.03	175.61
Transport and communications	33.70	36.18	31.69	32.12	34.33	35.41
Wholesale and retail trade	31.94	41.18	41.97	46.16	49.41	38.55
Banking and insurance	1.36	4.00	6.94	6.20	6.91	21.09
Ownership of dwellings	17.49	19.81	24.38	27.95	23.41	7.82
Public wage bill	39.38	39.38	35.63	31.89	31.03	25.28
Non-profit institutions	4.63	6.34	5.46	9.65	11.66	30.97
Hotels and restaurants	0.27	0.66	0.92	2.32	5.23	10.49
Other services	0.49	0.50	0.38	0.69	1.05	6.00
GDP at factor cost	494.34	566.09	607.29	627.96	672.16	707.10
Import duties	8.18	8.13	5.36	9.19	9.64	14.72
GDP at market price	502.52	574.22	612.65	637.15	681.80	721.82
Growth rate (%)	–1.8	14.3	6.7	4.0	7.0	5.9

Source: State Statistical Centre, Lao PDR.

providing agricultural, engineering, legal, financial, and medical services have also been established. A number of hotels have reopened and there has been significant growth in the transport of goods between Thailand and Unan in the southern province of China through northern Laos, Thailand, and Vietnam, and between Thailand and Cambodia through the southern part of the country.

Despite these favourable recent economic developments, the agricultural sector continues to dominate the Lao economy and

FIGURE 7.1
Lao PDR: Changes in Real GDP, 1988–93

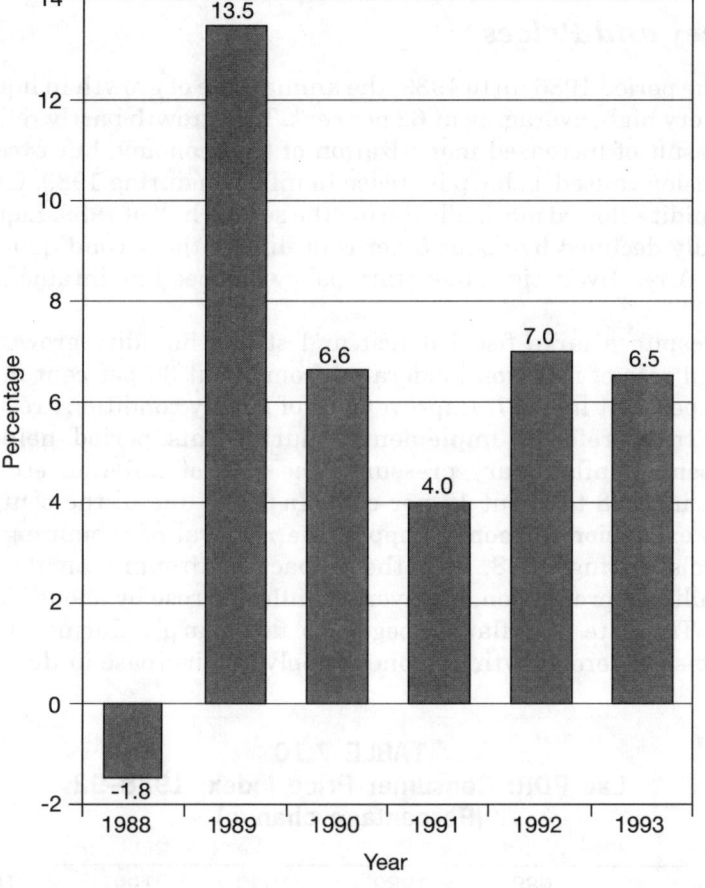

provides employment for about 85 per cent of the labour force. The impact of the reforms has been less visible in the rural areas, but there are indications of more intensive use of inputs to increase production of cash crops. Price and exchange rate reforms have been an important factor in reducing the terms-of-trade bias against agricultural products and providing incentives for increased and more diversified agricultural production.

Money and Prices

For the period 1986 up to 1989, the annual rate of growth in liquidity was very high, averaging at 62 per cent. This growth partly reflected the result of increased monetization of the economy, but excessive expansion caused a sharp increase in inflation during 1989. Growth in liquidity slowed markedly during the second half of 1989. Liquidity actually declined by about 5 per cent during the second quarter of 1990. A relatively tight monetary policy has been maintained since 1990.

Despite a large fiscal deficit and strong liquidity growth, the annual rate of inflation moderated from about 30 per cent in 1985 to 11 per cent in 1987. Improvement of supply conditions resulting from trade reforms implemented during this period helped in dampening inflationary pressure. The rate of inflation escalated again in 1988 to about 17 per cent. In 1989, due to the continued rapid expansion in money supply, the removal of remaining price controls during 1988, and the impact of drought on domestic agricultural production, the average inflation rose by about 58.4 per cent. The rate of inflation began to fall sharply during 1990 in response to zero growth in money supply and increase in the supply

TABLE 7.10
Lao PDR: Consumer Price Index, 1988–92
(Percentage change)

	1988	1989	1990	1991	1992
Total	13.0	82.1	17.7	10.4	6.0
Food	9.4	83.9	13.2	12.6	−1.1
Clothing	4.1	153.5	7.2	11.6	16.8
Services	28.1	43.2	93.6	20.8	28.6
Others	16.7	90.7	21.3	−1.7	7.7

Source: Bank of the Lao PDR.

of agricultural products because of good weather; the average inflation rate was brought down to about 40.4 per cent that year. The rate of inflation continued to decline throughout 1991 to about 19.4 per cent and to about 9.8 per cent in 1992. In 1993 the average inflation rate was only 6.3 per cent. (For more details see Table 7.10 and Figure 7.2.)

FIGURE 7.2
Lao PDR: Changes in Consumer Prices, 1988–93
(In percentages at year-end)

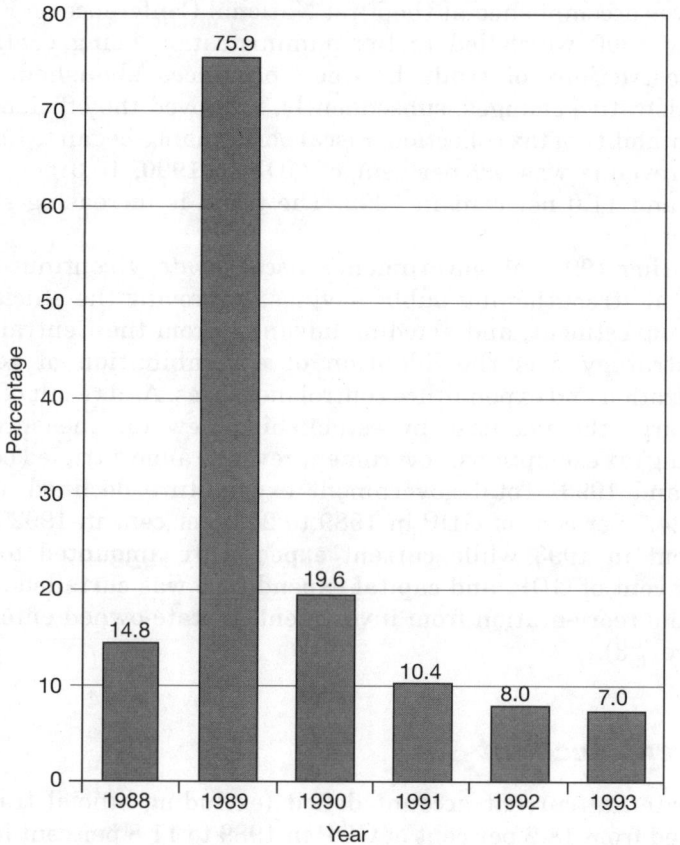

Source: Bank of the Lao PDR.

Public Finance

Government revenue fell from about 15.8 per cent of GDP in 1986 to 8.3 per cent in 1989, as direct transfers from state enterprises dropped sharply and were not compensated with increases in tax payments. The financial performance and tax contributions of state enterprises have suffered because of increased competition from private enterprises and imports under the more liberal trade regime. Changes were made to the tax system with the aim of increasing revenues with a broader and more encompassing tax system. The government's priority was to improve tax collection and monitoring. This was accomplished at the First National Conference on Finance of July 1990 which led to tax administration being centralized and restrictions of trade between provinces abolished. These administrative changes, subsequently, improved the efficiency and accountability of tax collection. Fiscal performance began to improve: fiscal revenue was 9.9 per cent of GDP in 1990, 10.3 per cent in 1991, and 11.0 per cent in 1992. The trend is increasing steadily (Figure 7.3).

During 1992 the government's fiscal strategy continued to be aimed at strengthening public savings, improving the efficiency of public investment, and avoiding advances from the Central Bank. The strategy was the adoption of a combination of revenue mobilization and expenditure control measures. As a result of efforts to enlarge the tax base by establishing new tax measures and reducing tax exemptions, government revenue almost tripled between 1989 and 1993. Total government expenditure declined steadily from 24.7 per cent of GDP in 1989 to 20.6 per cent in 1992 to 18.1 per cent in 1993 while current expenditure amounted to about 11 per cent of GDP, and capital expenditure was curtailed sharply with the reorientation from investment in state-owned enterprises (Figure 7.3).

Current Account

The external current account deficit (excluding official transfers) declined from 18.2 per cent of GDP in 1989 to 11.8 per cent in 1990,

FIGURE 7.3
Lao PDR: Budget Ratios

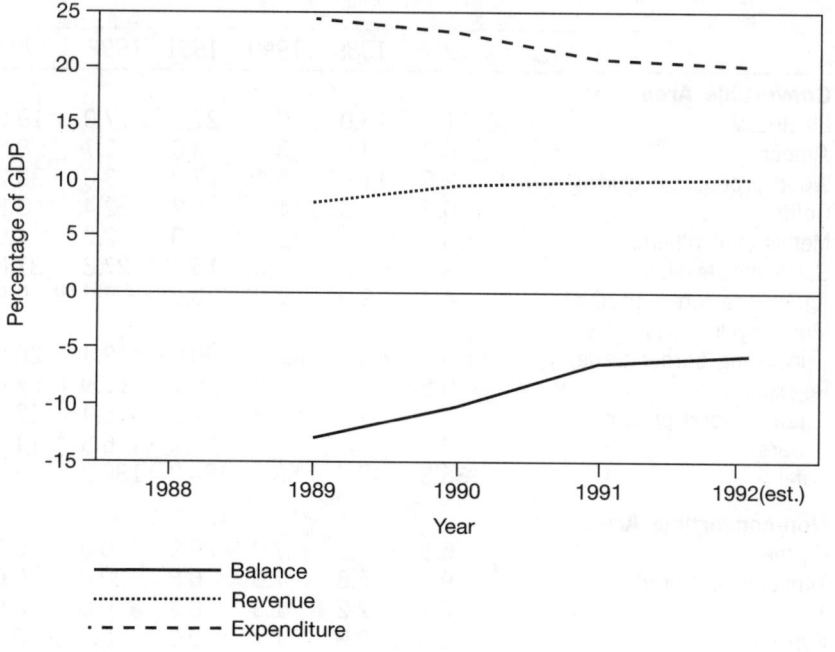

11.0 per cent in 1991, 8.8 per cent in 1992, and 8.5 per cent in 1993. The improvement in 1992 and 1993 was mainly due to an increase in net services, which reflected the growth in tourism receipts and increase in domestic spending by foreign embassies and international organizations.

Exports increased from US$57.8 million in 1988 to US$96.6 million in 1991, US$132.6 million in 1992, and US$209.4 million in 1993. The big improvement of exports in 1992 and 1993 was due to the increased export of garments, logs, and motor cycles as well as re-export of motor vehicles. On the other hand, electricity, which used to be the largest export of Laos, dropped to fourth largest (Table 7.11).

TABLE 7.11
Lao PDR: Composition of Exports, 1988–93
(In US$ million)

	1988	1989	1990	1991	1992	1993
Convertible Area						
Electricity	11.3	15.0	19.2	21.3	17.0	19.6
Timber	18.2	4.0	3.2	3.0	9.7	8.5
Wood products (including sawn)	2.6	11.6	15.4	17.9	33.0	38.2
Coffee	0.5	3.6	1.4	2.2	2.4	3.3
Metals (and others)	n.a.	n.a.	n.a.	1.3	2.2	4.0
Garments, textiles	n.a.	4.0	7.0	15.1	27.3	37.0
Agriculture/forest products	4.2	9.0	7.0	3.7	7.3	9.2
Motor cycles (assembly, including border trade)	n.a.	n.a.	n.a.	20.0	19.4	28.8
Re-exports	0.0	0.0	4.8	9.7	11.9	57.0
Logs, wood products			4.8	9.7	5.4	28.8
Cars					6.5	14.3
Total	36.8	47.2	58.0	94.2	130.2	205.6
Non-convertible Area						
Coffee	6.8	5.2	7.2	0.9	0.0	0.0
Timber/wood products	9.3	5.8	7.3	0.8	0.0	0.0
Tin	2.1	2.2	1.3	0.2	0.0	0.0
Gypsum	1.1	0.9	1.7	0.2	0.0	0.0
Others	1.8	2.0	3.1	0.4	0.0	0.0
Total	21.1	16.1	20.6	2.5	2.4	0.0
Total exports	57.8	63.3	78.7	96.6	132.6	205.6

Note: n.a. — not available.

Source: Bank of the Lao PDR.

Imports increased from US$162.4 million in 1988 to US$228.0 million in 1991, US$265.5 million in 1992, and US$375.7 million in 1993 (Table 7.12). However, non-aid related imports were more important in 1992 and 1993. Most of the increase in imports was of machinery and primary materials and, to a lesser extent, rice and other food products. (The main trends of development in the current account are depicted in Figure 7.4.)

TABLE 7.12
Lao PDR: Composition of Imports, 1988–93
(In US$ million)

	1988	1989	1990	1991	1992	1993
Convertible Area						
Rice and other food products	7.0	9.2	7.1	13.0	31.6	31.4
Provincial imports	10.9	15.4	11.3	15.4	n.a.	n.a.
Petroleum (including for tied aid projects)	6.3	12.2	7.3	21.1	24.3	19.7
Machinery and raw materials	10.5	11.2	29.2	61.3	94.7	191.2
For garment industry	n.a.	n.a.	n.a.	n.a.	20.4	31.5
For others (including garment industry)	n.a.	n.a.	n.a.	n.a.	52.3	62.7
For re-export (70 per cent of export value)	n.a.	n.a.	n.a.	n.a.	22.0	97.0
Other imports	29.6	30.7	20.4	48.1	50.5	56.2
Subtotal imports c.i.f.	64.3	78.7	75.3	158.9	201.1	298.5
Non-convertible area imports (rubles)	117.5	125.8	150.9	3.1	0.0	n.a.
Non-convertible area imports (US$)	53.4	57.2	68.6	1.4	0.0	n.a.
Petroleum, excluding re-export	16.8	12.4	21.2	n.a.	n.a.	n.a.
Total tied aid	44.7	75.0	57.7	67.7	64.4	27.2
Convertible area	26.1	57.1	55.4	64.5	64.4	27.2
Non-convertible area (US$)	18.6	17.9	2.3	3.2	0.0	0.0
Total imports c.i.f.	162.4	210.7	201.6	228.0	265.5	375.7
Convertible area	90.4	135.7	130.7	223.4	265.5	375.7
Non-convertible area (US$)	72.0	75.0	70.9	4.6	0.0	0.0

Note: n.a. — not available.

Source: Bank of the Lao PDR.

Exchange Rate

Figure 7.5 shows that the stability of the kip against both the U.S. dollar and the Thai baht has been maintained since 1989, a reflection of continued tight financial policies and relatively high real interest rates. The official rate of the currency depreciated slightly by less than 1 per cent per year from about 700 kips/U.S. dollar in 1990 to about 720 kips/U.S. dollar in 1992. As of December 1993 this rate still prevailed.

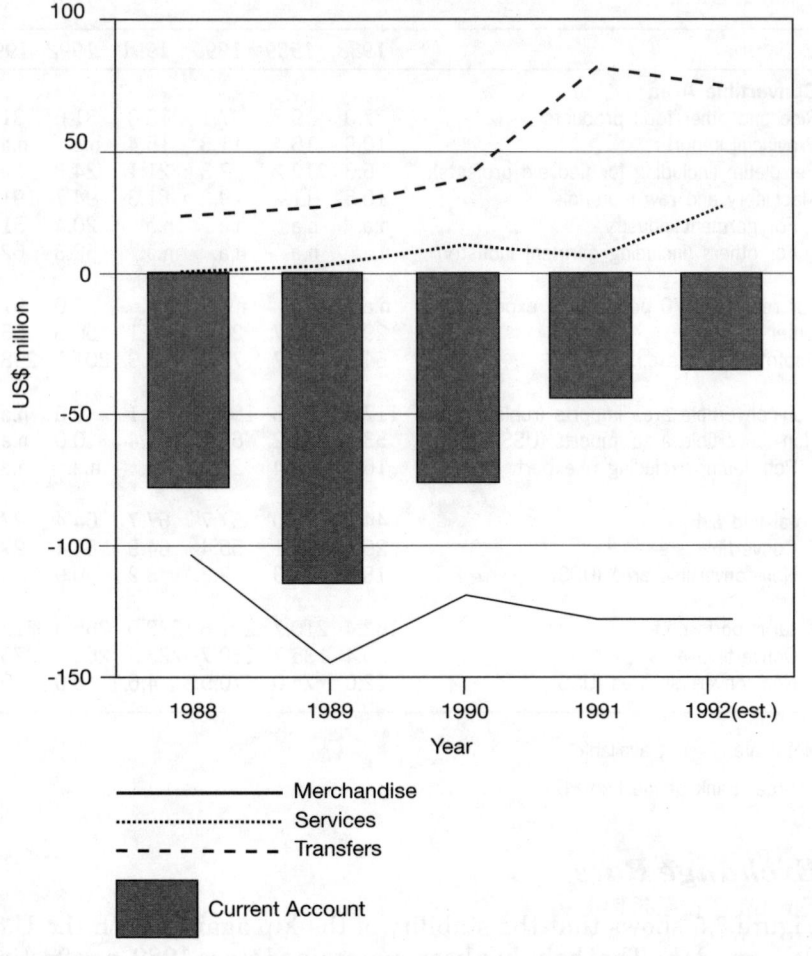

FIGURE 7.4
Lao PDR: Current Account

FIGURE 7.5
Kip Exchange Rates

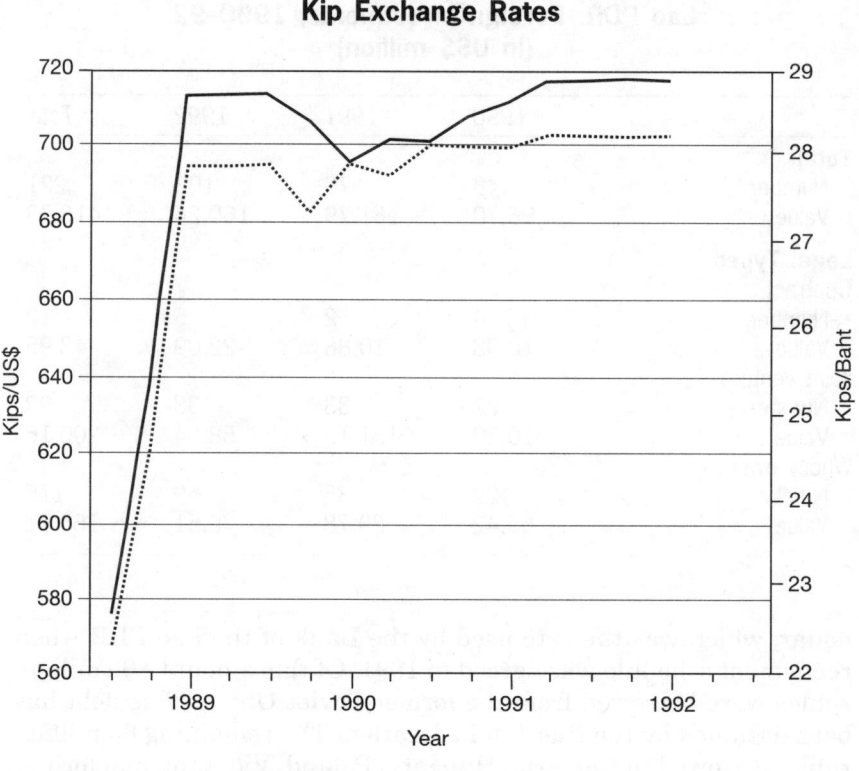

Year

US$ Official

Baht Official

External Debt

The total official external debt of the Lao PDR stood at US$1.148 million at the end of 1992. Debt to the convertible area has become more significant in recent years. The majority of this convertible area debt consisted of loans from multilateral agencies such as the World Bank and the Asian Development Bank (ADB). The total debt to the non-convertible area is 880 million rubles (US$734.4 million) when converted at the rate of approximately 1.2 rubles per U.S.

TABLE 7.13
Lao PDR: Foreign Investments, 1990–92
(In US$ million)

	1990	1991	1992	Total
Total				
Number	48	70	103	221
Value	96.70	161.79	160.24	418.73
Legal Types				
Contract				
Number	4	2	6	12
Value	10.98	10.88	22.09	43.95
Joint venture				
Number	22	33	38	93
Value	10.39	131.13	58.64	200.16
Wholly owned				
Number	22	35	59	116
Value	65.42	29.78	70.51	165.71

dollar, which was the rate used by the Bank of the Lao PDR when repayment schedule was agreed in 1991. Of this amount 800 million rubles were borrowed from the former Soviet Union. This debt has been assumed by the Russian Federation. The remaining 80 million rubles are owed to Bulgaria, Hungary, Poland, Vietnam, and former Czechoslovakia. As the bulk of the Russian debt has been rescheduled, interest free to the year 2000, and loans from multilateral agencies are on concessional terms, with an average interest rate of 1 per cent, the debt-service ratio in 1992 and 1993 was about 6.3 per cent and 4.5 per cent respectively.

Foreign Investment

The foreign investment law was introduced in mid-1988 and was amended in March 1994. The law authorized three forms of investment — business by contract, joint ventures, and wholly foreign-owned enterprises — before its amendment. But after its amendment only

TABLE 7.14
Lao PDR: Approved Foreign Investments by Sector, September 1988–December 1992
(In US$1,000)

Industrial Sector	September – December 1988	1989	1990	1991	1992	Cumulative Total	Percentage of Cumulative Total
Agribusiness	—	438 (2)	140 (2)	23,310 (5)	12,864 (18)	36,752 (27)	7.6
Garments/textiles	207 (1)	715 (3)	10,699 (9)	6,381 (12)	14,253 (23)	32,255 (48)	6.6
Wood products	619 (3)	4,217 (3)	4,011 (4)	4,521 (6)	32,420 (6)	45,788 (22)	9.4
Other manufactures	—	5,115 (13)	3,124 (6)	14,817 (18)	33,373 (20)	56,429 (57)	11.6
Total manufactures	826 (4)	10,485 (21)	17,974 (21)	49,029 (41)	92,910 (67)	171,224 (154)	35.2
Mining/petroleum	246 (1)	22,650 (4)	23,750 (2)	5,278 (3)	17,508 (7)	69,432 (17)	14.3
Import/export	2,200 (2)	7,462 (15)	2,299 (12)	7,566 (8)	7,008 (11)	26,535 (48)	5.5
Hotel/tourism	—	17,216 (5)	2,440 (5)	96,871 (9)	6,933 (5)	123,460 (24)	25.4
Retail/restaurants	—	—	—	25 (1)	492 (5)	517 (6)	0.1
Banking/finance	—	4,000 (1)	—	2,000 (1)	20,000 (4)	26,000 (6)	5.3
Consulting	30 (1)	100 (3)	418 (5)	210 (5)	119 (3)	877 (17)	0.2
Other professional services	—	—	—	—	511 (5)	511 (5)	0.1
Construction	—	2,639 (2)	—	—	7,080 (4)	9,719 (6)	2.0
Transport	—	—	44,160 (3)	314 (1)	2,681 (3)	47,155 (7)	9.7
Telecommunications	—	—	—	500 (1)	—	500 (1)	0.1
Hydro-power	—	—	5,750 (1)	—	5,000 (1)	10,750 (2)	2.2
Total approvals	3,302 (8)	64,552 (51)	96,791 (49)	161,793 (70)	160,242 (115)	486,680 (293)	100.0

Notes: 1. Figures in parentheses indicate the number of investments licensed.
2. The total number of investments by sector exceeds the total number of overall investments because some investments are bisectoral.

Source: AFIMC/LNCCI, Investment Opportunities in the Lao People's Democratic Republic (December 1992). Reproduced from UNIDO (April 1994), Table II.7, p. 27.

the last two forms remain. The law also guarantees that the capital and other assets of foreign investors will not be nationalized or requisitioned by administrative procedure and guarantees that profits from such investments can be repatriated. Tax holidays have been abolished and a low tax profit at a flat rate of 20 per cent has been introduced. From September 1988 to June 1994, 511 foreign investment (excluding large projects and hydro-power projects) licences were approved, amounting to US$780 million in aggregate value. The most attractive industries for foreign investors are identified as tourism, forestry, mining, hydroelectric power, petroleum, and garment. Initially, joint ventures had been the preferred structure for foreign investment in the Lao PDR (Table 7.13). But up to 1994, wholly foreign-owned investment had caught up and shared about half of the total approved licences. In terms of the number of licences awarded, garments, other manufacturing, and agribusiness were the preferred sectors. The most important sectors by value were wood-based industries and banking.

Foreign Investment Trends

The drive to attract foreign investment appears to have been very successful, although it is difficult to measure the actual foreign direct investment (FDI) flows into the country. Foreign investment is not fully captured in the balance of payments and the only information available through the Foreign Investment Management Committee (FIMC) is on licence approvals rather than project implementation. Estimates of the realized investment flows are not yet deemed reliable.

For the 1989–92 period, the sectoral pattern of investment (see Table 7.14) reveals that the largest share of investments is in manufacturing (garment, wood industries, and other manufacturing), accounting for one-third of the total licensed investments. Manufacturing investment has been primarily in export industries (garments) or assembly and export (motor cycles) with fewer investments aimed at the domestic market. Hotel and tourism account for about one-quarter of total investments, and petroleum exploration and mining for another 14 per cent.

The hydro-power sector presents potential for foreign investment because of the size of required investment and the nature of the market. Hydro-power projects worth about US$13.00 billion, or about ten times the national GDP in 1992, have been identified for potential development over the coming fifteen-year period. So far there have been already eighteen contracts and memorandum of understanding signed between the Lao Government and foreign investors. Hydro-power production will be primarily for export to Thailand.

Distribution of Foreign Investors

Investment licences have been awarded by the Lao PDR to twenty-three countries, including several countries in Southeast and East Asia. By far the largest source of investment is Thailand, which accounts for about 40 per cent of the total value of investment licences. Other Asian countries account for a further 21 per cent, making the total Asian investment in excess of 60 per cent. Of these countries Japan contributes a surprisingly small share, only 0.5 per cent of the total investment. The largest non-Asian investor, and second largest after Thailand, is the United States. It accounts for 18 per cent of the total investment value. The American investments are mainly in the petroleum and mining sector, and the investment size is nearly four times the average size for other countries.

Constraints and Prospects in the Reform Processes

Lack of Savings

The recent growth recovery in the Lao PDR needs to be consolidated. The sweeping reforms which have been undertaken under the NEM have greatly improved the incentive framework and the general conditions for development. They have already yielded positive production results. However, the return to normal weather conditions provided the main impetus to growth. Transforming the rebound into sustained growth will require tighter macroeconomic management and the development of new productive capacities,

TABLE 7.15
Lao PDR: Public Sector Account, 1986–89
(Percentage of GDP)

	1986	1987	1988	1989
Revenue	11.9	12.3	12.3	6.1
Fiscal revenue	11.1	11.2	12.6	8.6
Taxes	1.1	1.2	10.3	7.4
Non-taxes	10.0	10.0	2.3	1.2
Public enterprise savings	0.8	1.2	−0.3	−2.5
Current expenditures	9.6	9.7	13.0	10.3
Wages	3.0	3.1	5.5	4.2
Goods and services	6.3	6.5	6.9	5.3
Pensions	—	—	0.1	0.1
Interest	0.3	0.1	0.5	0.7
Public sector gross savings	2.3	2.6	−0.7	−4.2

Source: Ministry of Economy Planning and Finance, Lao PDR.

basic infrastructure, and the country's human capital. However, little will be achieved without mobilizing domestic savings in support of development expenditure. The public sector will need to mobilize additional fiscal resources and to restore enterprise profitability. Furthermore, there is a pressing need to expand the country's export base. Investments are already underway in some of these activities to expand productive capacities. They need to be complemented by a more supportive tax system, in particular the elimination of any anti-export bias in the sales tax and natural resource taxes.

The following key elements should be taken into consideration for further economic reforms to proceed in a fruitful manner.

Lack of Public Savings

The crux of the problem facing the economy is the lack of savings to finance its reforms. The implementation of the reforms has been accompanied by a severe reduction in public savings. Consolidated revenues mobilized by the public sector dropped by 6.5 per cent of

GDP compared to the pre-reform level (see Table 7.15), resulting from the deregulation of prices and wages, liberalization of trade, and floating of the exchange rate. At the same time public financing was burdened by additional transitional costs, such as a sharp increase in recurrent expenditure, in particular spending on wages and salaries, severance payments, and urgently needed modernization or rehabilitation of obsolete equipment. Due to lack of public savings, all investment was financed by external resources. In the absence of substantial additional savings in the private sector, this decline in public savings would lead to inflation.

The causes of this poor performance can be traced largely to previous inefficiencies in public resource management and the serious financial burden of supporting underperforming state enterprises. Under the former system of central economic management, public resource mobilization depended primarily on:

1. the forced procurement of goods and services at below market prices and exchange rates by government and state enterprises; and
2. the transfer to the budget of state-enterprise operating surpluses.

The vast inefficiency of the state enterprises was concealed by price distortions. The economic rents so captured allowed state enterprises to hide operational inefficiencies (overstaffing, weak management, poor quality, etc.) and transfer their cost to the rest of the economy. As part of the NEM, most prices and the exchange rate have been aligned with the market level and the government has given up control over the size of enterprise surpluses by giving full autonomy to state enterprises, including the setting of wage levels. With poor tax collection and poor tax administration, revenue declined. In addition, the most efficient source of public revenue, capturing the rents from hydroelectricity export, was undercut by the decline in hydroelectricity production and prices.

Public Enterprise Savings

State enterprise profitability suffered from the pricing policy and trade reforms. In the competitive sector the policy of liberalizing prices and floating the exchange rate, combined with trade liberalization, resulted in a reduction of the gross margin. Most state enterprises could not adjust their selling prices sufficiently to recoup the increased cost of their inputs and wage payments. For the manufacturing sector, the state industrial enterprises, handicapped by obsolete equipment and techniques, lacked the product quality and price competitiveness to match the increased competition from abroad, while in the services sector they were faced with the more dynamic private sector. This decline in profitability brought to light the fact that the former system of central economic management and regulation provided rents to state enterprises at the expense of the rest of the economy.

On the financing side, the change in the distribution of income at the expense of state enterprises was reflected in the deterioration in the operations of banks and the serious problem of accumulating bad debts in the banking sector. More than a third of the increase in bank credit to state enterprises during the first six months of 1989 constituted the accumulation of arrears from either (1) unrecoverable obligations of state enterprises which had been liquidated or dismantled; or (2) a bail-out of defaulting debtors.

In addition, the accumulation of arrears combined with a restrictive credit policy also created liquidity problems for the banking sector, which faced difficulties in meeting its own obligations to depositors. This undermined the confidence of the population in the banking sector, and hence limited its capacity to mobilize financial savings.

Private Savings

During the 1986–90 period, the increase in procurement prices of agricultural commodities generated a substantial increase in farmers' income, leading to a rise in their savings. Although there could possibly be about 35 per cent cumulative increase in private disposable income between 1986 and 1990, little private savings were mobilized to support public investment. This was due to three reasons:

1.   The private demand for consumption and housing had long been suppressed by the fear that conspicuous spending

would be a source of trouble. This pent-up demand began to catch up;

2. Households were reluctant to deposit money with the banks, due to the risk consideration; and

3. No other financial instrument existed at that time to mobilize private savings.

Hence, given the limited capacity to mobilize domestic savings, the public-sector financing requirement was met mostly by foreign capital inflows.

Lack of Administrative Capacity

The critically short supply of qualified managerial and professional staff as well as skilled technical manpower is likely to become a major bottle-neck in the implementation of the reform programme. In addition, the government lost a substantial number of staff as a result of the retrenching exercise it carried out in 1987. As a result, there is a critical shortage of skilled staff with theoretical knowledge or practical expertise in the management of a market economy. The unattractive public-sector remuneration (including salary level) is also a major cause of the shortage of capable and professionally qualified staff in the Lao PDR. Although government salaries had substantially increased in 1990 they remain very low when compared to the private sector.

Up to now there is still no well-functioning national professional training institute and pragmatic in-service training programmes to nurture a pool of high- or mid-level manpower with knowledge and expertise in financial and economic management.

The technical skill of the labour force is low. According to the census in 1986 the proportion of university graduates to total workers was only 0.3 per cent. Moreover in that year there were only 500 engineers and 1,500 technicians in the whole country. In recognition of this problem, the government, through its ministries, has launched training programmes concentrating, in the short term only, on high-priority areas such as public investment programming, budgeting technique, revenue and expenditure forecasting, and expenditure monitoring systems.

Lack of Capital Market

The Lao PDR is a capital-scarce economy with very underdeveloped financial markets. This is considered to be one of the most critical constraints on the growth of the private sector. Money supply (M1) amounted to only 8 per cent of GDP in 1990. Since the NEM was launched, several measures have been taken to restructure the banking system, develop the financial market, and introduce new monetary instruments. The mono-bank system was separated into the Central Bank and seven regional commercial banks in which one commercial bank was charged with handling foreign transactions. The government implemented an interest rate structure that has kept lending rates at real positive levels during the past five years, and also introduced short-term government directive to begin exercising more control over the money supply.

Although these measures represent a significant departure from the past, the financial system has many structural weaknesses that limit its ability to contribute efficiently to mobilize capital and provide financial services. The market remains highly concentrated regionally (concentrated in Vientiane and some southern provincial capitals).

Although agriculture contributes about 60 per cent of GDP, it accounts for a very small share of total bank-lending activities. The commercial banks were also under-capitalized and burdened by large shares of non-performing claims on state enterprises that effectively rendered them insolvent. (This matter has been corrected by capital injection from the government since September 1994.)

Despite some measures to deregulate the interest rates, they continued to be controlled by the Central Bank, to the extent that, in effect, they did not serve to reflect changing market conditions. At present, the commercial banks may set lending and deposit rates subject to maximum lending rate and minimum deposit rate guidelines established by the Central Bank. On the supply side, there are no significant long-term savings instruments. At present the only long-term credit available is through credit lines established with international aid.

A further feature of the Lao economy is the widespread use of foreign currency for domestic transactions, primarily Thai baht and U.S. dollars, although this has been illegal since late 1990. This makes it difficult for the monetary authorities to control the money supply.

Poor Physical Infrastructure

Transport

One of the Lao PDR's main development constraints is its weak transport and communications infrastructure. The creation of an integrated domestic market and the intensification of international trade, key objectives of the NEM, are seriously hampered because of these weaknesses. These deficiencies in infrastructure continue to be a major bottle-neck in the development of the minerals and hydro-power sector, which have the potential future export on which the growth could be based. However, the development of transport and communications, minerals, and hydro-power will rely heavily on success in attracting external public and private resources. Therefore, it is crucial that in planning for the development of these sectors careful and sustained attention should be given to efficient and effective resource mobilization, monitoring and regulation of private sector investment, and the co-ordination of multi-donor investment activities. During the period of command economy, the government's development policy focused on creating and subsidizing state-owned enterprises and on a number of large-scale infrastructure projects. The operation and maintenance of existing facilities were under-funded. The badly deteriorated infrastructure and low level of human resource development are the legacy of this policy.

The country's main transportation route is Road No. 14 from Udomsay (Chinese border in the north) to Pakse (Cambodian border in the south). Most of Road No. 13 is now being reconstructed or repaired. Other strategic links are the east-west links by Roads No. 6, 7, 8, and 9, providing access to sea ports through Vietnam and Thailand.

Telecommunications

The telecommunications sector in the Lao PDR is poorly developed, with only 0.16 telephone line per 100 inhabitants, one of the lowest densities in the world. Equipment is also obsolete and often not inter-connected due to the lack of investment to upgrade and expand the existing systems. This has hampered the development of trade, investment, commerce, and market in the country and is now recognized as a critical priority for development.

Power

The largest power plant in the Lao PDR is the Nam Ngum hydro-power station at the Nam Ngum River north of Vientiane. Its total installed capacity is 150 MW and energy generated is about 900 GWh per year, depending on the rainfall. About 70 per cent of the energy generated is exported to Thailand. Xeset hydro-power station in the south is the second largest in the Lao PDR, with an installed capacity of 45 MW and annual generation of about 180 GWh. There are currently three major distribution grids in the Lao PDR and some small isolated local supply systems. The largest grid is the northern grid, which covers much of Vientiane plain and is being extended to Luang Prabang with the main 115 kv transmission line. This grid receives power supply from the Nam Ngum power station. The southern grid, covering Champasak, parts of Saravan, and Sekong province, uses power from the Xeset power station. The grid is also linked to Thailand, providing it with the ability to export power in the wet season and as a back-up to import power in the dry season when Xeset's firm capacity is low. Savannakhet and Thakek also have small-scale grid and distribution networks dependent on power supplies from Thailand. But electricity is available only in a few cities. Expansion of the distribution network for electricity should be given high priority, because there is a high demand for electricity and it is essential for the development of other economic activities.

Lack of a Legal Framework

One of the basic problems facing the Lao PDR in its accelerated development is its lack of a legal framework for management of the emerging market economy and institutions to regulate and enforce the legal system in the country. A National Constitution was promulgated in August 1991. The development of a legal and regulatory framework has just begun with the promulgation of laws on foreign investment, land ownership, contracts, inheritance, property rights, banking and insurance, etc., and the penal code. Even with progress in these developments there is still much work that has to be done to promote private businesses, growth, and efficiency, and stimulate the general economic development of the country.

Legal reform in the Lao PDR still has an unfinished agenda. Many of the laws adopted at the start of the reform process have not been fully implemented, such as business law and land decree. In finance and banking especially, there exists a compelling need to equally develop banking supervision and regulatory capacity to oversee the activities of the commercial banks, particularly the newly licensed foreign banks, which are becoming active in Vientiane. Failure to adopt and implement more laws in a satisfactory manner could undermine Laos' objective of developing a market-oriented economy and discourage large-scale (foreign) investments requiring a more secure and transparent legal environment.

Prospects for Economic Development and Regional Co-operation

The Lao PDR is a country rich in mineral and forestry resources. It has vast electricity power potential, good quality land, and a favourably high land-to-population ratio. With its rich natural resources and geographical location of being surrounded by large external markets, Laos has good prospects for high economic growth in the future. But as a land-locked country, the Lao PDR is highly dependent on economic relations with neighbouring countries for access to critical supplies and international markets. For historical and geographical reasons, Thailand is Laos' predominant foreign trading partner and the main conduit for other external economic relations. However, cross-border flows with China, Vietnam, Myanmar, and Cambodia remain important, particularly to the northern and southern provinces of the Lao PDR, and would be the main engine for economic development of these provinces. Given these favourable economic prospects, Laos in all likelihood would be able to consolidate its relatively successful reform and sustain the economic development achieved thus far.

Forestry Potential

The Lao PDR is heavily dependent on its natural resource base to provide livelihood for its small population and to earn foreign exchange. A survey in 1989 by the Department of Forestry indicated that forests covered about 48 per cent of the total area of the country. In 1992, wood products accounted for up to 25 per cent of total exports, while the share of forestry in GDP was about 15 per cent. Log production volume has fluctuated from year to year, from about 160,000 to 250,000 cubic metres per year.

An annual allowable cut of some 280,000 to 300,000 cubic metres proposed by the Tropical Forestry Action Plan (the study conducted by the World Bank/United Nations Development Programme [UNDP] in 1990) was adopted by the government in 1990. With the introduction of a more sustainable natural resource management system and conservation of the country's forest resources, forestry will provide high potential for wood-processing industries and earn foreign exchange, given the high demand for wood products in neighbouring countries, namely Thailand and China.

Mineral Resources

The Lao PDR's geological structure indicates that the country is endowed with rich mineral resources. A geological map of 1990 identified mineral deposits, including those of gold, silver, tin, lead, zinc, copper, bauxite, iron ore, manganese, and gemstones. Moreover, deposits of limestone, marble, kaolin, gypsum, potash, salt as well as coal and lignite are known. Given the geological structure, the presence of petroleum and gas cannot be ruled out.

At present, mining activity in the Lao PDR is on a small scale. Gypsum mining in Savannakhet Province is the largest mining operation in the Lao PDR, with 100,000 tons of its annual output exported to Vietnam. The deposit at this site has proven reserves of more than 20 million tons. Tin mining in Khammouane Province has been yielding about 500 tons a year of concentrates (minimum metal content of 30–40 per cent). The proven reserve at this site is about 200,000 tons. A small coal-mining operation in Vientiane Province produces around 5,000 tons a year for domestic consumption. But there are substantial reserves at the site of about 5 million tons.

The government strongly commits itself to attracting foreign investors by allowing them to play a major role in mining operation in the Lao PDR. Presently, the government has secured the long-term presence of many multinational mining companies in the country by giving them concessions to explore mineral resources such as gold, oil and gas, lignite, gemstones, and coal. Such big companies include Newmont Gold Company, CRA Exploration, and Hunt Oil Company, among others.

Prospects are good in the development of gold and other precious metals and gemstones, for which the lack of infrastructure does not pose a significant barrier to development. For these high-value products, shipping costs are not significant, and export income can be expected within a few years of mine commissioning. The concessions for exploration will take some time and will not be realized until the late 1990s. By the year 2000, minerals can become a major export earner for the Lao PDR. So far the mining sector has also drawn increasing interest from foreign investors. Up to June 1993, seventeen foreign investments in different mineral resources had been approved.

Power

The Lao PDR has excellent hydroelectricity generation and thermal-power plant potential, and electricity can potentially be an even more significant export earner. Demand for electricity in Thailand is increasing at about 15 per cent per year, which would be a potential market for electricity generation from the Lao PDR.

At present the Lao PDR is optimistic about the contribution of hydroelectricity to its economic growth. The country's hydroelectric potential is estimated at 18,000 MW, of which only 200 MW has been developed so far. Electricity exports to Thailand account for one-fourth of Laos' foreign exchange earnings.

At present, 70 per cent of the electricity generated at the Nam Ngum Dam in Vientiane Province and at Xeset Dam in Saravan Province is sold to Thailand, earning about US$22 million in foreign exchange annually.

Cross-Border Trade and Development of Regional Markets

The Lao PDR, as a land-locked country, has a geographical location surrounded by external markets which can be used to help develop cross-border trade in manufactured goods, natural resources, and agricultural products, as it is located in the middle of the region encompassing Thailand, South China, and Vietnam.

Cross-border transactions in goods, services, and financial markets are playing an increasingly prominent role in the Lao economy and will be a critical factor in future economic development. The Lao PDR's trading partners, based on partial trade data for 1990–92, include on the export side Thailand (52 per cent), France (9 per cent), Germany (7 per cent), and China (5 per cent). On the import side the main partners have been Thailand (56 per cent), Japan (15 per cent), China (11 per cent), and France (2 per cent). Trade between the Lao PDR and China as well as Vietnam is gaining momentum as data for the first six months of 1993 released by the Ministry of Commerce of Lao PDR indicated that Vietnam imported about 25 per cent of Lao exports, mostly assembled or re-exported motor cycles.

Recent Lao trade with the non-convertible zone has not been significant. In 1991 Laos exported US$2.4 million worth of goods to and imported US$4.6 million worth of goods from the non-convertible zone. In 1992 such trade effectively diminished to insignificance.

To promote economic co-operation with neighbouring countries, the government of Lao PDR fully supports the Subregional Economic Co-operation organization initiated by the ADB which involved six countries in the subregion: Cambodia, the Lao PDR, Myanmar, Thailand, Vietnam, and Yunnan Province of China. The most important sectors for greater economic co-operation include trade, investment, transportation, communications, energy, and tourism. This Subregional Economic Co-operation organization would provide good prospects for economic development of the Lao PDR in the future.

Policy Issues on the Role and Function of Government for Further Reform Process

The government of the Lao PDR has put enormous efforts to implement the reforms in the country and considerable achievements have already been attained. These economic reforms have been supported by concessional loans and technical assistance from various international lending institutions, notably the World Bank, International Monetary Fund, ADB, and UNDP, and from bilateral grants. Such loans, technical assistance, and grants have substantially helped lessen the budgetary and balance of payments difficulties consequent upon the wide-ranging reforms undertaken by the government. The government should realize that the transition from one economic system to another is a long and complex process that will take much time and energies because of the prolonged period required for structural and institutional adjustments and changes as well as the inherent complexities involved in economic transformation. Some of the main elements of the reforms are being implemented without clear policy directives or operational procedures. For example, state subsidies to and transfers from state enterprises have ceased and privatization is well underway but the new fiscal system has not yet been established. This is a major cause of financial constraints, and could stifle some aspects of the reform process and the country would become increasingly dependent on external financing to cover both its investment programme and balance of payments deficit.

In order for the private sector to expand in an orderly fashion, and for the country to attract the kind of serious foreign investment that will contribute to long-term economic development, a regulatory framework conducive to the growth of the private sector needs to be established. Some work has been done in developing the legislation for such a framework but more work is required, particularly with regard to developing the institutions required to implement it. This area is of great importance as the government gradually moves away from direct involvement in the productive sectors of the economy towards a more regulatory role.

Changing the Role of Government

A central element of the ongoing economic reform process is the improvement in efficiency of the public sector in order to increase the effectiveness of support services. Three related activities which will be completed during the reform are:

1.   Restructuring of the role and functions of government;
2.   The continued divestment of non-strategic state-owned enterprises (SOEs), and improvements in efficiency and performance of strategic enterprises; and
3.   Further development of the legal and regulatory framework needed to facilitate the operations of an efficient market economy.

The shift to a market-based economy means that the primary role of the government is to provide an economic environment that will encourage the mobilization of public and private resources into productive areas and ensure the efficient use of those resources.

Restructuring the Role and Function of Government

The need for basic public administration reform has become increasingly significant since the introduction of the NEM reforms in 1986. The government has taken active measures to establish new public investment planning, reorganize the customs and tax collection, build a modern legal system, develop indirect instruments for money and credit control, and so forth. Many cadres trained under the former system have become redundant while there is a scarcity of civil servants familiar with the new procedures. In this changing situation there is an urgent need for a comprehensive strategy and vision of civil service restructuring to match the demands under the new policy environment emerging from the NEM programme.

Another reason to continue reform is the rising cost to the government of an inflated civil service, and the difficulty of meeting this cost in the budget. The entire civil service currently absorbs an estimated 1.65 per cent of the total population, which is excessive given the dispersed and rural nature of the population. Direct payment of wages and salaries now accounts for about 45 per cent of current government expenditures. Indirect costs, through housing, transport, and electricity provided to some civil servants, impose an additional burden. This reduces the balance available to finance operations and provide for maintenance expenditures.

Retrenchment

With respect to the retrenchment programme, the following priority measures are warranted to speed up implementation and minimize the cost of adjustment:

1. Selective retrenchment is necessary to reshape the civil service quickly and to ensure that the cuts are based on some rationale. Severance packages may need to be modestly enhanced to improve departure incentives, but must be kept within fiscally responsible levels and with a short time limit to encourage quick departure.
2. Improving the compensation system for the civil service and professionalizing it are essential. A clear link needs to be established between raising efficiency, staff commitment, and work performance. However, the bulk of retrenchment should be effected before compensation is raised to reduce the fiscal burden and disincentive to leave.
3. Careful assessment of the fiscal impact of the programmes on pension and social security liabilities is also essential. These programmes are still at an early stage and funding needs to be carefully prepared.

Priorities for Improvement to the Civil Service

The shortage of managerial, professional, and technical personnel is likely to become a major bottle-neck in the implementation of the reform programme. Intensive and systematic staff training is required. In the absence of a well-functioning national professional training institute for economics and finance, concrete and pragmatic in-service training programmes, focused on the development of operational skills, are the best vehicle for administrative upgrading. In view of the scarcity of human resources, a phased approach is preferable, concentrating, in the short term only, on high priority areas such as public investment programming, budgeting techniques, revenue and expenditure forecasting, and expenditure monitoring. Most of the training should be conducted in the country, as skills acquired in overseas training programmes tend to have less practical application. This form of training could be supported essentially through:

1. recruitment of experts with coaching ability and clearly delineated responsibility for on-the-job training; and
2. workshops for core and line ministries to discuss and disseminate knowledge of systems and methodologies.

Over the medium to long term, the upgrading of the civil service would need a more systematic civil service training plan, integration of training into career management, and improvement of working conditions in the civil service. This includes appropriate personnel management systems, career development policies, and adequate performance incentives.

In sum, the government needs to address this crucial development constraint arising from the pressing deficiencies of high-level manpower and the range of productive skills in the work-force required for the growth and development of the Lao economy. This perhaps will be the most decisive factor in determining the long-term success and sustainability of the reform effort of the Lao Government.

Continued Divestment of Non-Strategic SOEs

The government of the Lao PDR has embarked on a policy of

privatization. The main objective of the privatization policy is to increase enterprise efficiency. The government expects the following results from this policy:

1. the mobilization of domestic savings and foreign capital for machinery and working capital;
2. production and product technology as well as sectoral expertise;
3. access to export markets and closeness to local markets; and
4. stronger staff motivation, managerial performance incentive, and modern managerial skills.

While the privatization process has proceeded with extraordinary speed, its contribution to the objectives being pursued could be undercut if the process is not streamlined. Problems have emerged as to the valuation of assets, the forms of privatization, and the extension of privileges to private parties. They stem primarily from:

1. the limited administrative capacity of a broad privatization programme;
2. insufficient accounting standards and tax collection institutions;
3. weak private savings and willingness to invest; and
4. the underdeveloped legal framework for private sector activities.

At the end of 1992, no explicit privatization guide-lines had been defined. Supervisory agencies approached the issue pragmatically according to economic and political opportunities rather than following a fixed strategy and formal guide-lines. The choice between privatization form had also not been formally determined but was decided case by case. The terms of the privatization contracts did not follow fixed rules, either. Rent contracts, for example, varied in length from five years to thirty years. In the case of private investment, there was a problem that profit-sharing and decision-making power did not always follow the respective capital contributions; this could arise because of limited financial savings of the private party or in implicit recognition that the capital contributions were difficult to evaluate correctly.

To rectify this situation and protect against undercompensation for privatization of SOE assets, the privatization process needs strengthening.

The key issue to this process is to *develop privatization guide-lines*. Explicit and coherent central guide-lines for privatization should facilitate privatization activities of decentralized authorities, in particular by enhancing the effectiveness of staff with limited experience. Central guide-lines should also reduce redundancies in the formulation of concepts and rules by different authorities, and allow the pooling of the best expertise available for formulating such concepts and rules. Moreover, they could aim at making the privatization processes more transparent and decisions more objective in the pursuit of the public interest. Such guide-lines should be developed for all stages of the divestment process, including the choice of privatization form, partner search and assessment, enterprise and offer evaluation, formulation and negotiation of contracts, and contract implementation. Mandatory regulations should be warranted for: ensuring monopoly right or substantial duty protection from imports; restricting rental contracts over a longer period; and enforcing minimum enterprise evaluation standard.

Permanent staff capabilities at the central level should be available to review applications beyond a minimum ceiling, including the evaluation of assets, partner contribution and projected outflow, and conduct site verification as needed.

Further Development of the Legal and Regulatory Framework

When the Lao PDR was officially proclaimed in December 1975, the then existing constitution and legal system were completely abolished. Consequently, all previously existing laws were repealed. Although a new constitution was officially promulgated in August 1991, no entirely new legal system has been adopted, whether it be a common law or civil law system.

Since 1986 numerous important laws and decrees have been enacted to regulate different aspects of Lao's emerging market-oriented economy. For example, during the NEM period since 1986:

1. An electoral law was approved in 1986;
2. A law on foreign investment and regulations to implement it were issued in 1988 and 1989 respectively. Subsequently this

law was revised and passed by the National Assembly in March 1994;

3.   A decision on tax and customs and regulations to implement it were also issued in 1988 and 1989, respectively;

4.   Legislation on criminal law, criminal procedure, the People's Court, and the People's Judiciary Council was approved in 1989;

5.   A labour law was issued in 1990, followed by a decree in 1991. In March 1994 a revised labour law was passed by the National Assembly;

6.   Laws on central banking, enterprise accounting, and insurance were issued in 1990;

7.   Decrees governing foreign exchange transactions were issued in 1988, 1989, and 1990;

8.   Legislation on property ownership, contracts, civil procedure, nationality, inheritance, enterprise accounting, establishment of banks, and court fees was also approved during 1989–90; and

9.   A law prescribing the election process for the new National Assembly under the Constitution was adopted in 1991.

During this period executive decrees were also issued, such as the decrees on commercial banking, land use, and enterprises. The Law on the Budget, law on customs, and law on business were adopted in July 1994. Law on bankruptcy and law on guarantees were adopted in October 1994.

Although the Lao PDR has been making steady in adopting new commercial laws to develop a legal environment which is conducive to the operation of a viable market-oriented economy, several vital areas of its commercial law are still inadequately developed. Undoubtedly much remains to be done in order to fully create a legal environment that will effectively regulate and facilitate commercial transactions, promote private sector development, and stimulate national and foreign investment.

In addition other areas for commercial legislation are likely to become increasingly important in the medium term as growth in private sector transactions accelerates and more sophisticated instruments are developed. These include:

1.   Negotiable instruments law: this will help in developing Laos'

financial markets. For example, bills of exchange and promissory notes can be used as a convenient method of financing loan transactions.

2. Commercial agency and distributorship law: this is important to regulate the representation of foreign companies and the sales of their goods in Laos. It would also govern the relationship between these companies and their local agents and distributors.

3. Procurement law: this is essential to establish a uniform and fair domestic procurement system by public entities, one which conforms to international standards.

The absence of such laws often leads to bidding processes which are not competitive and thus open to abuse and economic distortions.

References

Bank of the Lao PDR. *Annual Report of Bank of the Lao PDR*. Vientiane, various issues.

Bourdet, Yves. *Laos Macroeconomic Studies*. The Planning Secretariat 11/1990. Lund: University of Lund, 1990.

–––. *Laos Macroeconomic Studies*. The Planning Secretariat 11/1993. Lund: University of Lund, 1993.

–––. "Laos: The Economic Mechanisms and After?" Mimeographed, no. 52/94. Lund: Department of Economics, University of Lund, 1994.

Chi Do Pham. *Economic Development in Lao PDR: Horizon 2000*. Report of IMF Resident Representative in the Lao PDR and Bank of the Lao PDR. Vientiane, 1994.

Committee for Planning and Co-operation, Lao PDR. *Annual Economic Report of the Lao PDR*. Vientiane, various issues.

Council of Ministers, Lao PDR. *Decree No. 17 of the Council of Ministers on the Conversion of State Enterprise Units to Other Forms of Ownership*. Vientiane, 1990.

Government of the Lao PDR. *Lao PDR: Socio-Economic Development Strategies*. Prepared for the Round Table Meeting at Geneva in 1990, 1992, and 1994. Vientiane, 1990, 1992, and 1994.

International Monetary Fund. *World Economic Outlook*. Washington, D.C., various issues.

Ministry of Planning and Finance, Lao PDR. *Annual Report*. Vientiane, various issues.

———. *First Five-Year Plan (1981–85)*. Vientiane, 1991.

———. *Interim Three-Year Plan (1978–80)*. Vientiane, 1978.

Statistical Centre, Lao PDR. *Basic Statistics*. Vientiane, various issues.

United Nations Conference on Trade and Development. *Lao PDR 1990*. United Nations Conference on the Least Developed Countries. Geneva, 1990.

United Nations Industrial Development Organization (UNIDO). *Lao PDR: Industrial Transition*. Vienna, April 1994.

8

Transitional Economy of Myanmar: Performance, Issues, and Problems

Myat Thein and
Mya Than

The world witnessed an unprecedented historic episode in the late 1980s. The formerly centrally planned economies (CPEs) of Europe and Asia started to transform their economies to a market-oriented system. The failure of CPE to generate growth and sustain development has been one of the main reasons for the transformation process. A cynical view suggested that reforms have been carried out only to stave off the crisis and ensure the survival of an authoritarian system. However, it is important to note that reforms in Central and Eastern Europe are quite different from those of the Asian CPEs due to their vast differences in economic, industrial, cultural, and historical characteristics.[1] Whilst the economies of the former Soviet Union and Eastern Europe have been undergoing continuing dramatic changes and upheavals as a result of *perestroika* (economic opening) and *glasnost* (political opening), developments in economic and political spheres in China, the Indochinese states, and Myanmar have been evolving slowly and steadily since the later part of the 1980s, which could be defined roughly as *perestroika* with delayed or little *glasnost*. Even within the Asian CPEs there exist different patterns of development in the transformation process. For example, unlike China, Vietnam, and Laos, Myanmar officially discarded the socialist economic system and even the country's name was changed from the 'Socialist Republic of the Union of Burma' to the 'Union of Burma' and later to the 'Union of Myanmar'. However, as in other transitional economies of Asia (TEAs) there is in Myanmar some degree of continuity of political culture which can facilitate the implementation of economic reform.

This chapter will try to examine Myanmar's transitional economy and identify the key issues for successful transition to market-oriented economy. Beginning with the motivating factors for change, it will examine reform measures and the process of economic reform which have taken place in the last couple of years.

This chapter attempts to analyse first of all, why the transition to a market-oriented economy became necessary for Myanmar, and then what measures have been taken in this regard, how successful or unsuccessful they have been, whether they were adequate, and what else still needs to be done. For a Myanmar, these are not merely matters of academic interest. These are matters which need to be under constant surveillance, examination, and re-examination. Nothing can be more disturbing for the people than to be lulled into complacency with whatever has been achieved so far. At the outset, it should be noted that this chapter is not an indictment or recrimination of any administration, past or present. It is essential that Myanmar understands why the transition to market economy became necessary, what has been achieved so far, and what key issues remain to be addressed.

Preconditions and Motivating Forces of the Transitional Economy

Before independence in 1948, during the colonial period, the Myanmar people were dominated not only by the British, but also eclipsed by other foreigners, mainly Chinese and Indians, who were more knowledgeable, more experienced, and somewhat ahead of the Myanmars in many fields of economic activities. This experience of having been relegated to the bottom rung of the plural society in their own country led the post-war Myanmar leaders to adopt socialist ideology and economic nationalism. Hence, following independence there was a land and tenancy reform, some industries and insurance companies were nationalized, and nationals were encouraged to be more actively involved in trade and industry. However, pragmatic considerations soon made the government ambivalent as regards the role of the state *vis-à-vis* the private sector in promoting economic development. As a result until 1962, in the period of transition from the colonial past, Myanmar had a mildly socialist, somewhat inward-looking, but basically market economy.

Political instability during March 1962 led the military to take over power. The following month, the military government issued its policy declaration, 'The Burmese Way to Socialism', which was a mixture of socialism, inward-looking strategy of self-reliance, and Burmanization. Faithfully adhering to that policy-mix, the government proceeded with great haste to lay the foundations for transition to a self-reliant socialist economy of Myanmar. Banks, businesses, and industries — all the vital means of production and distribution — were nationalized and foreign trade became the monopoly of the state. Through nationalization as well as by other means, the government also succeeded in ending the dominance of Chinese and Indian entrepreneurs and businessmen in Myanmar. By the early 1970s, all major economic activities except agriculture, small businesses, retail trade, and some road and river transport had been nationalized.

By then, the economic situation in the country was also becoming increasingly fragile after a decade of stagnation. The average annual gross domestic product (GDP) growth of 1.7 per cent for the preceding decade was below the annual population growth rate of around 2.1 per cent. This meant an absolute decline of 0.4 per cent per year in per capita terms. The main reason for the poor performance of the economy was the government's egalitarian policy of maintaining low and stable consumer prices by keeping prices of agricultural output low and unchanged, despite increases in other prices. This meant falling real farm income and lowered incentives for production and investment, as a result of which agricultural production stagnated. Its rate of growth at 1.76 per cent per annum was also below the population growth rate. Consequently, both exports as well as revenue for the central government declined. Falling exports and revenue in turn meant reduction in imports, investment, and overall supply, leading to inflation, thus further exacerbating the fall in real farm income. Table 8.1 clearly reveals the declining trend in economic performance.

The indicators shown in the table are very revealing about the state of the economy and are much more important than are commonly understood. The first three rows of Table 8.1 clearly show the declining trend in GDP growth and increasing rate of growth in money supply accompanied by increases in consumer prices. These indicators of economic ill health are not unconnected with the particular form of self-reliant strategy, which contributed to the stagnation in the agriculture sector, and which in turn led to the fall in exports and hence also imports. This led to shortages of consumer goods and the emergence of the huge black market. The economy was in shambles after a decade of autarky.[2] (See also Appendix Table 8.1.)

This poor state of the economy forced the government to take a number of reform measures. Government procurement prices for rice and other basic crops were raised in 1973 and 1974; commercial guide-lines were introduced to direct the operations of state economic

TABLE 8.1
Trends in Economic Performance in Myanmar, 1962–88

Years	GDP Growth	Money Supply	Consumer Prices	Exports	Imports
	Average Annual Percentage Change			Average in US$ million	
1962–65	4.9	11.0	3.2	248.3	222.8
1966–69	2.2	3.8	6.1	138.1	157.8
1970–73	1.3	17.6	7.8	128.7	167.4
1974–77	4.7	16.0	19.5	185.5	250.8
1978–81	6.5	12.9	0.1	399.2	719.6
1982–85	4.7	10.3	5.7	368.2	687.2
1986–88	−1.7	−2.4	17.4	215.0	272.0
1986/87	−1.1	14.5	9.2	351.2	549.9
1987/88	−4.0	54.4	23.9	257.7	623.9

Sources: Ministry of Planning and Finance and Ministry of National Planning and Economic Development, *Review of the Financial, Economic and Social Conditions, 1993/94;* and Tun Wai (1990).

enterprises (SEEs) a year or so later; and private investment, ownership, and operations in some 236 industries were encouraged. However, there was no follow-up by any specific measures. Most notably, the government abandoned its national self-reliance policy and was willing to accept development assistance and foreign loans. These reforms also coincided with the launching of the Second Four-Year Plan, which was actually the first of a series of Four-Year Plans which together constituted the Twenty-Year Plan (1974–93).

After these reforms, the economy began to move out of stagnation and economic growth accelerated. Unfortunately, these reforms neither came in time to prevent a series of protests and demonstrations, beginning with the workers' riots over rising prices in June 1974; nor did they change the economic system in any fundamental way. As in the past, government procurement prices for rice and other important crops soon began to lag behind free-market prices. Foreign trade was still the monopoly of the state. And although export promotion came to be emphasized, the overvalued official exchange rate remained intact. Then again, despite the fact that agriculture had been given priority over industry, industrial SEEs continued to have the lion's share of state capital expenditures. In short, government intervention in the economy was still very pervasive, and there was no systemic change and no marked improvements in the management of the economy.

Accordingly, the fairly high rates of growth achieved during the mid-1970s and early 1980s could not be sustained. In fact, the apparent success of the reforms was in large measure due to the temporary improvements in the incentives for agricultural production coinciding with the Green Revolution on the one hand, and to the large inflow of foreign capital on the other. Thus, when the Green Revolution effect faded and the government was forced to reduce the inflow of foreign capital due to mounting debts, the economy began to decline from the mid-1980s (Mya Than and Nishizawa 1990; Hill and Jayasuriya 1986).

Apart from the increasingly precarious foreign exchange situation, the government was also unable to mobilize sufficient savings for investment. As a result, imports had to be cut back and investments scaled down, thereby contributing further to constraints, shortages, and inflation in the economy.[3] The economic situation had degenerated into a "desperate" state.[4] By 1987 the foreign exchange reserves had fallen to an all-time low of 346.6 million kyats or about one month's worth of imports. The debt-service ratio had climbed to 58.24 per cent of export earnings and the consumer price index had risen by 23.9 per cent.

Perhaps desperation led the government to lift the twenty-one-year old restrictions on the procurement and domestic trade of rice and eight other major crops such as wheat, maize, pulses, cotton, sugar-cane, rubber, and virginia tobacco in September 1987. Then, just a few days later the demonetization rumour (officially denied), which preceded the decontrol of major agricultural commodities, became a reality when 25-, 35-, and 75-kyat notes were demonetized without any compensation. In retrospect, these measures in their own ways eventually contributed to the impending crisis.

Thus, the continued deterioration of the economy since 1962 becomes the motivating factor for Myanmar's transitional economy. However, purely economic aspects of a nation's life are by no means the only motivating forces for the transition to a market-oriented economy. The international scene at the time — economic reforms in China, *perestroika* and *glasnost* in the USSR and Eastern Europe, the success of the newly industrializing countries (NICs) — all these must also have had some influence in uplifting the aspirations of the Myanmar people and determining the decisions of their leaders.

Objectives and Reform Measures for Transition to a Market Economy

It was obvious to most that by 1987 or thereabouts, 'The Burmese Way to Socialism' had reached a dead end. It seemed there was nowhere to turn except back to the market. Thus, when the State Law and Order Restoration Council (SLORC) took over the reins of government in September 1988, the reform agenda, in a manner of speaking, was already on the table. What awaited the government was to continue with the unfinished agenda with specific policy initiatives and measures in a co-ordinated way and to tackle the practical problems that would inevitably arise in the process of transition from a socialist command economy to one driven by market forces and private enterprise. This, the SLORC has attempted to do although it has not been doing so in a co-ordinated manner.

The economic reform undertaken by the SLORC had three main objectives: (1) to transform the rigid and inefficient economic management of the planned economy into one suited to a market-oriented economy; (2) to encourage private investment and entrepreneurial activity at home; and (3) to open the economy to direct foreign investment and to promote exports. To achieve these objectives, an appropriate enabling environment and a whole set of supportive measures are necessary. As a requisite of an enabling environment, some would consider macroeconomic stability to be the most important. Others, however, may consider political stability to be even more important. As for measures, certain changes in the institutions, existing laws and regulations, and price reforms amongst others would be required. Table 8.2 provides the list of important measures taken so far in a chronological order.

The most important of these measures was the official revocation of the 1965 Law of Establishment of Socialist Economic System in 1989, which clearly reaffirmed the government's commitment to transform the command economy into a market-oriented one. Other measures were taken to facilitate private investment and entrepreneurial activity at home or to open the economy to direct foreign investment or to promote exports. The effectiveness of these reform measures in transforming the economy and promoting growth with stability as well as the identification of key issues to be addressed are discussed below.

Price and Market Reforms

It is obvious from the list in Table 8.2 that trade reforms constitute the bulk of reform measures. Apart from the trade liberalization measures of September 1987 mentioned earlier, the Ministry of Trade had by April 1993 issued fifty-nine notifications and fifty orders. In accordance with these notifications and orders, the corporations under the Ministry of Trade have been forming joint ventures with foreign enterprises, signing contracts to sell goods on consignment basis, and exchanging memoranda of understanding with foreign companies. Eleven corporations under the Ministry of Trade were also given new responsibilities and rights to enable them to operate as freely as possible according to the prevailing conditions of the market.

TABLE 8.2
Policy Reform Measures in Myanmar, 1987–94

1987	* Participation of private and co-operative sectors in foreign trade
	* Relaxation of government's monopoly in the domestic marketing of rice and some important crops
1988	* Removal of restrictions on private sector participation in domestic and foreign trade
	* Introduction of liberal Foreign Investment Law
	* Restitution of small and medium-sized establishments
1989	* Decontrol of prices
	* Official revocation of the 1985 Law of Establishment of Socialist Economic System
	* Regularization of border trade
	* Introduction of SEE law allowing private sector participation in economic activities
	* Relaxation of restrictions on private investment
	* Introduction of the Central Bank of Myanmar Law
1990	* Introduction of Myanmar Tourism Law
	* Introduction of 100 per cent retention of export earnings law
	* Introduction of Financial Institutions of Myanmar Law
	* Introduction of Myanmar Agricultural and Rural Development Law
	* Promulgation of Commercial Tax Law
1991	* Announcement of the Central Bank of Myanmar Rules and Regulations
	* Reestablishment of Myanmar Chamber of Commerce and Industry
1992	* Announcement to lease inefficient state-owned factories
	* Announcement of denationalization of nationalized saw mills
	* Announcement of sale of government palm oil firms
	* Announcement of establishment of four private banks
1993	* Introduction of foreign exchange certificate (FEC)
	* Announcement of establishment of four more private banks
1994	* Introduction of domestic investment law
	* Announcement of establishment of three more private banks
	* Announcement of licensing of representative offices of eleven foreign banks

As a measure to promote private sector participation in foreign trade, private companies had initially been allowed to retain 60 per cent of their export earnings. This was considered a great leap forward since it was the first time in a quarter of a century that the private sector was involved in foreign trade and allowed to retain some portion of its export earnings. The retention rate was raised to 100 per cent in March 1990. However, as the balance of payments position weakened following the regularization of border trade, import controls became more restrictive and exporters were then required to spend 25 per cent of export earnings to import "goods of high priority to the economy". Moreover, importers and exporters were required to obtain a licence from the Ministry of Trade for each category of goods specified in the Customs Tariff. The licences had to be renewed every year.

In November 1988, the informal border trade, which amounted to an estimated 50 to 100 per cent of the total official trade, was regularized firstly with China and later with Thailand and Bangladesh. However, the export of sixteen important products, including rice, teak, cotton, maize, rubber, and some varieties of beans and pulses, has been banned since 1990 (and ten more items, mainly metals and mining products, were banned again in 1993), although the list of exportable products for normal trade is less restricted.

Nevertheless, as a result of the reform measures, participation of the private sector in the economy increased significantly. In terms of its value-added contribution, it was particularly strong in the trade sector and, to a lesser extent, in the services sector. In the former it increased from 52.6 per cent in 1986/87 to 72.3 per cent in 1993/94, and in the latter, from 36.9 per cent to 41.1 per cent during the same period. In the directly productive goods sector, where its contribution was already large, the increase was marginal. Overall, the contribution of the private sector to GDP amounted to 76.0 per cent in 1993/94 as compared with 68.6 per cent in 1986/87. (See Appendix Table 8.1.)

Private sector involvement in terms of number of participants also increased significantly. To give just the most recent figures, between end February 1992 and end February 1993, the number of exporters/importers registered increased by nearly 32 per cent, from

3,577 to 4,721; business representatives by 35 per cent, from 735 to 993; Myanmar limited companies by 74 per cent, from 1,248 to 2,173; foreign companies and branches by 40 per cent, from 127 to 178; and so on.

As a result, great strides have been made in opening up the economy to private enterprise, especially in the trade sector. On the other hand, the above figures seem to suggest more than what the actual situation warrants, as many of the exporters/importers and business representatives are registered in name only and are not really very active. However, due to frequent changes in government trade policies, limited number of exportable products, uncertain and sometimes heavy tax burden including donations and bureaucratic hurdles, price and market reforms are still far from complete.

More fundamentally, liberalization or marketization measures have so far failed to touch the spiral of government interventions and other imperfections in the credit and product markets. To elaborate, farmers are still being supplied with subsidized fertilizer, credit, irrigation water, etc., although many of them could well afford to pay the market prices for these inputs since the liberalization of their product prices. In return, they have to sell a certain portion of their produce to the government at official procurement prices. The government then distributes the produce purchased to government employees at subsidized rates. There are also other types of intervention at the local or regional level. For example, individual farmers and private traders sometimes need permission from regional authorities to transport rice from one township to another.

However, according to a recent announcement, government intervention is likely to be reduced to some extent. Until the present season, rice farmers had to sell on the average 22 or 26 baskets per acre to three or four different organizations — Ministry of Trade (12), co-operatives (8), Joint-Venture Corporation (4), and the army (2) — at the official procurement price, which is roughly half that of the open-market price. But, in the present season the Ministry of Trade will be the sole purchaser at the official procurement price. And the amount that the farmers have to sell at that price has been reduced to twelve baskets per acre. However, unlike Vietnam where such a system (of rationing rice and other necessities to employees of state-owned enterprises) was abolished in 1988, Myanmar still has rationing and a dual-price system — the government procurement price and the free-market price.[5] For the sake of policy consistency and the promotion of economic efficiency, market-oriented policy of the government should not introduce measures which unintentionally might lead to market imperfections.

Rice is the most important of the various examples of the cycle of state intervention and price distortions. The system of subsidization and rationing prevails also in energy, power, and many other sectors. While there is no textbook *laissez-faire* economy in practice and while the poor need to be protected to some degree from the negative consequences of any reform, there are other less harmful ways of intervening in the market as well as protecting the poor than the ones being presently employed. According to the general principle of targeting in economic policy, intervention should be directed as closely as possible to the source of distortion, that is, to the prices paid by consumers rather that those earned by producers. Besides, the *raison d'être* for price and market reforms should not be forgotten. Unless prices are true and undistorted, profits and losses of productive enterprises cannot indicate efficiency and are therefore not a good guide for the allocation of resources in the economic system. In short, partial liberalization is likely to lose out on one of the most important benefits of a market economy, which is, allocative efficiency.

Nonetheless, one should also understand the typically Myanmar *cetana* (a combination of goodwill, benevolence, and hospitality) of the government in providing basic necessities to fixed and low-income earners at subsidized prices, as well as its desire to keep a lid on inflationary pressures by controlling the prices of energy, power, and so on. Then also, there is the bureaucracy, Findlay's "grey faceless tribe of today" who benefits from the dual-price system and who therefore has a vested interest in preserving it.[6]

However, as the experience of the 1960s has shown, the road to ruin could be paved with *cetana* if the basic policy is wrong. Furthermore, the policy of keeping a lid on some of the prices of essentials to check inflationary pressures, a micro-approach, is at odds with the expansionist macroeconomic policy which is fuelling inflation. Hence, unification of the dual-price system, involving as it does synchronization of many measures, is an issue which needs to be addressed if Myanmar is to advance further along the road to a market-oriented economy.

Foreign Investment Law

The Union of Myanmar Foreign Investment Law (FIL), promulgated on 30 November 1988, is historically a very significant step towards free-market mechanism. This law allows foreign investors to establish either 100 per cent foreign-owned enterprises or joint ventures in which the foreign partner would be required to take at least a 35 per cent equity stake. The new Foreign Investment Commission (FIC), comprised mainly members of the Cabinet, was appointed by the government to approve applications for investment projects. The foreign investors have, apart from the right to repatriate profits and to withdraw the legitimate assets on winding up of their businesses, the following tax incentives:

1. an income-tax holiday for three years from the beginning of operations, with a possible extension;
2. exemption or relief from income tax on profits for funds reinvested;
3. a grant of accelerated depreciations on capital assets;
4. 50 per cent relief from income tax accrued from exports;
5. customs duty exemption on capital goods and raw materials during the construction period;
6. right to carry forward losses for three consecutive years;
7. equal personal income-tax rates for non-residents and locals;
8. permission to pay income tax on behalf of foreign employees and include them as operating costs; and
9. deductions for research and development.

Moreover, there is also an unequivocal state guarantee against nationalization and expropriation. Priorities are given to projects which promote exports, exploit domestic natural resources, transfer high technology, increase employment, save energy, or contribute to regional economic development.

Although this law is the most liberal in Myanmar's economic history, it has some flaws. It does not mention long-term plans, at least, in terms of priority industries in which investors are encouraged to invest (for details, please refer to Mya Than 1990). There are also ambiguities in the FIL and the law on paper can be quite different from the law as practised. For instance, some potential investors were said to have complained that although the law allows 100 per cent foreign-owned enterprises, they could do business only as joint ventures with the government. That is not exactly true. What seems most likely is that different ministries interpret the law differently, depending on the outlook. It is possible that authorities in some ministries see Myanmar as a pretty maiden to be courted by international investors. On the other hand, authorities in some other ministries see themselves as fiercely competing for scarce investible funds available in the world. That seems to be the outlook in countries like Vietnam and Singapore.

The amount of total foreign investment in Myanmar since the introduction of the law, as of end August 1993, was only US$909 million, with oil exploration, hotel and tourism, and manufacturing sectors accounting for about 42 per cent, 24 per cent, and 9 per cent respectively. This amount seems to be very low if compared with Vietnam's foreign investment of more than US$4 billion in 1993. Both countries promulgated their foreign investment laws almost at the same time. One of the major differences between these two countries, apart from differences in political situation, was in the exchange rate. Vietnam in the middle of 1989 boldly floated its foreign exchange rate while Myanmar stuck to its unrealistically overvalued official exchange rate. The reluctance of foreign investors to invest in Myanmar also resulted from the uncertainties in political situation in the country, unpredictability due to frequent policy changes, ambiguities in legal framework, procedural delays in the processing of application for investment projects, lack of certain infrastructure, particularly electricity supply, and weakness in financial institutions.

Enterprise Reforms

In the more developed and industrialized CPEs enterprise reforms constitute the heart of the reform process. In Myanmar the SEEs are not important in terms of their contributions to the GDP. But they are very important in the sense that they are the major recipients of state capital expenditures and the main cause of budgetary deficits. There are more than fifty SEEs in manufacturing and processing, external trade, power, mining, energy, construction, and internal distribution. Since 1975/76, they have been run according to government guide-lines, which include yearly production, investment, and efficiency targets for each enterprise. About 45 per cent of the total investment and about 60 per cent of the public investment in the economy have been undertaken by the SEEs.

Although the previous government stipulated that the SEEs be operated on a commercial basis and were given greater autonomy over administrative and financial matters, they were still very much controlled. Even their product and input prices were set by the government. These SEEs were expected to be self-financing in that surpluses of profitable SEEs would be channelled to enterprises with deficits to finance their investment programmes. However, due to the centralized control, inefficient management, weakening of export markets, and rapid rise in investment expenditures, the SEEs had financial difficulties in the 1980s. "About one-third of their overall deficits have been financed by foreign loans and aids and two-thirds by bank financing" (Tun Wai 1990). This has led to inflationary pressure and deterioration in the balance of payments. Furthermore, capacity utilization in these industries declined drastically due to shortages of raw materials, spare parts, and power supply.

In November 1988, about three months after the present government took over power, announcements were made to the effect that SEEs were given greater autonomy in procuring their inputs, allocating their production, and deciding the prices of their products. Following these announcements, SEEs have been allowed to raise the prices of their products and services. But then, as in the past, infrequent changes in official prices soon led them to lag behind market prices. The SEEs are still being run on the basis of annual plans, operating ratios, and centrally allocated foreign exchange to buy much-needed imported inputs.

Nevertheless, intentional or unintentional marketization in varying forms had also taken place to some extent as a result of a shortage of foreign exchange. That is, some of the SEEs in the manufacturing sector producing easily marketable products were permitted to sell them in dollars; although how much of them would be sold and to whom, is still being decided by no less a person than the Minister concerned. Then again, some of the SEEs have also entered into contracts with local private entrepreneurs, who would find the necessary foreign exchange for importing raw materials and who in return would get the finished product for a service charge only.

While the above-mentioned forms of marketization have partly solved the foreign exchange shortage problem for some SEEs, the majority, however, are still afflicted by this problem. In fact, many of the SEEs in manufacturing are said to be running at well below their capacity due chiefly to lack of foreign exchange and shortage in power and fuel supply. Hence, what is needed is not simply legal or regulatory liberalization or decontrol, but actual restructuring of the ownership, management, and operation of these SEEs. Some of the SEEs, set up during the socialist era with the objectives of regional development, employment creation, or whatever, were not economically or financially viable to begin with. Either their technology was outdated or they were wrongly located. Thus, some of them need to be shut down while others need to be rehabilitated. In other words, nothing less than wholesale restructuring would be required in order to make them financially viable. Indeed, along with privatization (to be considered presently), financial viability rather than plan fulfilment or increased capacity utilization ought to be the overriding objective of SEEs in a market-oriented economy.

Privatization

Privatization can be considered in a broad sense, such as privatization of ownership, privatization of production, corporatization, and financial privatization. It also includes deregulation of the economy, that is, liberalization and marketization or removal of government regulations interfering with market forces. That being so, some aspects of privatization have already been considered in the preceding sections.

Although there was no transparent policy, the privatization process had already begun in Myanmar during the past regime of the Burma Socialist Programme Party (BSPP). In 1988 a number of small and medium-sized industrial establishments, mostly saw mills, rice mills, and oil-processing mills, were restored to the owners on an elective basis. However, very few had been taken back due to the existing regulations and lack of confidence. Even before this restitution, the government had announced that agricultural plantations (such as rubber, coconut) would not be nationalized for twenty years.

When the present SLORC government took over power in late 1988, the privatization of some SEEs had been on its agenda. This was mainly to reduce the financial burden of those enterprises which were incurring losses. However, no concrete programme for large-scale privatization has been formulated, although some of the SEEs have been earmarked for privatization on a case-by-case basis.

The conversion of SEE debt into equity in March 1989 and eventual writing off of debts could be considered as a move towards privatization. Following the promulgation of the FIL in November 1988, at least eighteen SEEs have entered into joint ventures with foreign firms or with local private investors. The Ministry of Trade played a pivotal role and had a lion's share in these activities, especially in the formation of six new joint ventures mainly engaged in local international trade. So far, their performance results are limited.

Resulting from the reform measures which tried to promote private sector development, the total number of private factories/ establishments increased from 39,059 in 1987/88 to 40,145 in 1993/ 94, which is about 2.7 per cent increase within six years. In September 1992 the government announced available for lease or joint ventures its fifty-five industrial establishments under the Ministry of Industry (No.1) dealing with textiles, food processing, pharmaceutical and household goods, metal processing, general manufacturing, paper and chemicals, and jute processing. Although negotiations are going on with local and foreign investors, only a few deals have been implemented so far.

In short, privatization in Myanmar has taken the following forms:

1. joint ventures between SEEs and private investors, both local and foreign;
2. joint ventures between Myanmar citizens and foreign investors;

3. management contracts to private enterprises without transferring ownership; and
4. leasing out factories and facilities owned by SEEs to private entrepreneurs.

The status of the privatization programme in Myanmar is shown in Table 8.3.

Many reasons have been given for the slow pace of privatization. One is that very few of the establishments are worth taking over, especially as the plant and equipment in most of them are outdated. Another reason is that prospective investors are reluctant to take on government employees; they are also uncertain about labour laws. Yet another reason is that local investors either lack the necessary funds or are afraid of tax burden.

While all of the above reasons have some elements of truth in them, they neither reveal the whole picture of the actual situation nor focus on the most important one. For instance, there are allegations that some of the deals may have broken down because of the unwillingness of prospective investors to make under-the-table payments in advance. Again, others may have broken down due to the fear of prospective investors that the sources of their funds may later be traced back to illegal channels. These could be some of the reasons.

TABLE 8.3
Privatization in Myanmar (as of July 1994)

Ministry	Lease	Joint Venture
No. 1 (Industry)	17	9
Forestry	3	2
Agriculture	9	–
Transport	1	–
Hotel and Tourism	9	3
Livestock and Fisheries	75	1
No. 2 (Industry)	3	1
Rail Transportation	–	2
Total	117	18

Source: *The New Light of Myanmar*, 8 July 1994.

However, the most important reason seems to be lack of awareness and understanding on the part of some members of the government as to the need for privatization. The need for and the method of privatization in Myanmar are quite different from those of former CPEs. In the CPEs privatization was needed because a market economy cannot function with a massive state enterprise sector. At the same time, because of the immense size of the state enterprise sector, representing between 50 and 90 per cent of the economy, and also because of lack of capital markets, the task of privatization was found to be formidable. In Myanmar, on the other hand, the size of the state enterprise sector is relatively very small. Because of that, privatization is not needed for the same reason as in the CPEs. But, it is needed because enterprise reforms have time and again turned out to be unsuccessful, and because Myanmar can ill afford to use its meagre foreign exchange and public resources for SEEs which are not equipped to survive the competition of the market. Moreover, because of the smallness of the size of the state enterprise sector, the conventional case-by-case approach to privatization seems to be quite feasible. In sum, as far as privatization in Myanmar is concerned, as of 1993, there was no overall policy and no clear institutional responsibility and co-ordination among the ministries involved.

Financial Restructuring

From 1948 to 1963, the Myanmar banking system consisted of the Central Bank (that is, the Union Bank of Burma), a state-owned commercial bank, a state-owned agricultural bank, and twenty-four private commercial banks, including fourteen foreign-owned. Since the nationalization of all banks in 1963, the financial management system in Myanmar was very much centralized until April 1989, when a new management system was introduced. This new system relieved the debt burden of the SEEs by converting the debts into state equity. According to World Bank sources, liabilities of SEEs towards the Myanmar Economic Bank (MEB) amounting to 49 million kyats were converted into state equity. The Central Bank has relieved MEB of part of the SEE loans while the rest may be written off.

Following the economic reforms introduced in 1988, the financial structure of Myanmar has been streamlined and restructured to be in line with the market-oriented system. For instance, the Myanmar Investment and Commercial Bank (MICB) was established in September 1989 as an initial step to facilitate the provision of banking services for local as well as foreign businessmen. Its aim is to provide credit and banking services to investors. Following the establishment of MICB, banking reforms were carried out, with various laws and regulations governing financial institutions and the Central Bank of Myanmar Law enacted in 1990. Thus, the banking system in Myanmar has changed from a mono-bank system to an independent central bank system.

These laws were introduced to develop the financial system and improve the efficiency in the performance of financial activities — to extend the scope of business in and outside Myanmar and to establish financial institutions such as commercial banks, investment and development banks, financial companies, and credit societies. These companies could be state-owned, joint ventures between the government and private investors, or privately owned. Following the enactment of these laws, central bank rules and the Myanmar agricultural bank rules were announced in 1991. Furthermore, since June 1992 eleven domestic private commercial banks have been established. Out of these, only four banks are allowed to handle foreign currencies. There has as yet not been any foreign private bank. However, the Central Bank of Myanmar has issued licences to eleven foreign banks to open representative offices in the country. Most of them are from Thailand and Singapore.

Foreign exchange certificates (FECs) were introduced in early 1993 with the objectives of facilitating tourism and increasing foreign exchange earnings. These certificates are exchangeable with foreign currencies such as U.S. dollars and pound sterling or with acceptable travellers' cheques. However, the FEC has become an instrument that provides the market rate of exchange for certain groups of people. As this is yet another way of getting around the problem of the overvalued official exchange rate, it should certainly help tourism. In other words, it has become a *de facto* devaluation of Myanmar currency to a certain extent. Some are of the opinion that this system, like in China, will serve as a shock absorber when the time comes for unification of exchange rates.

However, due to ambiguity in banking laws and the ever-present bureaucratic hurdles, financial restructuring in Myanmar does not appear to be really effective, as measured against the authorities' expectation, so far. The state-owned banks are still playing the monopolistic role as mere channels of state funds and remain risk-averse, inflexible, controlled rather than service- and customer-oriented. Although interest rates were changed in 1989 for the first time in twelve years, they continue to remain negative in real terms since inflation rate has been in the range of 20 to 30 per cent per annum. These negative interest rates continue to hamper the deposit growth, and foreign exchange deposit does not even carry any interest.

Although fiscal sector reforms and price-wage matters were dealt with by the SLORC government soon after it came to power in early 1989, it began to introduce financial reforms and macroeconomic management only in 1991. In this context the comments of U Tun Wai (1990) are illuminating: "While one can understand why the authorities could not handle all sectors simultaneously, it would not have been desirable if reforms for the financial sector and macroeconomic management had been introduced earlier. Even now, ... while the apparatus for reforms is in place, implementation is taking place only slowly."

Legal Reforms

As mentioned earlier, the 1965 Law of Establishment of a Socialist Economic System had been officially revoked in 1989. In the same year the State-Owned Enterprises Law was introduced to allow private sector participation in economic activities. Following these, exactly 100 laws enacted or amended in the past have been repealed (*Working People's Daily*, 20 February 1992 and 1 April 1993). Furthermore, many new laws, such as 100 per cent retention of export earnings law and the commercial tax law, have been promulgated in order to facilitate private enterprise in the emerging market-oriented economy.[7]

Nevertheless, some fundamental changes are still lacking. The most conspicuous amongst these are the laws regarding land tenure and ownership. As in the past, the state is the ultimate owner of land with cultivators having merely 'the right to work' on the land as individuals. They are thus prohibited to buy, sell, or mortgage the land on which they work. They could, however, pass it on to their sons and daughters. That this policy led to land fragmentation and the lack of improvement on the land had been noted by a number of scholars (Mya Than and Nishizawa 1990). Moreover, since it prevented efficient farmers from buying or taking over the land of inefficient farmers, inefficiency is at least theoretically 'locked in' the agrarian system by this policy. Whether and to what extent this policy is in effect hampering growth in the agricultural sector is, however, an empirical issue.[8]

Given the bitter experiences during the colonial period when many farmers became heavily indebted and nearly half of the total cultivated area came to be owned by absentee landlords, there should certainly be laws such as the Farmer's Rights Protection Law of 1963 to protect the rights of all farmers. Absentee landlordism should never be permitted. Also, there is nothing wrong with the state being the ultimate owner of land, all farm land as well as non-farm land. But, while retaining these laws in their essence, it should not be impossible also to amend them in such a way as to allow the dynamism of the market to work so as to enhance efficiency and growth in the agricultural sector. And agriculture, it should not be forgotten, is still the backbone of the economy. Although foreign organizations and persons are not allowed to own land in Myanmar, land may be acquired on long renewable leases (up to thirty years) and extendable on individual case basis, generally every ten years.

Laws governing the rights and responsibilities of workers as well as producers in other sectors of the economy are also very important. But here too some fundamental changes are still lacking. For instance, the 1964 law defining the fundamental rights and responsibilities of workers is presumably still in place. Similarly, both the 1966 amendment to the Trade Dispute Act, inserting a clause which enables the Labour Department to recover the amount payable to workers by employers as arrears of land revenues, and the 1970 amendments envisaging social security benefits to firms with five or more employees are still valid. In short, some fundamental laws enacted during the socialist era have not yet been revoked. While this in itself is not necessarily a bad thing in so far as some of these laws protect the rights of workers or enable women to work on equal footing with men, others which put employers at a great disadvantage need to be revoked.

In Myanmar neither workers nor employers pay much heed to existing laws. For example, casual labourers work fairly long hours (about ten to twelve per day), and most of them are paid according to the going market rate, which has been rising because of inflation.

Then also, because of its colonial past, Myanmar before 1962 already had an appropriate legal framework for a market economy. In fact, the Foreign Investment Commission is said to be using the commercial laws existing before 1962 as the basis for the assessment of the legality of investment projects. The Burma Companies Act used in post-independent days was amended in 1989 and the Special Company Act of 1950 still serves as a legal framework for companies. Most of the commercial laws, such as the Bankruptcy Law, Property Law, and so on, were introduced in Myanmar during the colonial period; however, Rana and Paz (1994) suggest that, as far as these laws are concerned, there is only little action in these days. Moreover, judges in the courts of law in Myanmar still refer to laws, commentaries, and rulings made since the 1940s.[9] Therefore, unlike the former CPEs of Europe, Myanmar does not need to create a completely new legal and regulatory system to protect property rights and regulate commercial relations. What is needed is to restore the pre-1962 legal framework and make some appropriate changes as required by the present situation.

However, as one scholar had noted, reforms must go beyond the macro level — that is, beyond better laws (Klitgaard 1991). According to him "the laws on the books in many developing countries are already state-of-the-art. But judicial systems tend to be cumbersome and corrupt. Police forces are often inept and sometimes predatory" (Klitgaard 1991, p. 232). The issue that needs to be addressed is not only, or even primarily one of, having a proper legal framework but also of creating a secure legal environment that ensures the enforcement of contracts and property rights and the effective operation of market dynamism. In this regard, the most vexing problem facing many businessmen today is the difficulty of taking effective action against absconders of business contracts — mostly swindlers.[10]

Macroeconomic Policy and Performance

The scope of macroeconomic policy is very broad. As succinctly put by Dr Tun Wai, it

> covers a broad spectrum of governmental attitudes and decisions on many questions, including the allocation of resources between current and future consumption or how to invest, establishing priority sectors for development, deciding upon methods for the mobilization of domestic financial resources, motivating people to work hard, ensuring the absence of inflationary pressure, and preventing balance of payments difficulties despite changing world economic conditions (Tun Wai 1990).

In other words, it covers all aspects of governmental decision-making — including political economy — concerning economic growth and macroeconomic stabilization.

Moreover, the interrelationship amongst various components of an overall macroeconomic policy, such as fiscal policy, monetary policy, and income policy, effecting aggregate demand and aggregate supply are very complex and their outcomes (depending as they do also on the timing and sequencing of measures) difficult to predict.

To begin then at the most basic level, and using past trends as points of reference, the first thing of note is that there has been not much change in terms of gross investment and savings in Myanmar. Between 1988/89 and 1993/94 rates of investment fluctuated between 9.5 and 15 per cent of GDP and those of savings between 11 and 14 per cent of GDP. On the average, Myanmar was investing about 12.0 per cent of GDP and saving 11.9 per cent of GDP. These rates of investment and savings were more or less the same as in the pre-1988 period, if one excludes the 1966-69 period when both were exceptionally low and the 1978-85 period when both were exceptionally high. Apparently, reform measures taken so far have neither succeeded in raising the rate of investment nor savings. Thus, on the basis of these two alone, no more than an average annual rate of growth of 4 or 4.5 per cent may be expected under normal conditions.

However, the shares of public and private sector in total gross investment have changed drastically in recent years. From the early 1960s, the share of public or state sector investment in total gross investment had been increasing along with the increasing participation of the state in the economy. By 1986–87, state sector investment came to constitute about 75 per cent of total gross investment. This trend has now been completely reversed. With the exception of 1988/89, which was an exceptional year, the share of state sector investment in total gross investment declined from 55.8 per cent in 1990/1991 to 42.6 per cent in 1993/94. This is yet another clear indication of the increasing participation of the private sector in the economy. And to the extent that private sector investment is generally more efficient than that of the public sector, better performance of the economy may be expected.

Then again, in contrast to the previous administration, investment priority of the present administration has shifted away from directly productive sectors, particularly industry, to services and infrastructural development (see Table 8.4).

As may be seen from Table 8.4, the investment priority of the previous administration was heavily biased towards the productive sector. This sector received more than 50 or 60 per cent of total state investment, while the infrastructural sector received from 20 to 25 per cent and the services sector from 10 to 18 per cent of total public investment. This trend has now been completely reversed. In line with a market-oriented strategy of development, the state now only devotes some 12 to 16 per cent of public investment to the productive sector. Also, in contrast to the past, the services sector is now the major recipient of public investment funds, followed by the infrastructural sector.

These investment allocations indicate that the state is now back to playing the classic role of providing needed services and infrastructure for private sector development. This is as it should be. And to the extent that specific investment projects are made on a sound basis and without much waste, they will have a positive impact on the long-term performance of the economy. In the short and medium term, however, private sector investment constituting two-thirds of total gross investment will largely determine the growth of the economy. Table 8.5 summarizes the changes in the overall economic performance in recent years.

The growth performance since 1985/86 has been anything but normal. First, the GDP at 34,300.6 million kyats in 1985/86 had been declining until it touched a low point of 28,004.6 million kyats after the crisis of 1988. This downturn in the performance of the economy

TABLE 8.4
Public Investment in Myanmar by Sector, 1974/75 – 93/94
(In percentage of total)

	1974-77	1978-81	1982-85	1990/91	1991/92	1992/93	1993/94
Productive Sector	55.6	69.0	60.7	16.1	12.0	15.2	14.5
Agriculture	10.6	9.2	11.0	5.3	4.3	6.6	7.9
Livestock and fishery	3.2	6.5	2.5	1.0	1.3	1.0	0.6
Forestry	4.9	3.6	2.7	1.9	1.1	1.4	1.4
Mining	11.1	13.3	8.5	1.8	1.4	1.3	1.8
Processing and manufacturing	25.8	36.4	36.0	6.1	3.9	4.9	2.8
Infrastructure	26.7	20.7	21.5	29.1	29.9	27.9	28.2
Power	6.2	5.3	8.3	6.9	4.5	5.0	4.1
Construction	3.1	3.0	4.4	10.0	15.3	13.4	12.2
Transport and communications	17.4	12.4	8.8	12.2	10.1	9.5	11.9
Services	17.7	10.3	17.8	54.8	58.1	56.9	57.3
Trade	—	—	—	4.1	2.7	3.8	2.7
Social and administration	—	—	—	49.4	50.7	51.5	52.7
Finance	—	—	—	1.3	4.7	1.6	1.9
	100.0	100.0	100.0	100.0	100.0	100.0	100.0

Sources: Ministry of Planning and Finance and Ministry of National Planning and Economic Development, Review of the Financial, Economic and Social Conditions 1992/93 and 1993/94; and Economic and Social Indicators, 1994.

TABLE 8.5
Trends in Economic Performance in Myanmar, 1988–94
(GDP changes in constant 1985/86 prices)

		1988/89	1989/90	1990/91	1991/92	1992/93	1993/94
Gross domestic product	% change	-11.40	3.70	2.80	-0.06	9.30	6.00
Agriculture	% change	-13.20	5.20	2.00	-3.90	12.40	5.40
Industry	% change	-15.90	11.30	0.10	-4.00	10.50	10.30
Services	% change	-3.30	-7.50	4.20	5.10	5.40	4.60
Gross domestic investment	% of GDP	9.57	9.49	14.69	15.14	12.50	10.52
Gross domestic saving	% of GDP	11.13	8.78	11.68	14.42	13.07	12.30
Resource gap	% of GDP	1.56	-0.71	-3.01	-0.72	-0.57	1.80
Inflation rate	% change in CPI	22.50	23.70	21.90	29.12	22.87	31.80
Merchandise exports	kyats million	2,193.00	2,846.50	2,961.90	2,931.80	3,655.40	4,071.20
	% change	10.70	27.70	14.50	-2.80	39.90	11.30
Merchandise imports	kyats million	3,443.00	3,395.00	5,522.80	5,336.70	5,365.30	7,218.20
	% change	-20.80	-8.40	48.00	-8.70	13.70	34.50
Trade balance	kyats million	-1,250.00	-549.00	-2,561.00	-2,405.00	-2,460.60	-3,147.00
External debt service	kyats million	738.00	1,186.00	433.00	544.00	763.00	603.00
Debt-service ratio	%	25.45	28.92	9.36	12.74	13.20	14.80

Sources: Ministry of Planning and Finance and Ministry of National Planning and Economic Development, Review of the Financial, Economic and Social Conditions, 1992/93 and 1993/94.

was then followed by a weak and rather erratic recovery until it surged in 1992/93 with a growth rate of 9.3 per cent, followed by 6.0 per cent growth in 1993/94. This erratic performance may have been due to uncertainties caused by the 'shuffling' back and forth between decontrol, partial control, then decontrol and the repeated adverse business conditions in the early years of reform.

At any rate, it is noteworthy that while there were skeptics who questioned the high growth rate in 1992/93 there were also others who regarded it as recaptured growth momentum if not the 'take-off' itself. Actually, the Myanmar economy is hardly at the threshold of economic take-off stage despite this apparent high growth. In fact, it was the third time since 1962 that such a high growth rate has occurred. The two previous occasions were in 1964/65 and 1967/68. Moreover, then as now, each time it took place after a major downturn in the economy. Such phenomena are not unusual in a supply-determined economy heavily dependent on agriculture and the vagaries of weather.

The high growth rate of GDP in 1992/93 may be seen more clearly in conjunction with the growth of the agricultural sector. The 'W'-shaped pattern of the decline and recovery for both the agricultural sector and the GDP as shown in Figure 8.1 not only attests to the close linkage between the two but also provides a reasonable explanation of the GDP level and growth in 1992/93. That is, as compared to 1986/87, Myanmar was utilizing somewhat more land but a little less fertilizer in 1992/93 to produce in equally good weather conditions nearly the same amount of agriculture output as in the earlier year. Agriculture accounts for about 40 to 50 per cent of GDP and employs two-thirds of the labour force. Therefore, a 15 per cent increase in the agricultural sector alone would boost the GDP by 6 or 7.5 percentage points. Adding to this its other indirect contributions to the GDP and recovery in other sectors, a 10 per cent rate of growth becomes really achievable.

It would be a mistake to rely entirely upon official GDP figures in assessing the state of the economy. For one thing the informal sector seems to have grown much larger than ever before. For another a lot of private transactions between Myanmar and abroad could not be fully recorded. Hence, one needs also to look beyond the GDP.

FIGURE 8.1
Myanmar: Changes in GDP and Agricultural Sector, 1986/87–92/93

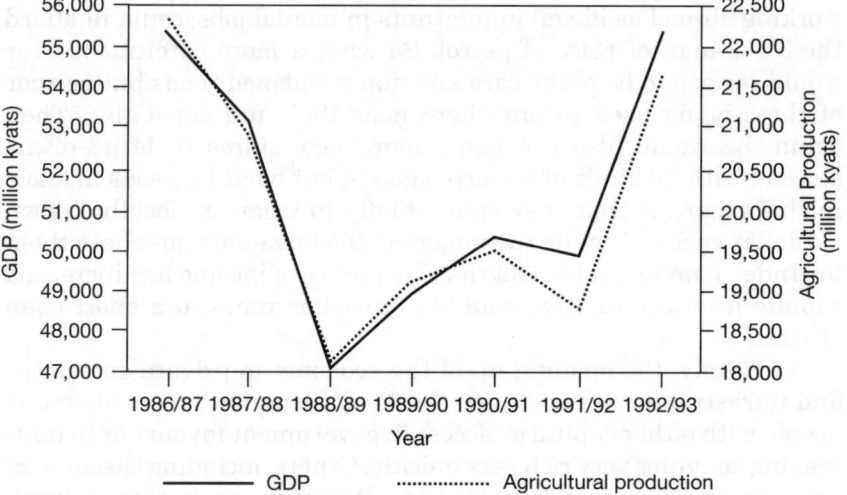

Looking beyond the GDP, some observers have noted many signs of affluence and indicators of an emerging market economy. Amongst the things they have noted:

1. an increasing number of motor cars in Yangon, Mandalay, and other big towns;
2. widened roads and highways with advertising billboards lining them at intervals;
3. new buildings and private houses in the urban centres as well as in new satellite towns adjoining them;
4. new stores stacked with all kinds of imported goods;
5. new and more sophisticated advertisements on television and in the press; and
6. numerous satellite dishes in many cities.

Certainly, not all of them should or could be dismissed, as in the Western media, as mere cosmetic improvements. On the other hand, not all of these, which may be called layman's indicators, can be taken at face value. Although there are many more private cars, few of them can be seen on the widened highways. This is largely because the owners of these cars, mostly parents of sons and daughters working abroad as illegal immigrants in menial jobs, could ill afford the black-market price of petrol. So what a more careful observer would see would be many cars and many widened roads but neither of them being used to anywhere near their full capacities. Then again, he would also see many more new stores in large towns stocked with all kinds of imported goods; but what he needs to know in this regard is that they cater chiefly to what are locally known as 'dollar earners', while the majority, the have-nots, just pass them by. Indeed, many people feel that inequality of income has increased rapidly from the relative equality of earlier years in a short span of time.

Certainly, the opening up of the economy to private enterprise and infrastructural investment by the government has made many people with either capital or access to government favours or to rent-seeking activities very rich very quickly. Others, including speculators and corrupt officials, who dared to cut corners or do things which were not strictly legitimate also became quite well off suddenly. However, very few of these *nouveau riche* are really entrepreneurs or innovators.

Official figures of national income also appear to support the general feeling of increasing inequality in income. The total output in 1992/93 was still slightly below that of 1986/87, let alone 1985/86. It caught up with the 1985/86 level only in 1993/94. Meanwhile the population had increased by some four and a half million people. This meant that income or output per head in 1992/93 had fallen even further than in 1986/87 or 1985/86. Therefore, the newly acquired affluence of some in combination with rising prices could mean greater income disparities and greater hardships for others.

But again, one needs to look beyond the official income per head as well as the official or formal income of people in different sectors and in different income brackets. Looking first at the farmers or rural families, there can be no doubt that the average and above-average farm families with four or more hectares have fared better because of liberalization and the relative increase in farm prices.

For example, a village called Ywatharnyunt near Nyaungdon, with approximately 275 households relying mainly on the cultivation of beans and pulses, had about thirty radios and two bicycles before 1988. Now it has one television set, over eighty radios and about fifty to sixty bicycles. It also has two cinemas, each with a capacity of 200 seats. More or less the same can be said of a smaller village with about 170 households called Kyontomar, also near Nyaungdon. Farmers in this village cultivate rice as well as beans and pulses as a second crop in the winter. This village too came to have one television set, one cinema, and many more radios and bicycles than before 1988.

On the other hand, the position of farm labourers and below-average farm families with less than four hectares who do not have much surplus produce left for sale in the open market seems to be no different than before. They are the ones who could not keep their houses in good repair and who do not possess much worldly assets such as radios and bicycles. More or less the same can be said of the majority of casual labourers in the private sector as a whole. The nominal incomes of most of them have probably just kept pace with the increase in the general level of prices.

As for fixed income earners in government service, the formal incomes of those in the lower-income brackets have probably kept pace with the increase in prices as their salaries had been increased by four or five times. The same cannot be said of those in the middle-income brackets, who enjoy neither fringe benefits like people in the higher-income brackets nor pay increase of the same magnitude as those in the lower-income brackets. However, even these middle-income people or a majority of them have been able to maintain their standard of living either by taking second jobs or by sending their children abroad to work.

Then again, the government has done much to reduce ethnic disparities in economic opportunities, especially through the development of border areas. It has disseminated agricultural techniques, set up pilot farms, provided roads, bridges, hospitals, schools, and communication facilities, and so on. This is something which can be overlooked by the casual observer, especially as these border areas are not easily accessible. Incidentally, these are also the sort of areas where market forces cannot be relied upon, at least in the initial stages, to bring about development.

On the whole then, the emerging pattern of income distribution and general welfare aspects of recent developments is somewhat mixed. On the one hand, the percentage share of the total national income going to the richest 5 per cent or 20 per cent of the income recipients could have gone up, being pulled up by 1 or 2 per cent of them becoming very rich overnight. On the other hand, this could happen without the share of the bottom 20 or 40 per cent going down, the sacrifice in relative terms, coming from people in the middle-income brackets. In technical terms, it means a change in the shape of the Lorenz curve without however affecting the Gini concentration ratio. Contrary to general feeling, increasing inequality of income seems to have taken place only in the urban sector, whereas it was probably the reverse as far as urban–rural income distribution was concerned.

Moreover, while most of those who became rich overnight can hardly be expected to be 'captains' of future development, the increases in rural incomes, by providing strong domestic demand, could be the basis for far-reaching, pluralistic, and hence self-sustaining development. Whether it will in fact become one is of course another matter. Depending as it does on many other factors, this requires examining some of the things which have already been examined here, such as the rate of saving and investment, progress made in putting market-oriented financial and other institutions in place, etc.; and some of the things which need to be examined further such as the state of internal and external balance and soundness of the macroeconomic environment.

It may be seen from Table 8.5 that Myanmar has been having an inflationary situation of over 20 per cent per annum for the past several years. To date the response of the government has been threefold. Firstly, it set up the Central Committee for Ensuring Smooth Flow of Commodities and Stabilizing Commodity Prices, presumably to tackle transportation and other problems of market imperfections on a commodity-by-commodity and case-by-case basis as well as through moral suasion, essentially a micro-approach. Secondly, the budgetary expenditures of government departments came to be scrutinized more strictly, although again on a piecemeal basis rather than in a comprehensive way on the basis of the annual plan. Thirdly, the government began to rely increasingly on donations for sporting, cultural, and many other activities. At first sight, donations by businessmen seem very attractive. Not only could the government undertake what it wants to do at the expense of businessmen, but donations could be also a form of progressive taxation. However, as the businessmen recouped their donations from consumers in the form of increased prices of consumer goods, they became regressive and could make the tax structure (which became very regressive during the socialist era) even more regressive (see Appendix Table 8.2). These initiatives suggest that the government has deliberately or otherwise failed to understand the macroeconomic problem, the solution for which requires appropriate fiscal and monetary policies.

Table 8.6 shows in a very simplistic way the internal imbalance and its outcomes. Total expenditure in current prices in the first row of the table may be taken to represent aggregate demand (AD), which between 1986/87 and 1993/94 increased by roughly six times. Output in real terms in the second row of the table may be taken to represent aggregate supply (AS), which during the same period remained more or less unchanged. For those who are familiar with macroeconomics, this implies an upward sloping aggregate supply curve parallel to the vertical axis representing the general price level. Increases in currency in circulation and money (M_1) in the following rows of the table can be regarded as manifestations of the increases in aggregate demand. The former in particular is consistent with the new equilibrium position of AD and AS. The result of all these changes in macroeconomic variables is a fourfold increase in the GDP deflator and consumer prices (Figure 8.2).

Figure 8.2 is a highly simplified diagram of macroeconomic adjustment. It is provided merely as an aid for visualizing the macroeconomic situation in Myanmar at two points of time, 1986/87 and 1992/93. The upward sloping vertical section of the aggregate supply curve is the same at both these points of time. However, unlike the usual textbook case, this is not because of full employment but because of rigidities in factor proportions, and in particular shortage of foreign exchange. The aggregate demand curves for 1986/87 and 1992/93 are represented by AD_1 and AD_4 respectively. As can be seen, given an unchanging aggregate supply, a fourfold increase in aggregate demand was accompanied by a fourfold increase in the price level. Obviously, both the increases in demand and price level were facilitated by the increase in money supply.

FIGURE 8.2
Demand, Supply, Money, and Prices

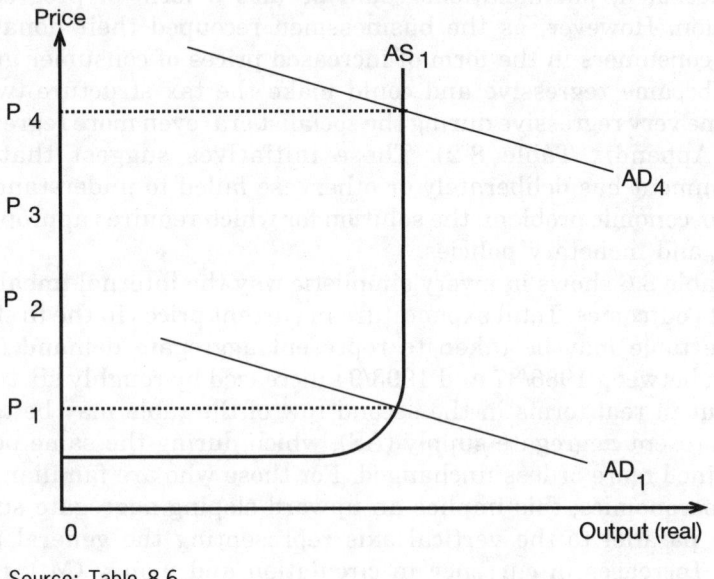

Source: Table 8.6.

The fact that the major cause of the increases in money supply has been the financing of public sector deficits by borrowing from the domestic banking sector is borne out by Table 8.6, which shows public sector accounts for 1993/94 and recent years.

As mentioned earlier, efforts had been made, especially in 1993/94, to reduce the deficits. But, as may be seen from the table, deficits still remain high. The relative importance of the sources of deficits has, however, changed. Until 1988/89 the deficits of the SEEs had always been higher than those of the government. In 1992/93, as in recent years, past trends were completely reversed. This was due partly to the contracting out of some SEEs to the private sector and partly to the increasing capital expenditures of the state administrative organizations.

In fact, capital expenditures of the state administrative organizations as percentages of overall deficits have been increasing progressively in recent years. Beginning from 1988/89, they increased

TABLE 8.6
Demand, Supply, Money, and Prices in Myanmar, 1986–94
(1985/86 = 100)

	1986/87	1987/88	1988/89	1989/90	1990/91	1991/92	1992/93	1993/94
Demand								
Total expenditure (current prices)	105.4	122.7	136.2	222.7	271.4	318.9	436.2	608.4
Supply								
Output (real)	98.9	95.0	84.2	87.3	89.7	88.8	97.5	103.3
Money and Prices								
Currency in circulation	112.6	62.0	92.9	144.6	211.0	284.6	400.4	504.9
Money (M1)	114.5	52.2	85.6	119.6	184.0	247.3	275.4	293.8
GDP deflator	106.6	129.2	161.7	255.0	302.3	358.9	454.3	586.4
Consumer price	114.7	140.1	171.5	212.1	258.5	333.9	369.0	489.3

Sources: Ministry of Planning and Finance and Ministry of National Planning and Economic Development, Review of the Financial, Economic and Social Conditions, 1993/94 and earlier; and selected monthly economic indicators.

from 29 per cent to 40, 58, 74, and finally to 75 per cent in subsequent years. This was because the government had been very active in providing widened roads, bridges, schools, hospitals, and so on. According to some, this was the SLORC's way of seeking legitimacy. Whatever it was, in so far as they were the main cause of the deficits, which in turn cause inflation, the important issue becomes one of balancing the infrastructural needs of the country with the need for providing price stability and a sound macroeconomic environment.

Expenditure is just one side of fiscal policy. The other side, the revenue side of fiscal policy, needs looking into also. Many economists regard fiscal balance as the key to the success of economic restructuring. And most would agree that in the efforts to achieve fiscal balance, along with cuts in expenditures, ways and means to increase revenues would need to be sought. When it comes to tax reform, it is easier said than done. As one scholar put it, tax reform is a topic about which more has been said, to less effect, than almost any topic in economic policy. Because of political and other difficulties, most governments shy away from making any genuine efforts to reform the tax structure. As a result most tax reforms remain in name only.

While this may be true, it is also a well-known fact that tax evasion is widespread in most developing countries. An extremely low tax ratio (that is, total tax revenue as a percentage of GDP) of 5.86 for 1991/92 coupled with high marginal tax rates suggest that tax evasion as well as tax avoidance (which is legal) must have been widespread in Myanmar too.[11] Therefore, there is plenty of scope for increasing tax revenues from existing sources, even at unchanged tax rates. This would, however, require better tax administration, visible and easily understandable penalties for tax evasion, simpler tax laws so as to make compliance more convenient, and, last but not least, minimal and equitable tax rates.

In market economies, fiscal policy and monetary policy can be separated because the central bank is to some degree independent of the executive branch. In Myanmar, however, the Central Bank of Myanmar (CBM) is directly under the Ministry of Finance, formerly a part of the Ministry of Planning and Finance. Therefore, the rate of expansion of the money supply is essentially determined by government spending in excess of its revenues.

There is an anomaly here in that the amount of budget deficits that the Ministry of Finance can cover through overdrafts on its accounts is limited in principle by the 1990 Central Bank of Myanmar Law. For the law expressly states that the advances to the government shall be limited to 20 per cent of the previous year's receipts. The CBM, under the Ministry of Finance, can hardly be expected to pressure the government to abide by this law by looking for ways to increase its revenues and savings on the one hand and by spending and investing wisely on the other. It is actually up to the government to bear that law in mind and to refrain from breaking it.

In this connection some scholars have raised doubts as to whether the government is in fact abiding by its own law. On the basis of data in Table 8.7, overall public sector domestic financing requirements for 1990/91, 1991/92, and 1992/93 were found to be 27.7, 23.2, and 23.2 per cent respectively of the receipts in 1989/90, 1990/91, and 1991/92. Thus, it would seem that the government had been unable to abide by the 1990 CBM Law.

Table 8.8 shows recent trends in the external position of Myanmar. As may be seen from the table (as well as from Table 8.5), Myanmar has been having deficits in its trade balance throughout the present transition period. As a matter of fact, looking further back Myanmar has had deficits in its trade balance ever since the late 1970s. However, there are important differences between then and at present. Firstly, foreign trade at present is no longer a state monopoly as it was then. This by itself is a big improvement, although as mentioned earlier, there are still many bureaucratic hurdles in the way of private exports and imports. Secondly, although an overvalued official exchange rate then has become even more overvalued at present, it is not an important impediment for exporting at present as many had expected. This is because of the 100 per cent retention system and also because border trade is usually conducted with local currencies; kyat/yuan rate changes from day to day as dictated by the market. As a result, exports have not been stagnant as in the past but have in fact been increasing. However, because of a fall in the terms of trade and because developmental needs for imports could not be curbed, balance of trade has continued to be negative.

To date, trade balance is still the most important item in Myanmar's external accounts. Nevertheless, there are other items requiring review, such as the services and private transfers — the 'invisibles' — in the current account and grants and foreign direct investment in the capital account.

As may be seen from Table 8.8, 'services' has become a positive and an increasingly important item. Judging by the mushrooming of hotels, inns, and other assorted guest houses in Yangon and elsewhere, this is probably due to tourism. However, as the figures in Table 8.8 indicate, it has still a long way to go to become a major foreign exchange earner. The other item in 'invisibles', private transfers, has become more and more an important foreign exchange earner. This stems from a relaxation in passport control that allows more Myanmar people to work abroad. While this earns foreign exchange, it also represents a brain drain.

With the exception of 1990/91, which was an exceptional year in many ways, the 'invisibles' were able to reduce the negative trade balance to a considerable extent. As a result, the current account balance in some years, particularly in 1992/93 and 1993/94, accounted for more than half that of the trade balance.

Official grants, shown in the capital account, usually amounted to 450 or 500 million kyats each year; 1989/90 and 1990/91 were two exceptional years. Foreign direct investment is a new item in Myanmar's capital account of the balance of payments. Arising as it does from the Foreign Investment Law of November 1988, it clearly reflects the opening up of the economy. However, after immediately picking up momentum in the first two years, it seems to be showing early signs of decline. Furthermore, although Myanmar's Foreign Investment Law is as liberal as that of Vietnam's Foreign Investment Code enacted in April 1988, the achievements of the former have been far less satisfactory than those of the latter. Apart from political factors, a major difference between the two, as mentioned earlier, was that Vietnam had boldly floated its currency, the Vietnamese dong, by the middle of 1989, so as to make it internationally convertible, whereas Myanmar held on to its unrealistically overvalued official exchange rate. Had the inflow of foreign direct investment in Myanmar been of the same scale as that of Vietnam, Myanmar would have not only enjoyed a surplus in its overall balance, but could have also dampened inflationary pressures by achieving internal balance.

Foreign exchange rate, as one commentator remarked, is a sovereign affair. At the same time, the same commentator as well

TABLE 8.7
Public Finance in Myanmar, 1988/89–93/94
(In millions of kyats)

	1988/89	1989/90	1990/91	1991/92	1992/93 (P.A.)	1993/94 (P)
State Administration Organizations						
Receipts						
Taxes	3,426.4	5,312.4	9,416.7	10,480.2	12,562.6	11,875.5
SEEs	1,557.6	2,141.6	3,433.8	3,341.9	4,996.8	6,489.5
Other	866.2	3,168.8	1,239.2	1,584.0	2,655.6	2,821.8
Total	5,850.2	10,622.8	14,089.7	15,406.1	20,215.0	21,186.8
Current expenditures	6,322.6	12,898.7	15,477.7	16,941.4	18,061.6	22,291.9
Current surplus/deficit	(-)472.4	(-)2,275.9	(-)1,388.0	(-)1,535.3	(+)2,153.4	(-)1,105.1
Financial account surplus/deficit	(+)152.7	(+)269.8	(+)314.1	(+)196.7	(-)102.5	(-)174.8
Foreign loans and aids	585.6	218.8	252.8	374.5	478.1	551.8
Capital expenditures	1,632.5	2,750.7	6,050.1	8,198.0	9,756.9	11,498.2
Overall surplus/deficit	(-)1,366.6	(-)4,538.0	(-)6,871.2	(-)9,162.1	(+)7,022.9	(-)12,226.3
State Economic Enterprises						
Current receipts	17,688.2	25,887.1	31,327.4	35,785.8	42,859.2	57,843.8
Current expenditures	20,467.9	25,596.4	32,219.1	36,054.4	44,169.6	60,810.9
Current surplus/deficit	(-)2,779.7	(+)290.7	(-)891.7	(-)268.6	(-)1,310.4	(-)2,967.1
Capital receipts	60.7	55.0	16.8	70.1	233.2	351.6
Foreign loans and aids	1,318.9	846.7	685.3	408.2	443.3	670.6
Capital expenditures	2,621.1	3,100.2	3,394.5	3,346.8	3,695.6	3,657.9
Financing requirement	4,021.2	1,907.8	3,584.1	3,137.1	3,617.4	—
Town and City Development Committees						
Receipts	390.0	986.1	1,879.3	2,401.9	1,727.3	—
Current expenditures	295.4	662.5	1,074.4	938.5	945.4	—
Current surplus/deficit	(+)94.6	(+)323.6	(+)804.9	(+)1,463.4	(+)781.9	—
Capital expenditures	112.1	647.4	765.3	156.0	46.8	—
Financing requirement	206.7	323.8	(-)39.6	(-)1,307.4	(-)735.1	—
Overall public sector domestic financing requirement	5,594.5	6,769.6	10,415.7	10,991.8	12,457.9	—
% of GDP	7.3	5.4	6.8	6.2	5.4	—

P — Provisional.
P.A. — Provisional Actual.

Sources: Ministry of Planning and Finance and Ministry of National Planning and Economic Development, *Review of the Financial, Economic and Social Conditions, 1992/93 and 1993/94.*

TABLE 8.8
Balance of Payments Summary for Myanmar, 1988/89–93/94
(In millions of kyats)

	1988/89	1989/90	1990/91	1991/92	1992/93	1993/94
Trade balance	−426.8	−789.6	−3,060.2	−2,583.4	−2,460.1	−3,147.0
Exports	2,036.7	2,806.7	2,966.3	2,702.0	3,711.0	4,071.2
Imports	−2,463.5	−3,596.3	−6,026.5	−5,285.4	−6,171.1	−7,218.2
Services (net)	−149.6	203.2	−256.2	148.0	555.8	997.4
Receipts	363.3	933.5	1,182.9	1,127.4	1,300.1	1,781.7
Payments	−512.9	−730.3	−1,439.1	−979.4	−744.3	−784.3
Private transfers	499.8	360.8	475.5	519.0	769.0	807.4
Current account balance	−1,076.6	−255.6	−2,841.9	−1,916.4	−1,135.3	−1,342.2
Non-monetary capital movements						
Official grants	465.3	193.2	181.2	404.4	453.3	552.5
Long-term capital (net)	941.4	95.1	443.3	180.4	48.3	50.6
Disbursements	1,394.1	893.8	757.8	385.5	643.1	668.8
Repayments due	−452.7	−798.7	−314.5	−205.1	−594.8	−618.2
Foreign direct investment	—	130.7	1,361.1	1,560.2	794.9	764.9
Other capital (net)	−95.7	2,037.2	−225.1	−221.9	161.9	—
International Monetary Fund (net)	−159.9	−70.3	−44.1	−27.7	72.6	−17.6
Subscription	−0.7	−0.5	−0.4	−0.4	−106.4	−3.7
Valuation adjustment (net)	−20.2	—	—	—	—	—
Errors and omissions (net)	236.0	53.5	—	—	—	—
Overall balance	289.6	2,213.3	−1,155.9	−21.4	−34.5	−2.1

Note: Figures for 1993/94 are provisional.

Sources: Ministry of Planning and Finance and Ministry of National Planning and Economic Development, *Review of the Financial, Economic and Social Conditions*, 1992/93 and 1993/94.

as many others have found Myanmar's foreign exchange rate regime to be puzzling, to say the least. According to them, advantages to be derived from the unification of the official exchange rate and the rates arising from the foreign exchange retention system are many. Apart from increased inflow of foreign investment, these include "reductions in explicit and implicit subsidies; improved government revenues, especially from customs duties; the ability to more realistically assess the market viability of state enterprises; and accelerating the development of the market economy through eliminating the licensing of exports and imports" (Asian Development Bank 1993, p.235).

Basically, exchange rate unification can be done in one of two ways. One way is to devalue the official exchange rate to such an extent as to reflect market conditions. The other way is to float it. Both involve hard choices or trade-offs. And the hardest are not economic but political trade-offs. Most governments with overvalued official exchange rates are reluctant to risk the destabilizing political effects of devaluation. On the other hand, there were governments which took the risk of doing what needed to be done. South Korea in the early 1960s propelled its export substitution phase with two large devaluations, of 104 and 65 per cent. Similarly, Brazil undertook a 100 per cent devaluation in 1964.

The Pace and Sequence of Reforms

There is a difference in the sequencing of reform measures undertaken in the TEAs and Eastern Europe. The East European approach is described as the 'big bang' or 'shock therapy' one whereas that of the TEAs is evolutionary and gradual. According to Rana and Paz (1994), the TEAs' approach to sequencing policy reforms involves a 'bottom-up' approach, with the implementation of most aspects of microeconomic reform (price reform, enterprise reform, and reform of the legal framework under which enterprises operate) coming earlier than macroeconomic reforms (fiscal, monetary, and foreign trade reforms). This approach differs from the 'standard approach' of the World Bank and International Monetary Fund which places macroeconomic reforms first. However, the performance of the TEAs proves that their approach is more appropriate. The pace and sequence of reforms in Myanmar are shown in Figure 8.3.

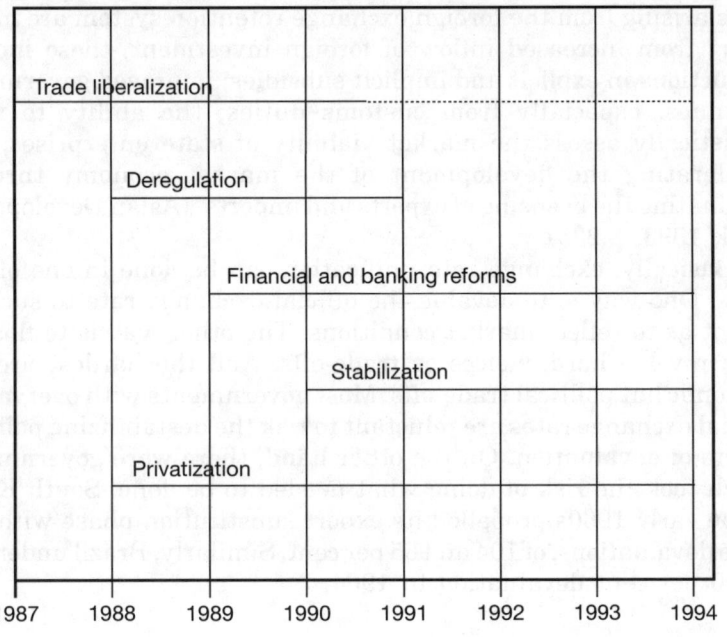

FIGURE 8.3
Pace and Sequence of Economic Reforms in Myanmar

The pace and boldness of reform measures do not depend only on the competence of the leadership (or the state) and the initial economic conditions facing the country, but even more so on the political situation. If one can safely assume a political precondition of genuine popular support, one can indeed take very bold measures and use 'shock therapy' rather than slow steps towards economic reform. Otherwise, one needs to proceed with caution, especially as much of the reform process is an uncharted territory. Look at what happened to the Soviet '500-day plan' which, on paper, was one of the most elaborate reform blueprints; and Poland's use of 'shock therapy' for which the government was thrown out of power by the dissatisfied populace.

The SLORC does not appear to have any Soviet-style reform blueprint as such. What it has is the knowledge of the pre-1962 market economy, the 1958–60 reform agenda of the caretaker military government, and inspiration from the success of that government.[12] Many, but not all, of the initial batch of reform measures given in Table 8.2 were either similar to those existing before 1962 or taken by the caretaker government. And many of them were certainly moves on the right track. However, compared to other TEAs the pace of these reforms seems rather slow. For the sake of brevity, this may be seen roughly in terms of Mya Than's *perestroika* and *glasnost* (International Centre for Economic Growth 1993). (See Figure 8.4.)

In Figure 8.4 Myanmar is placed at the left of both Vietnam and Laos, meaning less economic opening, chiefly but not only because of its unchanged and outdated exchange rate regime. Like Vietnam, Laos devalued its currency by 320 per cent in 1988. Since then its Central Bank has been adjusting the official exchange rate regularly so as to be in line with the prevailing exchange rate in the parallel

FIGURE 8.4
Economies in Transition

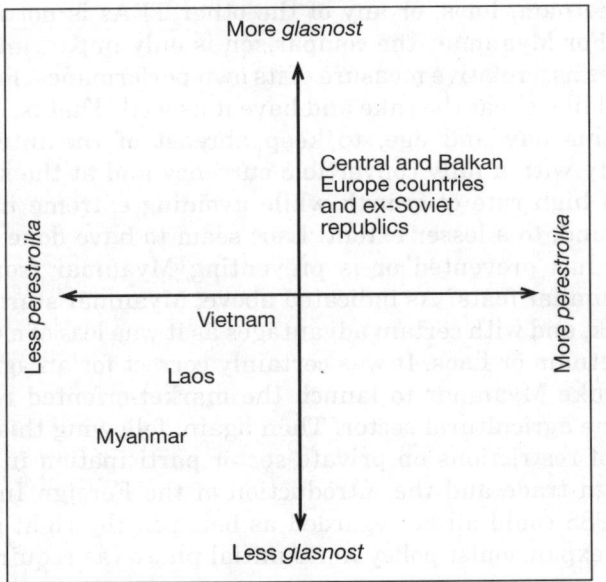

market. As for placing Myanmar below Vietnam and Laos in the matter of political opening, it is because most would consider people in the latter two countries to have relatively greater freedom of speech and freedom of press as well as their governments to be more tolerant of diverse views than Myanmar. Of course, if Myanmar could forge a genuine multi-party democracy on the basis of genuine social and political consensus with freedom of the press and so on in the near future, it would have to be placed above these two countries.

There are many variations to Figure 8.4 (Fischer and Gelb 1991). If one were to substitute less *perestroika* with less macroeconomic stability and less *glasnost* with less political stability and so on in Figure 8.4, the positions of the three Asian countries would probably remain the same. Both Vietnam and Laos, with annual inflation rates of 65 and 78 per cent respectively in 1990, had significantly reduced them to below 10 per cent by 1994. As for Central and Balkan Europe (CBE) countries and ex-Soviet republics, many of them should be placed in the same southwest quadrant as the three Asian countries.

More to the point, the fact that Myanmar seems to have lagged behind Vietnam, Laos, or any of the other TEAs is not important in itself. For Myanmar, the comparison is only important in so far as it serves as a relative measure of its own performance. For ideally, one would like to eat the cake and have it as well. That is, one would like, in this day and age, to keep abreast of the international community with a fully convertible currency and at the same time to have a high rate of growth while avoiding extreme instability. Vietnam and, to a lesser extent, Laos seem to have done just that.

What has prevented or is preventing Myanmar from accomplishing similar feats? As indicated above, Myanmar started on the right track, and with certain advantages as it was less of a CPE than either Vietnam or Laos. It was certainly correct for an agricultural economy like Myanmar to launch the market-oriented reforms in 1987 in the agricultural sector. Then again, following this with the removal of restrictions on private sector participation in domestic and foreign trade and the introduction of the Foreign Investment Law in 1988 could all be regarded as being in the right sequence. Even the expansionist policy in its initial phase (as required by the agenda of the caretaker government) could be considered as being useful in energizing private sector participation in the economy.

It should be noted that the macroeconomic policy accompanying the initial batch of reform measures in Myanmar was quite unorthodox. Instead of focusing on macroeconomic stability as many would have suggested (International Monetary Fund; Fischer and Gelb 1991; Lavigne 1992), Myanmar opted for expansionist fiscal and monetary policies, which would create jobs and thereby shore up at least short-term support. Of course expansionist policies may have been prompted by political rather than economic considerations. As Haggard and Webb observed: "An incumbent regime that believes its days are numbered will be strongly tempted to drum up support through expansionist policies and delays of reform, even if this policy is self-defeating over the long-run" (Haggard and Webb 1993, p. 147). Whatever it was, it has succeeded up to a point.

However, there is a price to pay for this 'success'. The success in terms of opening up of the economy and in generating employment through expansionist policies was achieved at the expense of macroeconomic stability and all the ramifications connected with it. Expansionist fiscal and monetary policies, by fuelling inflation, have prevented the dismantling of subsidies and rationing. They have also prevented the unification of exchange rates and dismantling of exchange controls and import licensing. And as a result of the latter set of measures, amongst others, sizable inflow of foreign capital needed for rapid development failed to take place. These are some of the reasons why many economists consider macroeconomic stability to be a prerequisite for a market-oriented development.

Apart from the above, some neglect in keeping track of the effectiveness of reform measures was also responsible for the slow pace of the reform process. Economic reform must be seen as an ongoing process of sound economic management. Each reform measure entails other supportive measures, including institutional changes, in a logical and coherent manner. For example, for the foreign investment law to be effective it needs to be supported by an internationally convertible currency. For marketization to be effective it needs to be backed up by an appropriate legal framework and environment. Then again, privatization could also be a means of achieving stabilization in so far as the sale of state assets could eliminate the monetary overhang. Therefore, it is very important to be constantly monitoring the effectiveness of reform measures so as to take corrective and supportive measures as and when necessary.

Concluding Remarks

Myanmar has certainly made some progress towards a market-oriented economy. But it has not yet fully achieved the three broad objectives of the government and, compared with the performances of its neighbouring countries, what has been achieved has not been much. And therein lie both the risk and the challenge facing Myanmar.

The risk is that at the present pace of reforms, Myanmar cannot hope to achieve more than a normal long-term average gross national product (GNP) growth rate of 4 or 5 per cent per annum at best. This means that, let alone catch up, it will be left behind in the backwaters of the Asia-Pacific basin. For the emerging countries like Vietnam and Laos are likely to emulate market economies such as Japan, South Korea, and Taiwan and achieve high rates of GNP growth of 10 per cent or more per annum on a sustained basis for at least fifteen to twenty years. It will be very bleak for Myanmar to be left behind as "a hewer of wood and a drawer of water".

The challenge for Myanmar is make the hard choices necessary for fundamental reforms and to develop a vision of the future. Reform measures so far taken, while yielding some positive results, are no substitutes for sound fiscal and monetary policies as a means of achieving macroeconomic stability. And, as indicated earlier, macroeconomic stability appears to be the key to unlocking the doors leading to other concomitant reform measures. But macroeconomic stability or a sound market economy alone will not guarantee high rates of GNP growth. For that Myanmar needs a vision of the future — to actively promote certain lines of activity and, if necessary, to intervene in the market in an optimal fashion.

Another important issue is the *sustainability of the reform*. It is a very complex case involving political, social, and economic factors; among them political stability, people's confidence in reform policies, macroeconomic performance, distribution of wealth, and scope of the reform. As far as political stability is concerned, Myanmar has more of it than at any point of time since 1988/89. Truce agreements have been signed between the SLORC and most of the armed dissident ethnic groups. The national convention for drafting the nation's much-needed constitution is being held although its conclusion has yet to be reached. In the economic sphere erratic performance since reform was introduced in 1988/89, frequent changes in reform policies, and continued high inflation may probably undermine the sustainability of the reform. Moreover, the trickle-down effect has yet to be seen.

Apart from these, the objective behind the reform is also significant for its sustainability. If reforms are carried out just to stave off the crisis, then sustainability is doubtful, as Haggard and Webb have rightly pointed out:

> A crisis in no way guarantees that any remedial actions taken will be sustained or institutionalized. As the crisis winds down, the urgency of reform lessens and the political forces resistant to reform typically revive. The outcome can be a cycle of policy deterioration, economic crisis, temporary or partial policy reform, recovery, and relapse. (Haggard and Webb 1993)

However, since the SLORC's three objectives (mentioned earlier) clearly stated its willingness to transform the inefficient economic system, sustainability of the reform will depend mainly on macroeconomic performance. If the trend of GDP growth of the previous two successive years continues with reduced inflation rate, the chances for sustainability of the reform are good.

Finally, the transition from a command economy to a market-oriented one requires not only innumerable reform measures — such as price and market reforms, enterprise reforms, institutional reforms, and legal reforms — and right pacing and sequencing of reforms, but also, equally important, a change in outlook and attitude. A commitment to change for the better requires an open mind; a sense of proportion and fairness; honesty to see the past for what it was; and tolerance for diverse views and individual initiatives.

APPENDIX TABLE 8.1
GDP of Myanmar by Ownership and Sector
(At 1985/86 constant prices)

Sector	Goods Kyats (million)	Percentage	Services Kyats (million)	Percentage	Trade Kyats (million)	Percentage	Total Kyats (million)	Percentage
1986/87								
State	4,057.1	11.90	5,213.8	60.60	4,342.0	33.90	13,612.9	24.60
Co-operative	1,812.0	5.40	216.3	2.50	1,732.0	13.50	3,760.3	6.80
Private	28,107.9	82.70	3,169.9	36.90	6,745.8	52.60	38,023.6	68.60
Total	33,977.0	100.00	8,600.0	100.00	12,819.8	100.00	55,396.8	100.00
1987/88								
State	3,515.7	10.90	5,378.2	60.70	3,592.8	29.90	12,486.7	23.50
Co-operative	2,049.9	6.30	222.8	2.50	1,374.6	11.50	3,647.3	6.90
Private	26,752.0	82.80	3,266.6	36.80	7,025.2	58.60	37,043.8	69.60
Total	32,317.6	100.00	8,867.6	100.00	11,992.6	100.00	53,177.8	100.00
1988/89								
State	2,803.6	10.00	5,153.6	60.80	2,889.0	27.30	10,846.2	23.00
Co-operative	1,646.0	5.90	153.7	1.80	718.6	6.80	2,518.3	5.40
Private	23,580.7	84.10	3,172.2	37.40	6,978.3	65.90	33,731.2	71.60
Total	28,030.3	100.00	8,479.5	100.00	10,585.9	100.00	47,095.7	100.00
1989/90								
State	3,398.5	11.39	4,563.6	57.50	2,890.6	26.00	10,852.7	22.20
Co-operative	1,111.9	3.73	117.6	1.48	611.5	5.50	1,841.0	3.80
Private	25,318.5	84.88	3,255.2	41.02	7,615.7	68.50	36,189.4	74.00
Total	29,828.9	100.00	7,936.4	100.00	11,117.8	100.00	48,883.1	100.00

Sector	Goods Kyats (million)	Percentage	Services Kyats (million)	Percentage	Trade Kyats (million)	Percentage	Total Kyats (million)	Percentage
1990/91								
State	3,599.0	11.76	4,857.4	58.74	2,960.0	26.00	11,416.4	22.70
Co-operative	806.5	2.64	123.7	1.50	637.5	5.60	1,567.7	3.10
Private	26,199.6	85.60	3,288.7	39.76	7,787.1	68.40	37,275.4	74.20
Total	30,605.1	100.00	8,269.8	100.00	11,384.6	100.00	50,259.5	100.00
1991/92								
State	3,705.9	12.34	5,136.8	59.50	2,769.6	24.98	11,612.3	23.40
Co-operative	578.0	1.93	146.3	1.70	630.9	5.69	1,355.2	2.70
Private	25,739.4	85.73	3,349.6	38.80	7,688.1	69.33	36,777.1	73.90
Total	30,023.3	100.00	8,632.7	100.00	11,088.6	100.00	49,744.6	100.00
1992/93								
State	4,061.5	11.95	5,394.3	60.23	2,962.6	24.22	12,418.4	22.50
Co-operative	488.6	1.44	132.1	1.47	718.1	5.87	1,338.8	2.40
Private	29,430.6	86.61	3,429.2	38.30	8,553.1	69.91	41,412.9	75.10
Total	33,980.7	100.00	8,955.6	100.00	12,233.8	100.00	55,170.1	100.00
1993/94								
State	4,274.6	12.06	5,505.2	57.43	3,048.3	23.81	12,828.1	22.20
Co-operative	410.9	1.16	139.3	1.45	499.0	3.90	1,049.2	1.80
Private	30,749.2	86.78	3,942.2	41.12	9,255.9	72.29	43,947.3	76.00
Total	35,434.7	100.00	9,586.7	100.00	12,803.2	100.00	57,824.6	100.00

Sources: Ministry of Planning and Finance and Ministry of National Planning and Economic Development, *Review of the Financial, Economic and Social Conditions*, various issues; and *Reports to the Pyithu Hluttaw*.

APPENDIX TABLE 8.2
Estimated Revenue from Taxes for Myanmar, 1994/95

Sources	Kyats (millions)	Percentages
Commercial tax*	4,312.2	34.4
Taxes on income and property	3,384.6	27.0
Customs duties	2,100.0	16.8
Taxes on the use of state property	874.5	7.0
Import licence, state lottery	1,854.0	14.8
Total	12,525.3	100.0

* Commercial tax normally includes sales tax, turnover tax, and value-added tax.

Source: Ministry of Planning and Finance and Ministry of National Planning and Economic Development, *Review of the Financial, Economic and Social Conditions, 1993.*

Notes

1. For details, please see Rana and Paz (1994).
2. As early as the mid-1960s a home-grown economist of international renown, Dr Hla Myint, pointed out the disadvantages of inward-looking policies which Myanmar (then Burma) and Indonesia were following (Hla Myint 1967). Then again, in the report of the Fifteenth Annual Consultative Meeting of the Colombo Plan, held in Yangon (Rangoon), Myanmar (Burma), in 1967, it was specifically noted: "Exports declined in India, Burma and Ceylon and these were the countries where there were low growth rates of GNP" (The Colombo Plan 1967, p. 4). These and other warnings by economists and other scholars went unnoticed or unheeded by the policy makers. On the contrary, the 1968/69 "Report to the People" proudly claimed that "Burma is no longer an export-oriented economy as it was in the past" "Report to the People 1968/69", p. 26).
3. According to Master's thesis by Htwe Htwe Aung the real-wage index of regular employees in manufacturing concerns had fallen from 100 in 1965 to 78.07 in 1972 (Htwe Htwe Aung 1975, p. 83). Note, however, that the relative sense of well-being as compared to one's neighbours may be even more important than the absolute decline in it. Moreover, although politicians are bound to exploit civil unrest, the basis for it will remain general discontent.
4. "Desperate" was the very word used by one of the high-ranking Burma Socialist Programme Party (BSPP) members to describe the economic situation around 1987.

5. The official procurement price for roughly half the amount of rice purchased by the government is actually a forward purchase price. At 850 kyats per 100 baskets it is about half the open-market prices of 1,700 to 1,800 kyats per 100 baskets.
6. For the rent-seeking behaviour of the bureaucracy see Findlay and Wilson (1984) and some of the references given in their study.
7. For the complete list of laws promulgated by the SLORC since it took over power see the three books in Burmese published by the Attorney-General's Office in 1990, 1991, and 1992.
8. Recently the authors undertook a brief field trip to two villages near Nyaungdon. They found that the cultivation rights of agricultural land could be bought and sold based on an understanding.
9. The authors found this out first hand at a law court when they came upon a judge hurriedly referring to a couple of law books of the 1940s just before going into session.
10. As one young businessman complained: "I have been swindled and I know by whom, but if I kill him I won't get any of my money back, and if I take legal action against him I am certain that he will be imprisoned and I still won't get any of my money back. So, I just have to tag along [with] him to get back as much of my money as possible." The same young man added: "It is people like [him] who are destroying Myanmar's business credibility. At one time I could easily get a letter of credit from my foreign business associates. Now I cannot get a letter of credit from them until they can actually see the consignment being shipped."
11. When the low tax ratio of Myanmar was noted and commented upon in an earlier paper by Myat Thein, it was even somewhat higher at 7 per cent of GDP than in 1991/92 (Myat Thein 1990, pp. 83–84).
12. During the eighteen months of its rule from May 1958 to January 1960, the caretaker government established law and order, cleaned up the cities by removing squatters and relocating them in new towns, abandoned unnecessary state projects, and encouraged the creation of joint ventures between the government and foreign firms.

References

Asian Development Bank. *Asian Development Outlook*. Manila, 1993.

Attorney-General's Office, Union of Myanmar. *Laws, Rules and Regulations, Martial Law and Notifications Promulgated by the State Law and Restoration Council* (in Burmese). Yangon, 1990.

———. *Laws, Rules and Regulations, and Notifications Promulgated by the State Law and Restoration Council* (in Burmese). Yangon, 1991.

— — —. *Laws, Rules and Regulations, and Notifications Promulgated by the State Law and Restoration Council* (in Burmese). Yangon, 1992.

Findlay, R. and John D. Wilson. "The Political Economy of Leviathan". Paper presented at the Third Sapir Conference on Economic Policy in Theory and Practice, 1984, in Tel-Aviv.

Fischer, S. and Alan Gelb. "The Process of Socialist Economic Transformation". *Journal of Economic Perspectives* 5, no. 4 (Fall 1991), pp. 91–105.

Haggard, S. and Steven B. Webb. "What Do We Know about the Political Economy of Economic Policy Reform?". *Research Observer*, July 1993, pp. 143–68.

Hill, H. and S.K. Jayasuriya. *An Inward-Looking Economy in Transition: Economic Development in Burma since the 1960s*. Occasional Paper, no. 80. Singapore: Institute of Southeast Asian Studies, 1986.

Hla Myint, Dr. "The Inward and Outward Looking Countries of Southeast Asia". *The Malayan Economic Review* 12, no. 1 (April 1967).

— — —. "A Perspective on Inward- and Outward-Looking Strategies in the Asian-Pacific Region". In *Development Strategies for the 21st Century*, edited by Teruyuki Iwasaki, Takeshi Mori, and Hiroichi Yamaguchi, pp. 1–12. Tokyo: Institute of Developing Economies, 1992.

Htwe Htwe Aung. "Socio-Economics of Labour Relations System in Burma". Master's thesis, University of Rangoon, 1975.

International Centre for Economic Growth. *The Newsletter* 6, no. 3 (January 1993).

International Monetary Fund. *IMF Survey*. Various issues.

Klitgaard, R. *Adjusting to Reality*. New Delhi: Tata McGraw-Hill Publishing Company Limited, 1991.

Lavigne, Marie. "Economic Reforms in Eastern Europe: Prospects for the 1990s". In *Development Strategies for the 21st Century*, edited by Teruyuki Iwasaki, Takeshi Mori, and Hiroichi Yamaguchi, pp. 270–91. Tokyo: Institute of Developing Economies, 1992.

Ministry of Planning and Finance and Ministry of National Planning and Economic Development. *Review of the Financial, Economic and Social Conditions*. Yangon, various issues.

— — —. "Report to the People 1968/69".

— — —. *Economic and Social Indicators, 1994*. Yangon, 1994.

Muskat, M. "The Political Economy of China's Future". *The Journal of East and West Studies* 19, no. 1 (April 1990), pp. 1–35.

Mya Than. "The Union of Burma Foreign Investment Law". In *Myanmar Dilemmas and Options*, edited by Mya Than and Joseph L.H. Tan, pp. 186–214. Singapore: Institute of Southeast Asian Studies, 1990.

Mya Than and Nobuyoshi Nishizawa. "Agricultural Policy Reforms and Agricultural Development in Myanmar". In *Myanmar Dilemmas and*

Options, edited by Mya Than and Joseph L.H. Tan, pp. 89–116. Singapore: Institute of Southeast Asian Studies, 1990.

Myat Thein, U. "Monetary and Fiscal Policies for Development". In *Myanmar Dilemmas and Options*, edited by Mya Than and Joseph L.H. Tan, pp. 53–88. Singapore: Institute of Southeast Asian Studies, 1990.

Rana P.B. and W. Paz. "Economies in Transition: The Asian Experience". In *From Reform to Growth*, edited by Chung H. Lee and Helmut Reisen. Paris: Organization for Economic Co-operation and Development, 1994.

The Colombo Plan. *Fifteenth Annual Report of the Consultative Committee.* Rangoon, 1967.

The New Light of Myanmar, 8 July 1994.

Tsutomu Murano and Ikuo Takeuchi, eds. *Indochina Economic Reconstruction and International Cooperation.* Tokyo: Institute of Developing Economies, 1992.

Tun Wai, U. "The Myanmar Economy at the Crossroads: Options and Constraints". In *Myanmar Dilemmas and Options*, edited by Mya Than and Joseph L.H. Tan, pp. 18–52. Singapore: Institute of Southeast Asian Studies, 1990.

Union of Burma. *The State-owned Economic Enterprises Law.* Yangon, March 1989.

Union of Myanmar. *The Union of Burma Foreign Investment Law.* Yangon, November 1988.

———. *The Central Bank of Myanmar Law.* Yangon, July 1990.

———. *The Financial Institutions of Myanmar Law.* Yangon, July 1990.

Working People's Daily, 20 February 1992 and 1 April 1993.

Mongolian Economy in Transition: Present Status and Problems

**Sakhiya Lhagva and
Tsedendambyn Batbayar**

Introduction

In many respects, the economic circumstances in Mongolia are quite special. A land-locked country surrounded by two gigantic neighbours — Russia and China — Mongolia has a land area of about 1.6 million square kilometres and a population of 2.1 million, about half of whom are under twenty years of age. Ulaanbaatar, the capital, accounts for about 25 per cent of the total population and about half the national production. Because of the country's northern location and high altitude, the climate is unusually severe and unpredictable, with average temperatures for half of the year typically below the freezing point. Mongolia has an abundant supply of agricultural land, but about 80 per cent of it is suitable mainly for extensive animal husbandry; intensive crop cultivation is limited.

After its zenith in the thirteenth century and a slow decline thereafter, Mongolia became a frontier province of China in 1691. The country declared its independence in 1911 with support from Russia, but it was not until 1921 that an independent state was firmly established. The economy at this point was based principally on nomadic pastoralism, and the industrial sector was represented by a coal mine, an electricity-generating station, a few small gold mines, and a few skin- and wool-processing plants, all of which were owned by foreigners.

Since 1921, Mongolia's economic, political, and social developments have been shaped largely by its close relations with the former USSR. Nonetheless, its domestic economy remained dependent on nomadic pastoralism until 1948, when the communist party secured a firm hold on the country's political power and instituted central planning and the collectivization of agriculture. Roads and railways were constructed, and the pastoral sector was divided into collectives. Investment in social and human capital increased sharply. The basic intent was to create an industrialized economy following the Soviet model and gain entry into the Council for Mutual Economic Assistance (CMEA) system. However, central planning in Mongolia led to the same economic problems that are commonly found in socialist economies, that is, growing inefficiencies and structural imbalances. In addition, the country's ability to maintain this economic system depended heavily on the largess of the Soviet Union.

To address these basic problems, Mongolia's authorities took a few tentative steps to restructure the economy in the mid-1980s, but it was not until after the first multi-party elections held in Mongolia (July 1990) that the transition to a market-oriented system actually began. Since that time, Mongolia has made rapid strides to remove price controls, liberalize the foreign exchange market, deregulate the financial sector, and privatize state enterprises. The pace of reform has been remarkable given the dire conditions created by the collapse of the Soviet Union and the abrupt cessation of its substantial financial support. Output dropped an estimated 30–60 per cent in 1991, and continued to decline in 1992 though at a slower pace.

This chapter will examine the economic reforms that have been taking place in Mongolia and some of the issues confronted by the reform. It will begin by providing a brief historical background. Major elements of the reform that are common for all countries implementing a transition from a centrally planned, command economy to a market-based one are then examined. The chapter concludes with the remaining problems and recommendations for future reform.

Mongolia's Pre-Reform Economy

The industrialization which began in the post-war period was based on the natural endowments of the country, primarily its animal raw materials and mineral resources. At the beginning of the 1960s, there were already more than 160 industrial enterprises, most of which were involved in the primary processing of animal raw materials. Industrial development accelerated after 1960, particularly in 1962, when the country joined the CMEA. The manufacturing sector processing animal raw materials and the mining sector were developed and served as the main exporting sectors of the economy. As a result, the country was able to process 70–95 per cent of all skins sold, 50 per cent of wool, and 50 per cent of meat in the mid-1980s. Several joint ventures with CMEA countries were established but it was the opening of the copper plant in Erdenet, a joint venture with the USSR, in the late 1970s that most affected the economic structure of Mongolia. With the plant copper ore became the most important industrial export, constituting approximately 40 per cent of total exports from Mongolia.

In addition to these industries some import-substituting industries, such as the construction material, wood-processing, clothing, glass, and food-processing subsectors, were also developed. The rapid expansion of industry increased the demand for power and physical infrastructure and thus several coal mines and coal-fired, power-generation stations were set up. Industrialization during this period resulted in significant economic and export growth and structural change. The industrial sector increased from 14.6 per cent of gross domestic product (GDP) in 1960 to 33.8 per cent by 1990 (see Table 9.1).

All of the above projects required capital expenditures far exceeding the country's capacity to pay. During the 1980s, the country's budget revenue averaged about one-half of GDP, while spending exceeded 60 per cent of GDP. These deficits were financed, and the projects implemented, with assistance from the CMEA, particularly the USSR. Traditionally, the financial assistance took the form of trade loans (that is, loans provided by the USSR to balance bilateral trade), loans for turnkey projects (that is, loans for purchases of Soviet plants including farms, houses, etc.), and loans for technical assistance (that is, loans for purchases of equipment

TABLE 9.1
Growth and Structural Changes in Mongolia's Economy during the Industrialization Period

	1960	1970	1980	1990
Growth Rates (in percentages at 1986 fixed prices)				
Gross social product	100.0	160.6	304.5	495.8
Gross industrial product	100.0	261.1	604.2	1,218.1
Gross agricultural product	100.0	128.2	123.2	179.6
Gross livestock product	100.0	113.3	191.2	154.2
External trade turnover	100.0	120.6	416.2	694.1
Structure of GDP (percentage of GDP at factor cost)				
Industry	14.6	22.6[a]	29.3[a]	33.8
Services	62.7	52.1[a]	55.7[a]	6.0

[a]As a percentage of national income.

Sources: World Bank (1993) and information provided by State Statistical Office, Mongolia.

and materials to implement investment projects by Mongolia). The inflow of funds for the above purposes averaged about 18 per cent of GDP annually, or about 30 per cent of the country's output, and were largely responsible for the stable growth of Mongolia's economy. The Soviet Union also supplied most of the equipment, technology, spare parts, and other critical inputs to the new sectors. In 1989, for example, 83 per cent of Mongolia's total imports were from the Soviet Union; imports from the Soviet Union and the CMEA countries combined formed 90 per cent of total imports (Appendix Table 9.1). In addition, Mongolia obtained 40 per cent of its consumer goods, 80 per cent of its supplies for the national economy, and 90 per cent of its technical machinery from the former Soviet Union. Exports were similarly directed to the CMEA group during this period (see Appendix Table 9.2). Therefore, with industrialization, Mongolia's economic structure became rigidly tied to the Soviet and CMEA countries' economies.

Moreover, the production structure of the economy was highly capital-intensive and the products were largely not competitive by world standards. The centrally planned management system created severe distortions in the factor and goods markets. Under the prevailing conditions, the only way to maintain economic growth was to obtain ever-increasing financiàl assistance from the USSR, primarily in the form of import subsidies. The share of foreign savings in gross domestic investment increased from 54.4 per cent in 1986 to 89.6 per cent in 1990. The inability to generate self-sustaining growth became the most disturbing trend of Mongolia's economy during this period.

Under these circumstances, the need for basic reform of the economy became obvious, and starting in the middle of the 1980s Mongolia's authorities took some limited measures aimed at economic restructuring. These measures included a reduction of profit taxes for enterprises coupled with more investment autonomy, differential price incentives to encourage exports to hard currency markets, less restrictions on privately held livestock, and selected retail price increases against fixed domestic prices. But the final acknowledgement of the necessity of a more complete transition to a market-oriented system came later, in 1990, by a new coalition parliament, formed as a result of the first multi-party elections (July 1990) in Mongolia.

The Dramatic Reforms of the 1990s

The Rationale behind the Reforms

Although Mongolia is considered to be an Asian transitional economy, it has more common features with the economies of Eastern Europe. Unlike Vietnam and Laos, political liberalization preceded economic liberalization in Mongolia. The reform process began with popular demonstrations in late 1989 and early 1990. The growing opposition demanded the end of the one-party monopoly, the establishment of a multi-party system, and free elections. Responding to the demands, the Mongolian People's Revolutionary Party (MPRP) amended the Constitution to delete its leading role and created a presidential post and an additional, more representative legislative body. By mid-1990, political parties were legalized and an electoral law was passed, leading to general elections in July of that year.

The elections maintained MPRP domination while giving the opposition an important voice. A coalition government was formed by the MPRP in September 1990. The Prime Minister from the MPRP, D. Byambasuren, invited two people from the opposition to be Deputy Prime Ministers. The rest of the Council of Ministers was composed of MPRP members. This composition of the Cabinet was highly instrumental in pushing market-oriented reforms forward.

The new coalition government implemented a three-year programme which attempted to dismantle the command economy and lay the foundations of a market-based economy. A drastic change was chosen by the government. Liberalization of prices, privatization, and banking reform were made the top priorities of government policy which aimed to establish a market economy in the shortest possible period of time.

Although MPRP candidates captured over 80 per cent of the 430 seats in the People's Great Hural, only 13 per cent of the People's Hural deputies were re-elected, bringing about wholesale changes within the MPRP. The MPRP won 62 per cent of the votes for the Small Hural (Standing Legislature), giving it thirty-one of fifty seats. The three main opposition parties won the remaining nineteen seats. The Small Hural, as a standing legislative body, became the main vehicle for promoting the democratization and market-oriented reforms in the country. During its two-year term, the Small Hural passed a number of laws urgently needed to carry out the reforms.

In March 1991 the Small Hural adopted a package of laws which were designed to promote a market-oriented process in Mongolia. That package included the Company Law, Law on Privatization, Tax Law, Customs Law, and Law on Banking. The Company Law clarified how a company should be set up, registered, and liquidated, and specified the rights and responsibilities of its members. The Company Law covered private businesses, co-operatives, and corporations, although a special chapter on state-run enterprises was included. The Privatization Law, enacted in May 1991, declared that an investment voucher would be issued and given to every citizen of Mongolia in order to transfer state assets to private ownership. The Small Hural during its two-year term enacted altogether fifteen laws and twenty decrees related to the establishment of market relations. Although all of them cannot be considered to be perfect, they have played a crucial role in introducing the basic elements of a market system in a short period of time.

At the same time the activities of a coalition government, although supported by the Standing Legislature, were not always consistent in implementing the reform policy. It undertook a premature decentralization of the banking system; the consequent loss of control over the flow of credit contributed to upsurges in inflationary pressure that seriously undermined the government's efforts to decontrol prices and liberalize quantitative restrictions in commodity markets. The same thing occurred in the 1980s in China, Hungary, the former Soviet Union, and Poland (McKinnon 1993, p.7). However, it should be noted that the massive credit to private citizens provided by the Byambasuren government was like seed money for them and helped to nurture the first generation of 'new rich' in Mongolia.

Why did Mongolia elect to undertake drastic reform? First of all, the results of the first free elections in July 1990 which brought a coalition government to power showed a popular support for change. It was a golden opportunity for all reformists who were eager to implement radical economic transformation in order to make political reform irreversible before the process was hopelessly politicized. Second, the ever-deteriorating external trade terms and increasing reluctance of the former Soviet Union to be Mongolia's creditor further spurred radical reform. For Moscow- or Budapest-trained young leaders of new democratic parties, ideas like those of L. Balcerowicz in Poland promoting 'shock therapy' were much more attractive than the *doi moi* approach in Vietnam. However, it should be noted that there was not a common awareness of what radical reform actually meant, even within the coalition government; this lack of a common idea on reform certainly contributed to inconsistencies between the reform plans and their implementation in later stages. Third, the ineffectiveness of the modest reforms in 1987–89 led many to feel the need for decisive, radical changes.

The Anatomy of the Reforms

The basic concept of the reform plan was to first dismantle the centrally planned system and then proceed with the creation of a market economy. In other words, the philosophy was based on the following: because a centrally planned economic system fully contradicts a market system, any attempt to introduce market deregulation without removing the centrally planned system first would fail.

Price Liberalization

The first major move to liberalize prices was taken in January 1991, by government Resolution No. 20 which sought to reduce the number of centrally controlled prices. Price controls were retained in only thirty-five retail categories and thirty-six wholesale groups of goods and raw materials. Items covered under the price control system included approximately 60 per cent of total sales. In addition, for goods remaining under government control, retail prices were doubled and farm-gate prices on agricultural raw materials and products were increased from 132 to 380 per cent. The elimination of subsidies from the state budget, which was necessary because of the increasing budget deficit due to external shocks, was the most important reason for the increase in the prices of goods remaining under government control.

Resolution No. 20 was also designed to set some anti-inflationary measures and to ease the impact of the price increases on the population. Ceilings for most wholesale prices were introduced and were 7–71 per cent higher that those established by the government. Most wages were doubled to compensate for the price increases and bank accounts for small savers (with less than 10,000 tugriks) were also doubled. In 1991 the government also issued an anti-monopoly resolution to prevent the establishment of monopolistic prices with the price liberalization reforms. In addition, rationing of a broad range of agricultural and industrial products was put in place in January 1991. In September 1991 the prices of half of the remaining thirty-five commodities that were still under government control were liberalized. During 1992 price controls on a large number of goods were eliminated while the prices of those goods which were still under official control were raised significantly to reflect changes in the official exchange rate, the cost of inputs, and world prices. By March 1992 only nine prices were left under government control and farm-gate prices were freed. By December 1993 the government supplied only flour, bread, and meat through the rationing system, and all other goods such as sugar, rice, and tea which were still formally under the system were supplied by private businesses at market prices. In March 1993 the ration prices of flour, bread, and meat were raised to near-market levels. At the beginning of June 1993 the government announced that it had completed all planned measures to liberalize prices. Now the government maintains control over only the prices of urban public transportation in Ulaanbaatar, retail electricity, some fees for public utilities and services, and housing.

Thus, the price liberalization was undertaken gradually, with due regard for its impacts on the economy. However, the effectiveness of the action on production was limited by the continuing privatization process.

Privatization

The development of the private sector in a transitional economy implies both privatization and the promotion of new private-sector activities. In Mongolia, as well as other former CMEA countries where virtually all economic activities were undertaken by the state, priority in economic reform has been given to privatization. Such an approach could also be considered a part of the priority placed on dismantling the old system.

There are two components in Mongolia's privatization programme: (1) privatization of small enterprises, which include some 1,600 small businesses, mostly agricultural assets and livestock; and (2) privatization of large enterprises, which include about 340 large state-owned enterprises that are to be privatized completely and about 360 state-owned entities that are to be partially privatized. The total book value of these assets was estimated to be about 20 billion tugriks, while the financial savings of householders at the inception of the privatization programme amounted to less than 1 billion tugriks.

Therefore, a voucher system was selected to give every citizen an equal opportunity to participate in the privatization process. According to this system, each citizen receives a voucher with a face value of 10,000 tugriks. The total value of the national vouchers is about 20 billion tugriks, which corresponds approximately to the value of the assets to be privatized. Each voucher has two parts: a violet voucher for the purchase of small assets or for 'small' privatizations; and a blue voucher for the purchase of stocks of large companies or for 'large' privatizations. The violet vouchers can be freely traded, but the blue vouchers can be monetized only upon the opening of the secondary market (which was scheduled to be opened in 1994). At this time, shares purchased with the blue vouchers may be sold.

The privatization programme started in July 1991 with the distribution of the vouchers and was initially scheduled to be completed in mid-1993. At the present time, almost all of the small businesses scheduled to be privatized, including livestock, have been privatized. As a result of the 'small' privatization, about 70 per cent of all livestock and small shops and service units have been transferred to private ownership. Nevertheless, about 25 per cent of the violet vouchers continue to be held by the population and the government is planning to exchange these through housing privatization.

The 'large' privatization move began in October 1991 with the opening of the Stock Exchange and trading of shares in companies for vouchers. By mid-1994 about 75 per cent of all assets to be privatized through 'large' privatizations had been privatized and the government expected to complete the programme by the end of the year. Thus, it could be concluded that the extensive privatization programme has been successful at distributing shares of companies to the citizens. There is no doubt that the privatization programme provided incentives and, coupled with trade liberalization, helped to develop market forces in the economy, especially in trade.

However, the impact of privatization on the economy as a whole, and growth of production in particular, has been less than expected. In our opinion, the rather insubstantial impact of privatization reflects the privatization scheme adopted and the lack of effectiveness of the newly introduced macroeconomic policy tools. In particular, while the vouchers were distributed, because of the wide dispersion of ownership, there was no single dominant owner in most cases. Also, the government has become the dominant shareholder of about half of the privatized companies, in particular, the largest and most influential companies. The management of these companies has not improved notably and some of them still incur losses and are able to continue operations only because of bank loans. Therefore, these companies respond only weakly to changes in the macroeconomic environment and together with the weak administrative control make newly introduced macroeconomic tools less effective.

Fiscal Reform

In a centrally planned, command economy, taxes and other instruments of fiscal policy play a secondary role in macroeconomic management since the state budget accounts for a large part of overall economic activities. Major shares of the national product are distributed through the state budget. In 1989, for example, Mongolia's state budget revenue equalled 60.6 per cent of produced national income (which was 49 per cent of GDP), while the budget expenditure equalled 81.7 per cent of produced national income and 65.8 per cent of GDP. However, as stated earlier, until the end of 1988, Mongolia's budgetary deficit, which amounted to nearly 20 per cent of GDP, was fully financed by the USSR through concessionary credits. Notably, this financing was counted as revenue (see Appendix Tables 9.3 and 9.4). However, with the slow-down and final cessation of Soviet aid in subsequent years, it became extremely difficult to finance the budget deficit. Therefore, to reduce the budget deficit the government sharply cut back its expenditure.

Expenditure Reduction

Expenditures that were related directly to business activities of economic entities, such as price subsidies and investment financing, were cut first. Drastic measures were taken in 1991–92, including the slow-down or complete stoppage of several large construction projects, the elimination of most price subsidies, and the sharp cut in subsidies and transfers to non-profit organizations. Capital expenditures were cut by 30 per cent (World Bank 1993). As a result, total budgetary expenditures were reduced by nearly 20 per cent in 1991 and more than 60 per cent in 1992 in real terms as compared to 1989. In 1993, however, expenditures began to increase, to about 26 per cent of 1989 expenditures in real terms.

The composition of expenditures also changed in 1991–93, reflecting the shift in government policy. The share of 'subsidies and transfers' and 'goods and services' in the total budget expenditure declined from about 25 per cent to 15 per cent and from 63 per cent to 51 per cent, respectively, in 1993 as compared to 1990. However, the share of capital expenditure more than doubled, mostly due to the increase in net lending.

Through the above measures, the government significantly reduced its expenditures; but clearly this was not a factor that promoted economic recovery. Since mid-1993, and especially in 1994, the above policy on budget expenditures has undergone some changes. Budgetary outlays connected with the government's social role, such as expenditures on social security, health, and education, are being rationalized. At the beginning of 1994, a health insurance system based on employer and employee contributions was introduced. In July 1994 the parliament passed a Social Security Law which instituted employee contributions to the pension scheme and set minimum retirement ages. Notwithstanding the above efforts, the budge expenditure still exceeds revenue.

Revenue Creation and Reform of the Tax System

The pre-reform Mongolian Government had two major revenue sources: taxes on corporate income and profits of state enterprises and co-operatives, and turnover taxes. The former consisted mainly of three elements: transfers of gross profits to a capital fund, a science and development fund, and a budgetary commission. In principle, each enterprise had its own tax rate. On average, enterprises paid taxes equivalent to 60–70 per cent of their profits. There were also several taxes on the income of individuals from selected activities.

The second major source of budget revenue, turnover taxes, amounted to 45 per cent of the total revenue and 90 per cent of tax revenues. Turnover taxes had two components: the import price differential, representing the difference between the import contract price and the fixed domestic wholesale price of the imported goods, and domestic turnover taxes. The share of revenue from import price differentials in the budget averaged about 35 per cent during 1980–89, but its volume declined during the 1980s because of increases in import prices.

Both of the above taxes were replaced by a more market-oriented system with the adoption of the Tax Law in 1991. The Tax Law established income tax rates ranging from 8 to 38 per cent. Taxable income included depreciation and wages, with special exemptions and deductions for certain types of enterprises. The 1991 Tax Law and Customs Law replaced the import price differentials with a customs duty at a uniform rate of 15 per cent.

Thus, the 1991 tax reform was intended to ease the tax burden on businesses and reduce government control. This change led to a decline in tax revenue. In addition, the change coincided with the collapse of the economy, which exacerbated the decline in tax revenues. As a result, tax revenues declined by nearly 65 per cent in 1992 as compared with 1989.

In December 1992 Mongolia's parliament passed a new package of tax laws: the General Tax Law, the Personal Income Tax Law, the Company Tax Law, the Sales Tax Law, and the Excise Tax Law. The package of tax laws specified twelve taxes and introduced four new taxes, among which the most important was a 10 per cent sales tax on domestically manufactured goods and imports. All excise taxes were converted to *ad valorem* rates. The Company Tax Law made labour and depreciation costs deductible from taxable income, and reduced the number of tax brackets and the ceilings of annual taxable income of each bracket. For instance, the marginal taxable income for the lowest bracket was reduced more than 300 per cent, but the tax rate was doubled. This change affected small businesses more severely, because the law established that the total amount of taxes paid should not exceed 40 per cent of taxable income. The 1993 tax reform thus became a factor which encouraged the consolidation of economic entities due to the tax rate ceiling. In November 1993 an amendment which tripled the marginal taxable income for all brackets, the Company Tax Law, was adopted. In general, the 1993 revision of the tax system attempted to broaden the tax base through the introduction of new taxes as well as a reduction in tax exemptions; the result was a doubling of tax revenue.

Nevertheless, the tax system reform has affected the government's budget revenue and overall economic development less than the increase in revenue from other sources, in particular from foreign sources. The tax revenue declined during 1990–93 more than total revenue: in real terms, approximately 22 per cent and 14 per cent, respectively. The share of the tax revenue in the total budget revenue declined from 86.5 per cent in 1991 to 75.4 per cent in 1993.

Financial Sector Reform

Prior to 1991, Mongolia's financial sector was based on a mono-bank system. The State Bank was empowered to carry out both central banking functions and commercial banking activities. Monetary policy, in general, consisted of allocating credit according to an annual credit plan so as to ensure the attainment of output and investment objectives. With the elimination of the state planning system and the liberalization of business activities and prices, the role of monetary and credit policies increased significantly. However, it is notable that the above reforms were undertaken when the financial system was not reformed and monetary tools were unable to play a significant role as macroeconomic policy instruments.

The initial step in financial sector reform centred on shifting from a mono-bank system to a two-tiered one. In May 1991 the new Banking Law legalized a two-tiered banking system. In accordance with the law, the State Bank was divided into two parts: (1) a central bank, called the Mongolbank, which is independent from the government; and (2) the commercial banking activities of the State Bank were transferred to seven commercial banks that were formerly State Bank departments. The Mongolbank's mandate is to implement monetary policy with the goal of maintaining the value of the domestic currency, provide settlement services for commercial banks, regulate commercial banks, and manage Mongolia's international reserves. In accordance with the law, bank lending and deposit rates have been freely determined by commercial banks with given guide-lines.

Since mid-1991, the Mongolbank has been tightening monetary and credit policies in order to contain inflation and improve financial discipline. Initially, the Mongolbank applied cash reserve requirements to non-bank deposit liabilities of commercial banks in

September 1991. In 1992 these requirements were reviewed and increased twice. The interest rate on the Mongolbank's overdraft facility was raised several times and in October 1992 it reached 160-214 per cent, making the real interest rate positive in terms of the official inflation rate. Also the Mongolbank has set direct regulations in banking activities such as the establishment of minimum interest rates on time deposits since November 1992 and quantitative ceiling commercial bank lending to non-banks since December 1992.

The development of indirect monetary management instruments remains an important element in banking reform. In 1991, 300 million tugriks of government bonds were issued, but the bonds carried only an 8 per cent interest rate and therefore did not have much of an impact. In late 1993 central bank bills were issued which were expected to become the principal instrument to regulate bank liquidity.

The above measures influenced commercial banks' interest rates and credit demand. Notwithstanding fluctuations in money aggregates during 1991–93 which were influenced by various economic and political factors, the interest rate has shown remarkable stability since the last quarter of 1993. In June 1994 there was a small decline in the commercial bank lending rate.

As a result of the tight monetary policy, inflation has slowed. The monthly average rate of inflation was 12.8 per cent in 1992, and in 1993 it was 9.1 per cent, despite the adoption in June 1993 of a floating exchange rate system. Nonetheless, the high interest rate has delayed investment activities. Therefore, taking into account the contractionary orientation of Mongolia's tax policy, it can be stated that the most important issues for monetary policy presently are the determination of policy objectives in connection with other policies and forecasting their impacts on the economy.

External Sector Reform

Until the beginning of the 1990s, all international operations of economic entities were under the government's control. Trade among the CMEA countries was conducted on the basis of five-year government-to-government trade agreements. To conclude the agreements, the government negotiated bilaterally for the quantity of the items to be exchanged annually during the five-year period and the general terms of trade. During the five-year period, annual government-to-government trade protocols were signed specifying the details of the commitments agreed to in the five-year agreements and fixing the trade prices, although the latter could be changed as an exemption. Under the five-year government and annual protocols, each government was to be responsible for delivering the agreed amount of items at the agreed prices to its trading partner. To fulfil its commitments, the Mongolian Government prepared plans for enterprises to produce and deliver to the foreign-trade enterprises specified amounts of certain items. Only foreign-trade enterprises were authorized to conduct foreign-trade operations. Seven foreign-trade enterprises were established for trade with CMEA countries, of which one specialized in export operations and the others in import operations.

Transferable rubles, which were not convertible and not acceptable for internal trade operations in a CMEA country, were used for payments of trade operations. The exchange rate between the tugrik and the transferable ruble was set by the State Bank through negotiations with the International Bank for Economic Co-operation (IBEC). The earnings of the export enterprises were recorded in the country's account with the IBEC and the export enterprises obtained their equivalent in tugriks. Import enterprises bought transferable rubles at the negotiated exchange rate, but within limits established by the plan.

A separate system was used for trade with non-CMEA countries. Trade with China, the Democratic Republic of Korea, and Yugoslavia was conducted through a bilateral clearing system. In the case of trade with a convertible currency area, the foreign company negotiated with the appropriate Mongolian state trading enterprise. Because Mongolia's external trade was conducted largely within the CMEA market, there were only two state trading enterprises operating for the purpose of conducting trade with non-socialist countries. The foreign currency earnings of these enterprises were sold to the State Bank at the exchange rate set by the latter, and these enterprises were allowed to buy convertible currencies from the Bank according to a centralized plan.

Under these circumstances, the foreign-trade enterprises were not able to balance trade operations so the balance-of-payments situation was set up beforehand at the government level. Within the framework of the modest reforms of the late 1980s, some large enterprises were allowed to handle foreign trade. The new Law of State Enterprises implemented in 1989 eliminated monopolies enjoyed by state foreign-trade enterprises. A Law of Foreign Investment was passed at the same time. A new foreign exchange retention scheme was also adopted under which foreign exchange earned by enterprises above state orders could be retained by them.

After 1990 the reform process was extended and under the Company Law adopted in 1991 all businesses, irrespective of ownership, were allowed to handle foreign trade. The government exercised export licensing in 1991–92, but continuously reduced the categories of items covered. At present only about ten categories of items are subject to licensing, most of which are for cultural, conservation, or security reasons. A certificate of registration is required to export goods. There are no export taxes or minimum prices established for exports. All imports are subject to a uniform customs duty of 15 per cent. However, exemptions are in place for thirty-three categories. Import prohibition and licensing apply only to categories for health and security reasons.

All foreign-trade operations are conducted, in principle, at world prices on the basis of convertible currencies. There are no restrictions on the use of foreign currencies for that purpose. The official barter trade agreements with Russia and China were abolished in April 1994, and similar agreements with Afghanistan and the former Socialist Republic of Yugoslavia are currently inactive.

The foreign exchange retention scheme has since been reviewed and under a Foreign Currency Law, effective from May 1994, all foreign exchange earned by economic entities may be retained and used for any purpose without restriction. However, foreign exchange surrender requirements are currently still applicable for a few public enterprises.

The reform of the foreign exchange regime was the most complicated part of the transition because of the heavy external dependence of the economy. Therefore the government transformed the regime gradually, through a series of devaluations of the tugrik. In June 1990 the first devaluation occurred which resulted in the exchange rate falling from 3 tugriks = US$1 to 40 tugriks = US$1, as the commercial rate, and 7.1 tugriks = US$1 as the rate for barter trade. In January 1993 these rates were unified and established as 150 tugriks = US$1. In May 1993 a floating exchange rate was adopted and the interbank market for foreign exchange was established. This led to immediate price changes because the new, market-defined exchange rate devalued the tugrik by almost 200 per cent. However, the exchange rate was stabilized and sharp price increases were avoided. The stabilization of the official rate close to the rate in the parallel market of about 400 tugriks is considered a sign of the improved macroeconomic conditions in the economy. The exchange rate is currently set on the basis of foreign exchange transactions, in which the central bank acts as an intermediary to match bids and offers made by banks.

The Foreign Investment Law was renewed in June 1993 with more liberal provisions on ownership, and simplified administrative procedures for registration and approval of new investment. Thus, all areas of economic activity involving overseas business were liberalized through the lifting of government control. Thus, the basic instruments of external sector management that are appropriate in a market economy were introduced in principle.

Impact of Reforms

The coalition government faced very serious problems because of drastically changed internal and external factors during this period. With the modest reforms taken in the mid-1980s to improve economic management and reduce central control, the government drew on its contingency reserves at the State Bank in 1989, causing a 10.5 per cent increase in the amount of currency in circulation. The situation deteriorated further in 1990 and early 1991, and real economic growth is estimated to have decreased over that period.

More importantly, at the end of the 1980s, the Soviet Union was no longer willing to be Mongolia's sole creditor. As stated earlier, Soviet credits played a dominant role in the pre-reform Mongolian economy.

Further, the elimination of the CMEA trade regime in January 1991 had dire impacts on the Mongolian economy, leading to a substantial decline in both the volume and value of Mongolia's foreign trade. In November 1990 Mongolia and the Soviet Union reached an agreement to value trade and to effect settlement in convertible currencies beginning in 1991. With the adoption of world prices for exports and imports, prices of most export commodities dropped while import prices rose. For instance, the price of copper, Mongolia's principal export, fell by 21 per cent relative to the price of petroleum products. The decline in the purchasing power of Mongolian exports is estimated to have been US$70–80 million or 6–7 per cent of the country's GDP. Since Mongolia's imports of petroleum from the Soviet Union accounted for 35 per cent of Mongolia's total exports in 1990, the changing prices had a severe negative impact on the trade balance of the country. There were also many cases of non-delivery of petroleum products, spare parts, and other imported inputs from Russia because both Mongolia and Russia required that payment be made in convertible currency, which neither side had.

Declining Production

The impact of the dramatic reforms on the Mongolian economy was thus unclear. There are various factors, including the external shocks caused by the termination of financial assistance from the USSR and CMEA countries and the deterioration in Mongolia's terms of trade which certainly exerted a drastic impact on the Mongolian economic activities. Together all of these factors led to clearly a sharp decline in the output of the Mongolian economy in the early 1990s (see Table 9.2).

As shown in Table 9.3, the fall in industrial output continued into 1993. The drop in some sectors had been so large that they were close to collapsing. Sectors more dependent on the import of inputs — for instance, building materials, metalworking, textile, glass industries, and construction — declined more than others, reflecting the impact of the severe external changes. The smallest declines were in the livestock sector not only because it was less import-dependent, but also because of the greater ability of small entities to adapt in a market environment than large enterprises.

Consequently, if liberalization is undertaken initially in sectors where small businesses dominate, then the reduction in overall economic activities caused by the reform process may be lessened.

TABLE 9.2
Index of Main Indicators of the Mongolian Economy, 1990–93
(1989=100)

Indicator	1990	1991	1992	1993
GDP	97.5	88.5	67.7	—
Per capita GNP	94.7	84.5	67.7	—
Gross industrial output	94.3	80.1	75.6	65.8
Gross agricultural output	96.3	89.1	83.8	80.3
Gross volume of construction work	90.9	69.2	17.2	—
Foreign trade turnover	94.1	42.1	47.9	—
Inflation rate (January 1991=100)	—	152.7	649.8	1,838.7
Unemployment rate (percentage at year end)	5.5	6.5	6.3	8.7

Source: State Statistical Office, Mongolia.

TABLE 9.3
Index of Industrial and Agricultural Output in
Mongolia by Sectors, 1990–93
(1989=100)

Sector	1990	1991	1992	1993
Industrial, Total	94.3	80.1	75.6	65.8
Energy	99.5	97.2	90.8	88.6
Fuel	89.0	87.4	77.6	100.7
Metalworking	84.8	63.0	72.0	5.1
Non-ferrous metals	100.8	74.4	88.6	217.2
Building materials	96.4	60.8	40.0	7.2
Wood processing	82.3	75.0	47.1	11.9
Textiles	89.9	73.0	57.4	29.9
Clothing	90.7	78.2	29.4	12.3
Leather, fur, and shoes	104.5	87.4	63.2	29.1
Printing	86.5	85.2	51.0	15.1
Glass and china	82.6	65.8	52.4	7.3
Food	91.6	86.6	55.0	47.2
Chemicals	94.7	81.7	—	60.1
Gross Agricultural Output	96.3	89.1	83.8	80.3
Livestock	100.0	99.7	97.4	92.8
Crop farming	87.3	64.8	52.6	51.5

Source: State Statistical Office, Mongolia.

It was expected that price liberalization would favour growth of output because the new, more realistic prices which emerged as a result of price liberalization would stimulate producers, although it might accelerate inflation. Instead, the economy responded to price liberalization with high rates of inflation and a decline in output. The main reason for such a response is, obviously, an increase in import prices of critical inputs. Further, mostly due to expectations of upcoming privatizations, the management of state-owned enterprises did not respond to price liberalization by making efforts to increase production or restructure enterprises.

Inflation

The drastic reform in the Mongolian economy, based on a philosophy of breaking down the existing economic structure in order to build a new one, influenced production and other economic activities more negatively than it did positively. The first visible consequence of the overall dismantling of the state planning system, and the trade and price liberalization efforts, was a decline in production and acceleration of inflation (see Appendix Table 9.5).

The acceleration of inflation was also stimulated by other actions, such as the elimination of price subsidies, a devaluation of the national currency, a wage doubling and subsequent elimination of wage control, and an increase in money in circulation. It is interesting to note that while the main reason for the January 1991 doubling of retail prices was to adjust prices closer to world prices, in fact, together with other measures, this increase in retail prices gave impetus to the inflation process. For example, personal saving deposits above 10,000 tugriks and bank balances of all economic entities were not doubled. This was intended to have an anti-inflationary effect but instead caused a mass money outflow from the bank, partly owing to the absence of a flexible interest rate mechanism. In addition, the loans made to private persons and co-operatives for the purpose of promoting private-sector development stimulated inflation because a considerable amount of these loans were monetized and, moreover, subsequently became bad loans.

Nevertheless, inflation is an inevitable process in transitional economies, reflecting the distortions and imbalances created by a centrally planned system. In the case of Mongolia, the inflation was also a reflection of the shrinking of surplus aggregate demand that had been supported by external sources.

The external shock which arose with the collapse of the CMEA system immediately affected the financing of the budget deficit and, as a consequence, required a cutback in budget expenditures. The budget deficit was covered, especially in 1990 and 1991, by increases in the money supply, thus leading to inflationary movements. Currency in circulation more than doubled in 1991 as well as in 1993, as compared to the annual average rate of 9 per cent during 1985–90 (see Table 9.4).

Under these circumstances, anti-inflationary measures became the top priority of the stabilization policy. It included a tight monetary policy strengthened by the creation of institutions of money management as well as a fiscal policy that was targeted towards reducing the budget deficit. As a result, the rate of inflation slowed down notably and for the first half of 1994, averaged 3.7 per cent. However, a tight monetary policy coupled with a contractionary fiscal policy implemented for a relatively long period of time can become a factor which delays the recovery of the economy.

TABLE 9.4
Mongolia's Money Development, 1989–94

	1989	1990	1991	1992	1993	1994 (31 March)
Currency in circulation (millions of tugrik)	581.1	742.7	2,003.0	2,896.4	10,786.1	13,655.6
Annual change (percentage)	110.5	127.8	269.7	144.6	372.4	126.6
Domestic credit (millions of tugrik)	7,953.1	8,418.6	12,854.2	19,129.9	31,603.7	36,404.5
Annual change (percentage)	99.5	105.9	152.7	148.8	165.2	115.2

Source: Mongolbank.

Economic Structure

The drastic changes in the economic environment created by the reform changed the structure of the economy (see Table 9.5). In a sense, it could be said that there has been a movement towards 'de-industrialization'. The share of agriculture doubled during the last three years with declining shares occurring for other sectors. A modest decline of agricultural output in comparison with other sectors caused an increase in its share of gross output of the economy. The decline of 19.7 per cent in agriculture in 1993 as compared with 1989 is explained by a reduced dependency of its main subsector, livestock, on external factors.

Changes in industrial production follow the same direction as those of the overall economic structure. Table 9.6 shows that because of the larger decline in the output of the manufacturing subsectors, the share of primary subsectors rose significantly. In particular, the non-ferrous metals subsector, which largely involves the mining of copper ore, increased its share of total industrial output from 9.1 per cent in 1989 to 37.7 per cent in 1993.

TABLE 9.5
Composition of Mongolia's Gross Social Product, 1989–92
(In percentages, at current prices)

Sector	1989	1990	1991	1992
Total	100.0	100.0	100.0	100.0
Industry	48.0	48.9	46.9	45.4
Agriculture	15.4	15.7	16.7	30.7
Construction	11.5	9.9	6.9	3.5
Transport and communications	10.7	10.6	9.0	7.9
Trade	13.4	13.8	19.6	10.9
Others	1.0	1.1	0.9	1.6

Source: State Statistical Office, Mongolia.

TABLE 9.6
Composition of Mongolia's Industrial Output, 1989–93
(In percentages)

Sector	1989	1990	1991	1992	1993
Industry, Total	100.0	100.0	100.0	100.0	100.0
Energy	13.5	13.2	13.0	13.4	15.7
Fuel	3.6	3.2	3.5	3.9	5.8
Metalworking	3.0	2.9	1.7	1.2	2.3
Non-ferrous metals	9.1	9.9	10.8	17.8	37.7
Building materials	8.8	9.0	4.9	2.7	1.2
Wood processing	5.5	5.0	4.1	3.2	1.3
Textiles	10.4	10.8	9.8	10.8	5.5
Clothing	4.4	4.5	4.6	2.0	0.9
Leather, fur, and shoes	10.6	10.9	13.9	13.1	4.2
Printing	0.9	0.9	0.8	0.6	0.2
Glass and china	0.4	0.3	0.3	0.2	0.1
Food	24.6	24.1	27.3	24.4	13.4
Chemicals	3.9	3.7	2.0	2.3	3.8

Source: State Statistical Office, Mongolia.

Trade

The above changes are also reflected in the export structure of Mongolia. The commodity composition of exports has undergone significant change although copper concentrate, cashmere, and leather products remain the main Mongolian exports. However, the direction of change is opposite of that in the 1980s. At the beginning of the 1980s, agricultural raw materials, including wool, hides, and skins, accounted for the largest share of total exports, while in 1989 minerals contributed the largest share of total exports. Also, the export volume of manufactured consumer goods such as cashmere, camel wool knitwear, leather goods, and carpets increased in the 1980s. In contrast, exports of these products dropped sharply during 1990–92, while exports of most raw materials increased (see Table 9.7).

Nevertheless, the composition of imports did not change notably during the 1990–93 period compared to the past decade, excluding

TABLE 9.7
Principal Exports of Mongolia, 1990–92

	Unit	1990	1991	1992	Ratio of 1992 Exports to 1990 Exports (percentage)
Copper concentrate	'000 tons	261.9	201.5	261.5	99.8
Molybdenum concentrate	tons	2,931.7	1,661.3	1,925.7	65.7
Fluorite concentrate	'000 tons	85.7	96.1	86.5	100.9
Sawn wood	'000 cu.m.	22.8	—	41.8	183.3
Intestine	'000 rolls	1,325.8	237.0	2,252.1	170.0
Sheep skins	'000 pieces	125.0	—	565.9	452.7
Washed wool	tons	1,923.7	121.6	997.0	51.8
Cashmere	tons	311.1	71.8	676.0	217.3
Cashmere tops and dehaired	tons	27.0	24.4	83.0	307.4
Cashmere knitwear	'000 pieces	217.0	—	23.4	10.8
Sheepskin coats	'000 pieces	56.6	81.7	21.9	38.7
Leather goods	'000 pieces	87.0	—	70.1	80.6
Carpets	'000 sq.m.	1,355.7	27.0	218.6	16.1

Source: State Statistical Office, Mongolia.

the slight increase in the share of petroleum and petroleum products and the decrease in the share of industrial raw materials. As a result of these changes, the trade balance deficit declined and in the first quarter of 1993, Mongolia registered a trade surplus. Also, international reserves rose slightly in 1993 after a significant decline during 1990–92.

The open-economy policy and the new trade regime resulted in notable shifts in the direction of trade of the country (see Table 9.8). Although Russia remains the major trading partner of Mongolia, trade volume with China is increasing rapidly. Within a span of two years, China became Mongolia's second-largest trading partner. China's share of Mongolia's imports increased from 1.2 per cent in 1989 to 21.2 per cent in 1993. Oil and spare parts are the principal imports from Russia while consumer goods are the main import items from China. Mongolia's main exports to these two countries also differ: agricultural raw materials to China and consumer goods to Russia. Japanese exports to Mongolia are increasing rapidly, placing Japan third among Mongolia's trading partners.

TABLE 9.8
Mongolia's Direction of Trade
(As a percentage of total exports and total imports)

	Exports		Imports	
	1989	1992	1989	1992
Total	100.0	100.0	100.0	100.0
Former CMEA countries	91.3	61.6	96.7	55.6
Former USSR	76.9	57.8	87.1	52.8
Northeast Asian countries				
China	0.4	17.0	1.2	12.3
Japan	3.0	5.1	0.5	10.1
South Korea	—	0.5	—	2.0
EC countries	0.7	8.2	0.7	8.4
United States	0.2	1.1	—	0.4
Others	4.4	6.5	0.9	11.2

Sources: Data provided by Mongolian authorities.

It is widely acknowledged that a rapid move to free trade could instigate a widespread collapse of domestic manufacturing — no matter how the exchange rate is set, and no matter that part of this sector might eventually be viable at world market prices (McKinnon 1993, p.9). In Mongolia the centralized state-trading company was dismantled in 1990 and hundreds of individual enterprises were authorized to negotiate their own foreign trade contracts. This change was made before domestic commodity prices were rationalized and decontrolled, and before the system of multiple exchange rates was unified. In such a chaotic situation, with hundreds of inexperienced traders, it is not surprising that foreign trade was not handled efficiently.

Employment

The economic slowdown naturally led to greater unemployment and a sharp drop in the living standards of the population. As a centrally planned, command economy, Mongolia had not previously experienced open unemployment. Thus until 1991 official unemployment data referred to the number of people not employed in the state and co-operative sectors, which was negligible. Since 1991 the official data refer to the number of registered, unemployed persons, which increased from 45,700 at the beginning of 1991 to 73,600 in June 1994, resulting in an unemployment rate of 6.6 per cent and 8.7 per cent, respectively. However, it should be noted that the data understate the problem because a number of persons seeking jobs do not register. Nevertheless, self-employment opportunities, in particular private trading businesses, have eased the problem to some degree. In the near future, however, considerable growth in unemployment is expected as a result of the limited possibilities associated with the expansion of self-employment and the increasing active-age population.

Currently, about 25 per cent of the population has an income lower than the officially announced minimum level of standard of living. Health and education indicators are worsening. On the whole, the economy's decline continues to cause a reduction in the living standards of the population.

Prognosis on Future Development of the Reform

The major result of the reform undertaken in Mongolia is the removal of the centrally planned system of economic management and the introduction of basic elements of macroeconomic management inherent in a market economy (see Table 9.9). The macroeconomic policy tools which were adopted during the reform period are becoming more effective. However, the economy is still in a recession and signs of recovery remain weak. One key factor that has delayed the recovery and which is becoming the most urgent problem of the reform is enterprise reform. As discussed earlier, privatization did not result in significant development of private ownership and, because of this, the behaviour of the largest enterprises has been difficult to manage with common macroeconomic tools.

Therefore, one of the objectives of the reform for the future is the completion of the privatization programme with the current, voucher-based scheme and the fostering of greater efficiency in privatized entities, especially in the improvement of their management. The government had intended to complete the privatization of the economic entities by the end of 1994 and then start the sales of housing units in Ulaanbaatar. The government plans to retain full ownership of no more than thirty entities upon completion of the privatization programme. Nevertheless, the management of privatized economic entities could be improved significantly after the emergence of the 'real owners' through sales of shares in the secondary market. Towards this end, the opening of the secondary market would have an important impact not only on financial development and ownership, but also on enterprise management. A Security Law was expected to be enacted at the end of 1994 during the parliamentary session.

Another factor which will influence the reform process is the structure of the economy. As was described earlier, the existing structure of the economy is inefficient and without structural changes any reform of economic management will have limited impact. In the above respect, support for increases in investment which could lead to recovery of the economy has become the basic objective of the present reform. Structural measures must be implemented which will increase investment, mobilize greater domestic savings, and encourage the expansion in exports, together with the development of legal and institutional reforms. These measures could include increasing public investment, especially to develop infrastructure and export potential, and encouraging private investment in the government investment programme through development of various forms of partnership. Measures also have to be taken to promote foreign direct investment.

TABLE 9.9
Pace and Sequence of the Economic Reform in Mongolia

Policy Areas	Date of Introduction	Implementation
A. Deregulation		
Price liberalization	January 1991 –June 1993	Completed
Foreign investment	1990, 1993	Revised
Privatization	1991–94	Voucher one programme is nearly completed
Banking	1991	Two-tiered system was introduced
B. Trade liberalization		
Company law	1991	All units allowed to handle foreign trade
Import tariff	1991	Uniform 15 per cent tax introduced
Export taxes	1991	Licensing in very narrow areas
C. Stabilization		
Fiscal policy		
Tax reform	1992	Progressive taxation was introduced
Control of public expenditure	1982–92	Reduced by half in real terms
Monetary policy		
Money supply	1990–91	Imperfect control
Credit to public sector	1991–94	Controlled
Exchange rate policy		
Devaluation	June 1990	
Unification of the exchange rate	January 1993	
Floating exchange rate	June 1993	

However, any action to expand public investment should be reviewed in conjunction with its possible consequences on financial development and budgetary realities. Also, efforts to develop the monetary system should focus on the development of indirect monetary instruments and rationalization of interest rates.

In our opinion, a number of political factors appear to have slowed down the reform process, notwithstanding its optimistic expectations. In particular, the government has been strongly criticized by the opposition, which led a hunger strike in March 1994. With the reform measures attacking high inflation, other problems such as the growing unemployment and the increasing gap between the rich and the poor have emerged; this has resulted in a nostalgia about the old, happy days when everyone had an equal share of public goods — a sentiment that is becoming apparent to the government. Responding to the demands of some urban segments, the Mongolian Government appeared to be reforming less enthusiastically and from time to time making difficult choices concerning the pace of reform and the distribution of adjustment costs.

The effectiveness of the reform as a whole will depend to a large degree on social development. Measures should be taken to reform the social safety net, increase social benefits to the vulnerable groups, support self-employment and job training, and enhance human resource development.

Agriculture

The major agricultural activities in Mongolia are animal husbandry and crop farming. Livestock is the dominant sector, representing 70 per cent of agricultural value added and accounting for 94 per cent of land use based on extensive semi-nomadic grazing. The remaining 6 per cent of the agricultural land is cultivated and crop production accounts for about 44 per cent of total exports, which consist mostly of livestock products. The main agricultural exports are meat, leather goods, camel wool, and cashmere.

Limits on private herd ownership were partially relaxed in 1987 and eliminated in 1990. The state farms and pastoral co-operatives

were privatized under the small-scale privatization programme
adopted in 1991. By late 1993, over 95 per cent of the national herd
was in private hands. Most of the state farms were broken up into
smaller production units specializing in a single crop. The high
degree of industrial concentration in Mongolia, where several lines
of products have only a single outlet — for example, the single dairy,
flour mill, or slaughterhouse in a large city — has compounded the
problems of privatization. As of mid-1993, state orders had officially
been eliminated for all products except meat, where they applied
to only about half the volume affected in 1992. Government control
over distribution of goods has shrunk as all bans on private exports
of agricultural products have been lifted.

Pending the passage of a land law, all farm land remains state
property. The possibility of long-term leasehold is being considered
for crop land. Delay in passing the land law has created uncertainty
about land use rights. Pastoral land, probably, will remain under
state ownership, although consideration is being given to charging
usage or grazing fees.

Manufacturing

Manufacturing in Mongolia is characterized by (1) outdated
equipment, technology, and management practices; (2) industrial
concentration where a small number of large enterprises account for
all or most of the output; and (3) dense location in the three largest
cities. At the end of 1990, there were more than 400 large public
enterprises, most of which were incurring losses.

Mongolia's manufacturing subsector is inefficient and heavily
dependent on imported inputs. The capital/output ratio steadily
increased between 1940 and 1990, indicating the capital-intensive
nature of investment. While this policy might once have been desirable
to import technology, the present number of uncompetitive enterprises
and their low productivity suggest that past investment has not
always been efficient. Since the productivity of key export industries
influences the efficiency of the economy as a whole, this is a source
of concern. In order to compete internationally, Mongolian industries
will need to improve their efficiency and cost-effectiveness.

Energy

Electricity, generated with domestically mined coal and imported diesel fuel, is the principal source of energy in Mongolia and is produced by two distinct systems. The Central Electricity System (CES), fed by five coal-fired thermal power stations, supplies electricity to the three main cities and to six *aimaks* (provinces) where 50 per cent of the population resides. The CES is connected to the Russian grid by a 220 kv line to Irkutsk. Supply in the remaining twelve *aimaks* is decentralized. Two projects are being identified as priorities for specific long-term investments. The Egiin Hydropower project in north-central Mongolia is one option under consideration, providing Mongolia its first peak-load capacity plant. The second option involves three *aimaks* in western Mongolia — Uvs, Hovd, and Bayan-Olgii — which were originally planned to be supplied by a transmission line from Krasnoyarsk in Russia.

Mining

Mongolia is well-endowed with mineral resources, with over 600 known deposits and more than eighty types of minerals. Large-scale operation is concentrated in the mining of copper, coal, fluorspar, and molybdenum. Silver, gold, tin, tungsten, and precious stones are also mined in small-scale operations. There are also 170 deposits of construction materials, such as granite and marble, some of which are extracted.

Coal is the primary energy source for electricity production and the most intensely mined in Mongolia. The fourteen open-pit mines account for 95 per cent of total supply, with the two largest mines at Baga Nuur (4 million tons annually) and Sharyn Gol (1.6 million tons annually) accounting for over 70 per cent of total output. The government is seeking foreign investment to support major expansion of the three largest existing mines, as well as the development of a new coking-coal deposit (Tavan tolgoi) believed to have an annual production capacity of 20 million tons.

The Mongol–Russian copper venture at Erdenet is Mongolia's largest industry and the source of close to half the country's foreign exchange earnings. Until recently, it produced exclusively for the Russian market and was dependent on Russian sources for spare parts and energy. With small shipments to Japan in 1991, market diversification has already begun. However, the complex faces increasing transport and grinding costs, coupled with an expected deterioration in its copper concentrate grade. Survival is unlikely without managerial improvements and new technology.

Other non-ferrous metals also offer attractive new investment opportunities in Mongolia. A recent study lists nineteen specific mineral deposits or groups as warranting further investigation. A widely held view is that gold offers the most favourable near-term prospects and could rapidly increase its share in Mongolia's mineral exports above the present 4 per cent.

Petroleum

Mongolia currently produces no petroleum, importing all of its needs almost exclusively from Russia. Imports of petroleum products have been decreasing sharply since 1990, but still require about 25 per cent of the country's export earnings. Two oilfields are known to exist in the East Gobi basin of southwestern Mongolia; one of these was developed during the 1940s but was abandoned in the 1960s.

The Mongolian Petroleum Company (MPC) was formed in 1990 with the objective of attracting foreign investment to develop production not only to meet domestic demand but also for export. Two related studies have been carried out with American technical assistance: (1) an appraisal of oil and gas resources and the financial attractiveness of oil exploration; and (2) an evaluation of Mongolia's petroleum law with recommendations to improve the climate for investment in the sector.

The MPC, in co-operation with Exploration Associates as technical adviser, formulated a petroleum law that was ratified in February 1991. Regulations for implementing the law and a model form of a production-sharing contract were subsequently drafted and adopted. Petroleum exploration contract areas within Mongolia were then delineated and designated. The areas were open for application as Round One commenced on 1 May 1991.

To conclude, Mongolia has some impressive assets which could greatly contribute to its development, including:

1. an abundance of mineral resources;
2. broad opportunities to utilize solar and wind energy;
3. the fact that it is a young nation, with 75 per cent of the people of age 35 or less;
4. a high literacy rate of 85 per cent;
5. a large livestock economy with 25.4 million head;
6. an agricultural area totalling 130 million hectares;
7. a geographical bridge between Central Asia and Northeast Asia;
8. a location between two huge markets, Russia and China;
9. a strong commitment to a market economy; and
10. a relatively stable political situation.

On the other hand, Mongolia suffers from some disadvantages, such as its land-locked location, low population density, and extreme continental climate. Perhaps the most challenging problem Mongolia faces is the poor state of its transportation facilities with access to Mongolia possible only through Russia and China. Thus, goods from other countries must be carried to either Chinese or Russian ports and then transported by rail some 2,000 kilometres to Mongolia. This situation must be improved by greatly expanding the transportation network.

APPENDIX TABLE 9.1
Sources of Mongolian Imports
(As a percentage of total imports)

	1985	1986	1987	1988	1989	1990	1991
Total	100.00	100.00	100.00	100.00	100.00	100.00	100.00
USSR	86.86	86.76	87.24	85.96	82.78	77.51	66.03
CMEA	7.44	6.68	5.52	6.86	6.54	8.95	4.05
Hungary	1.17	1.19	1.13	1.19	1.24	2.22	0.89
Poland	1.39	1.48	1.20	1.35	1.63	1.43	0.08
Romania	1.65	1.40	1.07	1.19	1.15	0.68	0.17
Czechoslovakia	2.65	2.39	1.89	2.97	2.15	3.68	2.69
Yugoslavia	0.58	0.22	0.23	0.16	0.37	0.94	0.22
Bulgaria	0.99	1.15	0.96	0.97	1.43	1.84	0.36
Europe	3.23	3.42	2.98	3.34	5.24	6.75	11.28
Austria	0.28	0.50	0.31	0.36	1.00	1.08	4.82
Belgium	0.01	n.a.	0.01	0.01	0.01	0.04	0.03
United Kingdom	0.06	0.03	0.04	0.26	0.44	0.27	0.22
Italy	0.01	0.03	0.12	0.11	0.51	0.39	0.58
Netherlands	n.a.	0.13	0.01	0.01	0.01	0.01	0.14
Denmark	n.a.	n.a.	n.a.	0.02	0.11	0.01	0.17
France	0.04	0.03	0.03	0.02	0.04	0.26	0.03
Germany	2.71	2.40	2.34	2.24	2.69	4.05	3.46
Switzerland	0.12	0.30	0.12	0.31	0.43	0.64	1.83
Asia	0.61	1.14	1.67	1.64	2.83	3.94	7.79
Hong Kong	n.a.	n.a.	n.a.	0.01	n.a.	0.29	0.22
South Korea	n.a.	n.a.	n.a.	n.a.	n.a.	0.10	2.02
Singapore	n.a.	n.a.	n.a.	0.02	0.04	0.08	0.25
China	0.45	0.84	1.43	1.16	2.07	2.41	4.52
Japan	0.16	0.30	0.24	0.45	0.72	1.06	0.78
Other countries	1.46	1.68	2.01	1.86	2.06	2.44	0.69
North Korea	0.47	0.53	1.05	0.89	0.63	0.60	0.33

n.a. — Not available.

Source: State Statistical Office, Mongolia.

APPENDIX TABLE 9.2
Destination of Mongolian Exports
(As a percentage of total exports)

	1985	1986	1987	1988	1989	1990	1991
Total	100.00	100.00	100.00	100.00	100.00	100.00	100.00
United States	0.01	0.01	0.06	0.20	0.01	0.14	0.09
USSR	77.01	78.66	77.96	75.59	73.24	78.33	67.59
CMEA	12.25	9.76	10.35	12.40	11.97	10.25	4.52
Hungary	2.15	1.87	1.78	1.88	2.48	2.07	2.64
Poland	2.76	1.98	2.12	2.53	1.98	1.70	0.06
Romania	2.29	1.82	1.87	2.50	2.07	1.53	0.03
Czechoslovakia	4.57	3.80	4.08	4.14	4.10	4.53	1.24
Yugoslavia	0.48	0.29	0.50	1.35	1.34	0.42	0.55
Bulgaria	n.a.	n.a.	n.a.	n.a.	2.99	2.53	0.43
Europe	6.11	5.60	5.85	4.88	6.20	4.17	5.61
Austria	0.04	0.01	0.01	0.01	0.25	n.a.	0.03
United Kingdom	0.41	0.39	0.54	0.22	0.68	0.45	0.55
Italy	0.13	0.01	0.04	0.01	0.25	0.83	1.35
Netherlands	1.00	0.52	0.64	0.41	0.80	0.23	0.14
France	0.04	0.06	0.04	0.05	0.01	0.41	0.32
Germany	3.53	3.44	3.41	3.04	3.12	2.07	2.93
Switzerland	0.96	1.17	1.17	1.14	1.09	0.18	0.29
Asia	1.49	1.34	1.69	3.38	3.98	3.14	20.60
Afghanistan	n.a.	n.a.	n.a.	n.a.	n.a.	0.23	0.92
Hong Kong	n.a.	n.a.	n.a.	n.a.	n.a.	n.a.	1.12
Singapore	n.a.	n.a.	n.a.	n.a.	n.a.	n.a.	0.03
China	0.39	0.46	0.52	0.42	0.58	1.76	15.17
Japan	1.10	0.88	1.17	2.96	3.40	1.15	3.36
Other countries	0.80	1.77	1.10	0.78	3.82	3.71	0.75
North Korea	0.80	1.77	1.10	0.78	0.83	1.18	0.32

n.a. — Not available.

Source: State Statistical Office, Mongolia.

APPENDIX TABLE 9.3
Summary of Mongolian State Budget
(Millions of tugrik)

	1980	1985	1989	1990	1991	1992	1993[a]
Total revenue	3,452.6	4,918.0	5,243.3	5,328.7	6,065.1	11,301.2	61,096.9
Total expenditure	3,988.6	5,700.9	7,062.3	6,812.3	8,929.3	11,741.4	61,934.1
Overall deficit	−536.0	−782.9	−1,819.0	−1,483.6	−2,864.2	−440.2	−632.9
Overall deficit as a percentage of GDP	6.0	9.2	17.0	14.2	15.1	1.1	0.4
Percentage of foreign financing in covering overall deficit	100.0	100.0	89.3	77.8	99.7	85.1	n.a.
Total revenue in percentage of GDP	51.1	52.5	48.9	50.9	32.1	21.9	43.7

[a] Preliminary data.

Source: State Statistical Office, Mongolia.

APPENDIX TABLE 9.4
Mongolian State Budget
(Millions of tugrik, at current prices)

	1988	1989	1990	1991	1992
Total revenue	4,650.6	5,211.3	5,294.7	8,964.5	11,799.5
Current revenue	4,649.0	5,208.5	5,288.4	8,964.5	11,799.5
Tax revenue	4,202.6	4,835.9	4,262.2	5,053.1	9,839.4
Corporate tax	1,976.3	2,290.5	2,043.0	2,485.9	5,035.9
Individual income tax	40.5	46.7	45.1	100.0	227.6
Excise tax	—	—	371.9	813.6	2,018.2
Customs duties and import surcharges	—	—	—	294.7	1,543.8
Fees, charges, and others	32.1	30.8	22.7	93.2	103.8
Social security	270.0	300.3	209.3	842.0	623.6
Non-tax revenue	144.3	164.8	794.2	886.3	1,139.0
Capital revenue	1.6	2.8	6.3	—	—
Total expenditures	6,660.9	7,012.3	6,710.6	10,796.6	16,965.5
Current expenditures	5,146.1	5,382.8	5,434.5	9,778.0	11,142.0
Wages	877.1	902.2	904.3	1,848.3	2,862.5
Subsidies	1,554.4	1,665.5	1,674.2	1,234.2	1,140.2
Transfers	821.8	808.7	865.4	3,635.1	2,766.5
Social security	722.7	729.5	793.0	2,166.8	2,392.6
Reserve fund and others	295.3	417.1	142.3	785.8	725.3
Capital expenditures and net lending	1,514.8	1,629.5	1,276.1	1,018.6	5,823.5
Budgetary investments	1,514.8	1,629.5	1,276.1	1,018.6	1,053.8
Overall current balance	−495.5	−171.5	−139.8	−813.5	657.5
Overall balance	−2,010.3	−1,801.0	−1,415.9	−1,832.1	−5,166.0
Financing	2,010.3	1,801.0	1,415.9	1,832.1	5,166.0
Foreign, net	2,016.1	1,607.9	1,097.8	1,825.7	4,398.0
Domestic Borrowing from the banking system	−5.8	193.1	318.1	6.4	768.0

Sources: Ministry of Finance, Mongolia, and various International Monetary Fund publications.

APPENDIX TABLE 9.5
Consumer Price Indices of Mongolia

Year	Month	General Index (16 January 1991=100)	Monthly Index
1991	September	134.90	n.a.
	October	139.19	103.1801
	November	146.34	105.1369
	December	152.72	104.3597
1992	January	158.18	103.5752
	February	173.69	109.8053
	March	230.78	132.8689
	April	262.42	113.7100
	May	274.29	104.5233
	June	340.13	124.0038
	July	371.10	109.1053
	August	377.24	101.6545
	September	409.70	108.6046
	October	531.49	129.7266
	November	585.16	110.0980
	December	649.79	111.0448
1993	January	823.29	126.7009
	February	888.61	107.9340
	March	978.96	110.1676

Source: State Statistical Office, Mongolia.

References

Asian Development Bank. *Mongolia: A Centrally Planned Economy in Transition.* New York: Oxford University Press, 1992.

Batbayar, Tsedendambyn. "Mongolia in 1992". *Asian Survey* 33, no. 1 (1993).

―――. "Mongolia in 1993". *Asian Survey* 34, no. 1 (1994).

Denizer, Cevdet and Alan Gelb. "Mongolia: Privatization and System Transformation in an Isolated Economy". World Bank Policy Research Working papers, no. 1063. Washington, D.C.: World Bank, 1992.

Gonzales, John J. "Mongolia's Reform: Experiences and Prospects". Paper prepared for the East-West Center / Organization for Economic Co-operation and Development seminar From Reform to Growth: Countries in Transition Compared, 16–17 December 1993, in Honolulu.

Hahm, H. "Mongolia: Development of the Private Sector in a Small Economy in Transition". Mimeographed. World Bank, China and Mongolia Department, July 1993.

Hirono, R. "Mongolia's Struggle to Create a Market Economy". *Japan Review of International Affairs* 6, no. 2 (1992).

Kuribayashi, S. *Mongolia: Issues in Creating a Development Strategy. Rethinking Development Strategy in Northeast Asia.* Tokyo: The Sasakawa Peace Foundation, 1993.

McKinnon, R.I. *The Order of Economic Liberalization.* Baltimore: Johns Hopkins University Press, 1993.

Milne, E., J. Leimone, F. Rozwadowski, and P. Sukachevin. "The Mongolian People's Republic: Toward a Market Economy". International Monetary Fund Occasional paper, no. 79. Washington, D.C.: International Monetary Fund, 1991.

Mongolia, Ministry for National Development, National Working Group. "Mongolia's Economic Situation, the Government's Reform Programme, and the Role for External Aid: A Policy Statement". August 1991.

―――. "Mongolia Policy Framework". Paper presented at the Mongolia Meeting of Donors, 13–14 September 1993, in Tokyo.

―――. "Recent Economic Developments on Short- and Medium-Term Objectives of the Government". May 1992.

Murrell, P., G. Korson, and K. Dunn. *Price Policy in Mongolia: A Chronology of Developments.* IRIS Working Paper Series, no. 6. Maryland: College Park, 1992.

World Bank. *World Tables 1993.* Baltimore: Johns Hopkins University Press, 1993.

Contributors

The Editors

SEIJI FINCH NAYA is Director, Department of Business, Economic Department and Tourism (DBEDT) of the State of Hawaii and Professor of Economics since 1971 (currently on leave of absence) at the University of Hawaii, Porteus Hall, Honolulu, Hawaii. He holds a Ph.D. in economics from the University of Wisconsin. Professor Seji Naya's activities have focused on the international economic problems of Asian countries and issues of economic co-operation in the Asia-Pacific region. He has organized, chaired, and participated in numerous collaborative research projects and international conferences on Asian economic development. He serves as senior advisor to the non-profit International Center for Economic Growth (ICEG), San Francisco. He has also served as advisor and/or consultant to such organizations as the ASEAN Secretariat, the UNDP, UNCTAD, USAID, and the International Development Center of Japan. He was formerly Chief Economist of the Asian Development Bank and Vice-President and Institute Director at the East-West Center. He has written many professional books and articles that have appeared in such journals as the *American Economic Review*, *Economic Development and Cultural Change*, *Economic Record*, *Journal of the American Statistical Association*, and *Developing Economies*.

JOSEPH L. H. TAN is Senior Fellow at the Institute of Southeast Asian Studies, where he has served as the Co-ordinator, ASEAN Economic Research Unit since 1985. He received his undergraduate training at Brandeis University and obtained his doctorate from Harvard University. He has been Editor-in-charge of the *ASEAN Economic Bulletin* since mid-1987. His recent publications include: *Vietnam Dilemmas and Options: The Challenge of Economic Transition in the 1990s* (joint contributing editor with Mya Than, 1993); *Regional Economic Integration in the Asia-Pacific* (contributing editor, 1993); and *"Strengthening Subregional Linkages between ASEAN and Indochina"* (forthcoming).

The Contributors

TSEDENDAMBYN BATBAYAR is Director, Institute of International and Oriental Studies, Mongolian Academy of Sciences, a post he has held since 1990. He received his undergraduate training at Leningrad University and his postgraduate training at the Institute for Far Eastern Studies, Moscow. His research interest covers a wide range of issues, including Mongolia's development strategy. His most recent publications are year-end articles on Mongolia in *Asian Survey*; and an article on Mongolia's economic reform in *Sekai* (July 1992).

S. STANLEY KATZ is currently a Visiting Fellow at the East-West Center, Honolulu. He has previously served as Senior Advisor to the President, European Bank for Reconstruction and Development (London, 1990–93); Vice President for Operations, Asian Development Bank (Manila, 1978–90); Deputy Assistant Secretary, U.S. Department of Commerce, and Foreign Service Officer, U.S. Department of State (Washington, D.C., 1967–78); Senior Economist, International Bank for Reconstruction and Development (Washington, D.C., 1965–66); Economist, Organization for Economic Co-operation and Development (Paris, 1962–65); Economist, U.S. Bureau of the Budget, Agency for International Development, and the Development Loan Fund (Washington, D.C., 1955–62). Dr Katz was a Professorial Lecturer, George Washington University (Washington, D.C., 1975–78). He holds a B.A. in Political Science, Syracuse University, M.A. in Economics, Maxwell Graduate School, Syracuse University, and a Ph.D. in Economics, American University. He has published one book and numerous articles in the fields of economic development and international finance.

PANOM LATHOULY is presently Senior Economist in the Economic Research Department, Central Bank of Lao PDR. His previous positions include Deputy Director of Planning and Price Department (September 1982 – April 1989); and Head of Section for Capital Investment, Department of Planning and Statistics, Ministry of

Industry and Trade (August 1980 – August 1982). He holds a B.A. in Economics from the Australian National University.

LE DANG DOANH is currently President of the Central Institute for Economic Management and responsible for Vietnam's economic relations with Japan and other OECD countries. Mr Doanh assisted in the drafting of important laws such as the Labour Code, the Law on Bankruptcy, and the Law on State-Owned Enterprises. He has, since the beginning of *doi moi*, been part of the economic policy team that set the parameters for Vietnam's economic growth into the 1990s. Educated in Hanoi and Germany, Mr Doanh has written and travelled extensively and speaks several languages fluently.

SAKHIYA LHAGVA is Deputy Director of the Institute of Economics, Academy of Sciences, Mongolia. He received his economic science degree in 1989 from the Mongolian State University. Since 1990, he has been a senior research fellow studying problems connected with macroeconomic management and delivering lectures at the Institute of Administrative Management, Development and Technical University, Ulaanbaatar. In 1991–92, he was a visiting researcher at the American University, Washington D.C., where he studied macroeconomics and international economics.

ADAM JOHN MCCARTY completed his doctorate in Development Studies at the Australian National University. He is a free-lance consultant, and in 1993 was Resident Project Co-ordinator and World Bank Consultant for UNDP's technical assistance project to the Vietnamese State Planning Committee, Hanoi. In 1992 he was Survey Expert and World Bank Consultant for the Vietnam Living Standard Measurement Study, Hanoi.

MOHAMED ARIFF, a specialist in International Economics, is Professor of Economics and Dean of the Faculty of Economics and Administration, University of Malaya, Kuala Lumpur. He also holds the Chair of Analytical Economics. He has authored, co-authored, and edited many books and monographs, in addition to publishing numerous articles in academic journals and mass media. His book *The Malaysian Economy: Pacific Connections*, published by Oxford University Press, won the prestigious Tun Razak Award in 1993.

MYA THAN is a Fellow and Co-ordinator of the Indochina Programme at the Institute of Southeast Asian Studies. He was formerly a staff member of the Department of Research and Management Studies, Institute of Economics, Yangon. He was educated at Yangon, Myanmar, and did his postgraduate studies in Prague, Czechoslovakia. He has written extensively on the economic and social aspects of development in Myanmar and the three Indochinese countries.

MYAT THEIN is currently Professor of Economics and Acting Rector of the Institute of Economics, Yangon. He was educated at Rangoon University and did his postgraduate studies in economics at Warsaw University and Cambridge University. His fields of specialization include macroeconomics, development economics, economic planning, trade, and welfare.

PETER A. PETRI is Carl Shapiro Professor for International Finance and Dean of the Graduate School of International Economics and Finance at Brandeis University. His research focuses on trade and investment, with specific applications to the Pacific Rim. He frequently acts as consultant for the World Bank and was a member of the research teams involved in the East Asian Miracle project and the *East Asian Trade and Investment* report. He has published numerous books and articles and is an editor of the *Journal of Asian Economics* and *Singapore Economic Review*.

CHANTHAVONG SAIGNASITH is currently Director, Department of Public Investment Programme and a member of the Committee for Planning and Cooperation. He received his training at the East-West Center, Honolulu, Hawaii; the Economic Development Institute (EDI) of the World Bank, New Delhi, India, and Washington D.C.; and the Institute for High Economic Planning, GosPlan Moscow, USSR. He has also been a member of the technical committee of the New Economic Mechanism Board responsible for economic reform in the Lao PDR.